THE MAHOGANY TREE

LONDON:
PUBLISHED FOR THE PROPRIETORS, BY R. BRYANT,
AT PUNCH'S OFFICE, WELLINGTON STREET, STRAND.
AND SOLD BY ALL BOOKSELLERS.

THE MAHOGANY TREE

An Informal History
of PUNCH

Arthur Prager

HAWTHORN BOOKS, INC.
Publishers/NEW YORK
A Howard & Wyndham Company

79-28341

Frontispiece: *Punch*'s first cover. By Archibald Henning, 1841.

Cartoons by kind permission of *Punch*.

To the men and women of *Punch*.

Introduction

n 1841 a group of hearty, genial topers got together in a London tavern and decided to start a magazine. They set high quality standards for its contents, and in time it became a power in politics and a financial success. Then it drooped a bit and became a bland little joke book. Then it became a power again. Then it nearly vanished.

The magazine, of course, was *Punch*. This book is a history of its progress, and, more important, of the people who guided its destinies: the editors, writers, and artists who made it an institution. The Mahogany Tree is the editorial table that still sits in the *Punch* offices. It was given that name in a laudatory poem by William Makepeace Thackeray, who was a *Punch* writer for many years. Many of the most celebrated figures of English literature sat at the *Punch* Table and were invited to carve their initials on it for posterity.

Writing a book about *Punch*, according to the late P. G. Wodehouse, gives me the right to ''wear corduroy trousers and grow a short beard and speak as an authority on trends and cycles and the differences between wit and humour.'' I have no intention of doing anything of the kind. Nor do I intend to fall into the hoary trap of trying to distinguish between the English and the American senses of humor. There isn't any difference, and don't let anyone ever try to tell you there is. As for Victorian humor, well, that is another story.

The following pages are illustrated with a number of excerpts and cartoons, some of which may strike the reader as not at all funny. I included them, not because they were the cream of 138 years of superlative comedy, but because they were typical of their period and because the people who lived when they appeared in *Punch* thought they were funny. Because of space limitations, I have had to leave out many things that are funny in order to have room for those which have historic value. For example, purists will complain at once that I have not included a locomotive by Rowland Emmett, a child on a fat pony by Thelwell, or a satanic schoolgirl by Ronald Searle. These are so well known in our day that there really is no reason to omit a Victorian cartoon by John Leech or Charles Keene in order to show them. We all know what they look like.

I also have tried to include new material not found in the numerous histories of *Punch* and its writers and artists. Would you like to know what William Makepeace Thackeray did on those little trips to Paris? Are you curious about the bitterness between P. G. Wodehouse and A. A. Milne and how the creator of Jeeves chose to revenge himself on the creator of Pooh? Do you want to know which editor, after a Homeric struggle with the board of directors, was the first to insert a rude four-letter word in a *Punch* article? Read on. Do you want to know which *Punch* editor wrote the play that Abraham Lincoln was watching when he was assassinated, or which editor wrote musical comedies with both Gilbert and Sullivan before they formed their partnership, or which editor married the daughter of the man who discovered that the duckbill platypus lays eggs? Do you know which *Punch* writer invented the Double-Crostic and which cartoonist invented the Enfield rifle? Read on.

And, of course, there is the Curious Affair of the Forged Letter, revealed herein for the first time. Until he reads this paragraph, *Punch's* editor Alan Coren will not know that the letter inviting him to enjoy the pleasures of Africa as a special VIP guest of Uganda's President Idi Amin was an excellent forgery cooked up by the extraordinarily pretty girls who make up the magazine's clerical and administrative staff and who are the real backbone of the organization. If Alan Coren tells you he knew it all the time, don't you believe him. That goes for his editorial predecessor, William Davis, too, who quoted the letter in an article about Coren in *Vogue*.

The true purpose of this brief introduction is to offer my thanks to the *Punch* people for their help and their patience. Special thanks to William Davis, who invited me to the Wednesday editorial lunches at the famous *Punch* Table. Thanks to the busy staff, Alan Coren, Sheridan Morley, William Hewison, Geoffrey Dickinson, Miles Kington, Jonathan Sale, and Philip Hood. Many thanks to Basil Boothroyd, and to Chairman and Managing Director A. V. Caudery, who let me use the original Henry Silver diary. Special thanks to the *Punch* women Mary Anne Bonney, Olivia Grogono, Caroline Cook, and Pamela Todd, who let me sit in Sir

Bernard Partridge's chair and invited me to lunch at *their* table. Thanks to Albert Barnes, who emerged from the secret cave where he has reigned as ''maintenance'' for forty-nine years and who told me about the days when he delivered proofs to the homes of Sir Owen Seaman, A. P. Herbert, and E. V. Knox on his bicycle each week, receiving for his pains a shilling from Knox, a sixpence from Herbert, and a hearty ''Thank you very much'' from Seaman.

Thanks to former Punchites who helped me by remembering anecdotes of the old days, Bernard Hollowood and Anthony Powell, Peter Dickinson, Peter G. Agnew, and *Punch*'s new proprietor, Lord Barnetson; and to Dan O'Shea and Josephine Reidy, who cleared my way to American sources.

Special thanks to Susan Jeffreys, now Susan Hood, who assumed responsibility for me and waved away my requests for books and documents, offering always ''something much better'' from the library files. Extra special thanks to *Punch* historian R. G. G. Price, who was kindest and most helpful of all, feeding me information about behind-the-scenes matters and hitherto unpublished items in spite of the fact that my book can only compete with his own excellent *A History of Punch* published by Collins in 1957. There is really no way I can thank him enough.

Most especially thanks to those people alive and dead whose names I have not been able to mention. There just isn't enough room to include everyone who counted over a period of 138 years. It takes a great many hands to build a National Institution, and time and space have forced me to skim surfaces and stick to highlights. Thanks to all of you just the same.

THE
MAHOGANY
TREE

Why is a chestnut horse going at a rapid pace up an inclined plane like an individual in white trousers presenting a young lady in book muslin with an infantile specimen of the canine species?

Because he is giving a *gallop up*. (A gal a pup.)

—Punch (*1841*)

leet Street has not changed appreciably in the past century. Sir Christopher Wren and Grinling Gibbons are now tightly juxtaposed with (and somewhat overshadowed by) aluminum, steel, and tinted glass, but it takes more than architecture and façades to alter the character of a London district. The buildings, old or new, still house the survivors and ghosts of the palmier days of the British press—the *Times*, the *Illustrated London News*, the *Standard*, and, of course, *Punch*, standing proudly among the newcomers.

The area still teems with writers-for-hire, any one of whom might easily be taken for Prince Florizel of Bohemia in his favorite disguise, "painted and dressed to represent a journalist in reduced circumstances"; or perhaps for *Punch*'s own perennial butt, the wretched Jenkins of the *Morning Post*. They can be found at any time of day, wolfing down sandwiches at Wimpy Bars and trattorias, side by side with impeccable but impecunious young barristers from the nearby Inns of Court.

Nowadays not many members of the working press (nor, for that matter, of the legal profession) can afford to eat at the historic pubs—the venerable Cock or the Cheshire Cheese—where they would in any event be crowded out by noisy American tourists. The rich and successful still stroll up to the Strand on a pleasant day to lunch at the Savoy Grill as their predecessors did in the days when Edgar Wallace made it the locale of his fictional intrigues. Romano's, favorite of the Savoyards and the staff of the *Pink 'Un*, is gone forever.

On a bright September day in 1977 I emerged from the Chancery Lane tube station and headed south toward Tudor Street for my first visit to the

3

offices of *Punch*. I had written to the editors from New York, explaining that I wanted to write a book about the magazine and asking permission to use their library. A reply from A. V. Caudery, chairman and managing director of Punch Publications Ltd., offered his personal help in my project and added an invitation to lunch. It was to meet Mr. Caudery that I now found myself cautiously squeezing my way past bellowing workmen and enormous flatbed vans loaded with giant rolls of newsprint, down the narrow length of Bouverie Street toward *Punch*'s latest resting place in the United Newspapers Building.

With time to spare I walked around the neighborhood to see if I could absorb a little of the historic atmosphere. *Punch* was first published in Wellington Street, later occupying premises at Numbers 92 and 85 Fleet Street and 10 and 11 Bouverie Street. Thus, from the first day of its existence in 1841 to the present, the magazine has never moved more than a few hundred yards. It was at 85 Fleet Street that the staff and their friends climbed to the roof annually to watch the Lord Mayor's Show. It was there that the editors and their families and guests assembled on the balcony to see the wedding procession of the Prince of Wales and Princess Alexandra of Denmark in the spring of 1863. Of course, the *Punch* wags with their reputation for sublime buffoonery could not resist a comic gesture. They dressed up a statuette of Mr. Punch, festooned it with flowers, and articulated it with ropes, so the leering puppet could be made to execute an absurd bow when the royal carriages drove by. The result is described in the diary of Henry Silver, *Punch*'s drama critic and writer-of-all-work, who never tired of chronicling the doings of his colleagues.

> I was between the Misses Lemon with Mrs. Leech at the corner and Mrs. Sothern next behind her husband, Lord Dundreary by my side and Shenton pulling the string that made Punch bow his greeting—funny to see the fat old Aldermen and stiff military swells all gradually burst into broad grins as they passed. And . . . how smilingly the Princess herself looked up at Punch and what a good view of her the Punchites obtained. Somewhat of a cross between a beadle and a ballet girl was Mr. Punch, crowned with a white rose and well covered with white flowers.*

The magazine moved its operations to 10 Bouverie Street in 1900. The building was demolished in 1930 and replaced with a new one, described

---

*The Misses Lemon and Mrs. Leech were the families of the editor and principal cartoonist. "Lord Dundreary" was the actor E. A. Sothern, who had scored a tremendous success in the role of the silly peer in the play *Our American Cousin* (1858) by Tom Taylor. Long, drooping whiskers have been called "Dundrearies" ever since.

PUNCH AT THE PROCESSION.

MERRILY, merrily clang the bells,
  And the gay flags flutter around,
While the boom of the cannon in thunder tells
  That Her foot is on English ground !

Lustily, lustily cheers the street,
  As she passeth its crowd among,
" Welcome, fair Bride ! may thy life be as sweet
  As the Spring-flowers o'er thee flung ! "

Flash the glad tidings along the wires
  To the heart of old London town,
Bid a welcoming peal from her hundred spires,
  And——

Thus far had *Mr. Punch* proceeded with his Ode, and was doubting
a moment what rhyme to use for "town"—"Bid the LORD MAYOR
in his gown" seemed rather too Tupperian, and "Let every joy be
own," although it looked a rhyme when written, did not at all sound
e one,—thus sat *Mr. Punch*, in a prodigiously fine frenzy rolling his
etic eye and staring at the ceiling to assist his inspiration, when in
ne a Royal footman, whom from his scarlet livery *Mr. Punch* was
ry near mistaking for a postman, and who carried a deliciously rose-

scented *billet doux*, which, in the prettiest of handwriting contained
these gracious words :—

> " *Bricklayers Arms, Saturday, a quarter to two.*
>
> " DEAR MR. PUNCH,
>
> " WILL you excuse a hurried notice, and join us in our carriage.
> Papa and ALBERT EDWARD say they can make room for you.
>
> " Sincerely yours,
> " ALEXANDRA."

" P. S. Please bring *Toby*."

To throw aside his pen and poem, to put on his Court Suit (which
for such emergencies hangs always at his elbow), to dress up *Toby* in
his knickerbockers and his best frilled collar, to bid good bye to *Judy*
and his other guests in Fleet Street, and to reach the Bricklayers'
Arms by the nearest way accessible (which, as the City was blocked up,
was *via* the back streets and over Vauxhall Bridge), was to loyal *Mr.
Punch* but five short minutes' work. Ere two o'clock had struck he
was seated in the carriage with the Princess smiling at him as only she
can smile, and *Toby*—lucky dog !—was reclining in her lap.

It is needless to observe that throughout the seven miles *Mr. Punch's*
loyal eyes were never once removed from the fair face of the Princess :
but the following, he has heard, was the

ORDER OF PROCESSION.

One Policeman, to clear the way (which he didn't).

A whole regiment of Black Guards, mostly with their caps knocked off.

Some weak-legged Supernumeraries staggering with big banners.

Band of the Ten Stunners (City), all in full blow.

Another Policeman.

A score or two of old and seedy-looking carriages, all propelled by Screws, and filled
with tailors, drapers, grocers, goldsmiths, salters, skinners, tallow-chandlers, fish-
mongers, coach and harness-makers, blacksmiths, chimney-sweeps and cooks ;
arrayed in their Court Suits (bright blue gowns with mangy fur),

Banners and Big Drums.

Some very Jolly Young Watermen (ætat. 65 at least) with pewter plates upon their
bosoms and carrying enormous Flags,

The City Commissioners of Lieutenancy and Lunacy ; the latter dressed like Jack
Tars of the period, in top-boots.

Banners, Bassoons, and Big Drums.

Another Live Policeman.

Officers of the Corporation ; all of them elected apparently by weight.

Aldermen (ditto, ditto), Sheriffs and Under Sheriffs, crammed four in a carriage,
with two footmen and three small boys hanging on behind

The Reception Committee and other City Flunkeys.

Banners, Beadles, Banjoes, Bassoons, and Big Drums.

Another live Policeman attended by his Staff.

" His Honourable Royal Highness " (see French press) THE LORD MAYOR, drawn
by Eleven Horses, and attended by the Common Crier, in full cry

Band playing the City Anthem : " ROSE, thou art the fairest flower ! "

A fifth Policeman, mounted.

Gentlemen of the Press, on foot, in muddy boots.

A Royal Trumpeter, blowing his own Trumpet.

Six Royal Carriages, the Sixth conveying ALBERT EDWARD, ALEXANDRA, Rose of
Denmark, her Royal Pa and Ma. His Excellency TOBY ! and the illustrious
PRINCE PUNCH.

Messieurs Tag, Rag, and Bobtail, and other distinguished followers, upon their
ten toes.

A Strong force of Two Policemen, trying to do the work of twenty, in keeping back
the crowd.

How the Procession looked, for reasons before stated *Mr. Punch* must
not be asked. How the PRINCESS ALEXANDRA looked is quite another
question, and *Mr. Punch* in his enthusiasm would like to fill a volume
by way of a reply. Photographs ! poob, nonsense, BROWN ! don't talk
to us of photographs. No photograph can fairly picture her fair face.
Mr. Punch believes that Phœbus was so dazzled by her beauty that
when he tried to take her portrait he was forced to hide his face. And,
what is better than mere beauty of feature or complexion, there is
lovingness and cleverness and goodness in her face. Well may our young

---

*Punch on the royal wedding. The statuette bowing to Princess Alexandra was
presented to the magazine by the German sculptor G. A. Fleischmann. It now
stands in the editor's office at 23 Tudor Street. (Drawing by George du Maurier,
poem by Shirley Brooks, 1863)*

in 1955 by R. E. Williams (who spent what Malcolm Muggeridge called "the best part of his working life" at Number 10) as "a modest red brick building of five stories."

> Once through the door of *Punch* there is a country-house peace, and it is rather a surprise that no butler greets you but rather a commissionaire who himself looks a little like Mr. Punch. He will unhurriedly get your name wrong, and should you have legitimate business lead you up the graceful sweep of dangerously polished stairs. You may catch a glimpse of the present editor-in-chief [Muggeridge] who after less than three years in the chair also looks like Mr. Punch.

The new building figured importantly in the eventual purchase of the magazine by United Newspapers in 1969 for a complicated exchange of shares but not much cash. The sale of the premises at Number 10 brought United almost as much money as they paid for *Punch*, so, strictly speaking, it could be said that they got the magazine for practically nothing. Lord Barnetson, head of United Newspapers, has not yet begun to look like Mr. Punch.

I looked into the lobby of Number 10 to see, if not the original, at least the 1930 replacement for that famous staircase up which P. G. Wodehouse, A. P. Herbert, Milne, and other immortals had hurried, clutching their manuscripts. There was no commissionaire. The building, if its directory is to be taken seriously, now houses a number of what seem to be nonjournalistic enterprises with strange, faintly sinister names that sound like obscure branches of a clandestine intelligence service. Rubyriver Ltd., Fadebray Ltd., and Dunmist Ltd. hint vaguely at political assassination or mysterious disappearance (or perhaps cemeteries for pets). Most alarming of all are the NBC Staff Superannuation Scheme and the Mineworkers Injuries Scheme, suggesting bureaus dedicated to prematurely aging television executives or maiming miners. The names might have been concocted by Gilbert à Beckett for one of the broad practical jokes that so delighted *Punch* staffers a century ago.

A. V. Caudery was a distinguished, gray-haired man dressed in a dark, conservatively cut suit, the prototype of the British businessman, quite the opposite of what one would expect the senior executive of a comic paper to look like, but a casting director's dream of the persona that goes with the title "Chairman and Managing Director." His office, although it was situated in a comparatively new building by Fleet Street standards, had a faintly Victorian air, possibly due to gold-framed oil paintings and a complete leather-bound set of *Punch*. He greeted me, unsmiling, with slightly chilly courtesy. Our meeting was brief and conducted in such a way that all my questions were answered politely, but I found myself out in the corridor again with great speed, somehow under the impression that I had completed my business and terminated the interview myself. It was masterfully done, obviously the result of many years of experience. I realized suddenly that Mr. Caudery had not really given me any assurances of anything at all, not the right to use cartoons and *Punch* excerpts, or even the library.

As I left the chairman's office, I was intercepted by R. G. G. Price, a staff member and contributor of more than three decades standing, and Mary Anne Bonney, Mr. Caudery's secretary, a lovely, deceptively shy young woman with blond hair and a rosy complexion. They had been deputized to take me to lunch at the Fleet Street Bistingo.

This odd combination of escorts, a senior and internationally known humorist and literary critic, and a pretty young secretary, illustrates the unique position held by the women of *Punch*. Although they are hired for and expected to carry out the usual typing and filing chores, they are definitely members of the official family and wield considerable power in the magazine's operations. Their opinions are valued by writers and editors, and they are often expected to assume assignments at a diplomatic level rarely reached by their American counterparts or, for that matter, their British equivalents outside of *Punch*.

In return they are left alone and allowed to do as they please. As a result, they work much harder and their productivity is incredibly high. "The money's so bad," one of them said to me later, "we say we'll take the job for a year, you know, and then go on somewhere else. But there's something about *Punch*. It's so easy to work here. Sometimes when there's a special—a book coming out or something like that—we work very late, but usually nobody checks when we come and go. If you want to take a long lunch and go to a gallery or something, nobody says a word. They just want to know that you've done something interesting."

In the matter at hand, Mary Anne Bonney had been delegated to accompany Richard Price on a delicate mission that included both protocol and intelligence duties, that of checking me out carefully to see what I was up to and what ought to be done about me.

The three of us engaged in superficial conversation over an excellent lunch and a first-class bottle of wine. ("Might as well be a good one; it's on the firm," Price said gleefully as he and Mary Anne ordered from the right side of the menu.) I was not aware of any special scrutiny on their part, or of anything more than a normal, social meal shared by people of marginally similar interests who don't know each other very well. Nevertheless, at some point before the coffee arrived, I seemed to have passed the test, whatever it was. An imperceptible change came over my hosts.

On our return to Tudor Street, I found that the frost had melted from

Mr. Caudery's manner, although there was no way he could have talked to them between our departure and our return. Some vibration or signal had passed through the magazine's corridors. I was given the freedom of the office, the files, and the library. Mr. Caudery himself suggested that I might like to use the diary of Henry Silver, the mid-Victorian Pepys of the early *Punch* days, a document always kept under lock and key in his office. The *Punch* girls, to whom I had hitherto been invisible, all smiled at me as I passed.

In time I realized that Price and Mary Anne had been assigned, not to report on my good points, but rather to winkle out my bad ones. What they had discovered at the restaurant was not that I was a paragon, but rather that from the *Punch* point of view I could be considered relatively harmless and could be turned loose with no fear that I would behave badly or steal the first editions. How they had come to this conclusion only a Briton could ever understand. I don't know what Richard Price said to Mr. Caudery, but I did find out what Mary Anne later reported in secret to the powerful female clique in the secretaries' room. ''We've got another American,'' she said to the girls, ''but this one is all right.''

With such a tribute echoing down the corridors of a National Institution, how could my project fail? I was far too pleased with myself until I found out that her approval was based on a comparison with a previous American who was *not* all right. I never found out exactly what he did or who he was, but apparently whatever test had been given him, he had failed it. Like the unfortunate Widmerpool, whose life was colored by the fact that he had worn the wrong sort of overcoat at school, my predecessor had blotted his copybook in some irrevocable fashion, a misfortune for him but a blessing for me. The following morning I was given a small table in the library and a cup of Nescafé and left, like any other Punchite, to work as I pleased in my own way and my own time.

My interview with William Davis, the editor in chief, came soon after my meeting with Mr. Caudery. A passionately kinetic character, Davis gave the impression, even when sitting behind his wide, cluttered desk, of being in constant rapid motion or about to dash away at full speed. He greeted me in his shirt-sleeves, his tie slightly awry and an unruly lock of hair over his forehead. He shook my hand, dropped it, and began to lope nervously around the office, pausing occasionally to deliver the answer to a question about himself or the magazine that I might consider germane to my project, although in actual fact I had not had time to ask any questions at all.

The antithesis of Mr. Caudery, who is the kind of Englishman often portrayed in the movies directing with gentle, unruffled calm the activities of a hollow square under attack by maniacal dervishes, Davis has an air about him that is vaguely un-British. Thackeray and John Leech would have disapproved of him. Shirley Brooks and Mark Lemon would have respected his abilities. Sir Francis Burnand would have fired him. Sir Owen Seaman would never have hired him in the first place. I was not at all surprised when he told me that his background was not, in fact, English at all but German. He was born in Hanover. His mother had married a soldier in the British Zone of Occupation. He had not spoken English until he was twelve years old.

"If you'd been born in a different zone you might be editing the *New Yorker* now," I said, the sort of joke I would never have ventured with Mr. Caudery.

"Or *Krokodil*," he said, grinning.

As much an expert at controlling interviews as Mr. Caudery, Davis took mine over and steered it into the channels he thought most appropriate. Like a schoolmaster guiding a favorite but slow student, he saw to it that I absorbed exactly the knowledge he thought should be put in my book and not a bit more. From time to time I opened my mouth to ask a question that never got asked because Davis, lowering his voice to show that what he was about to say was terribly important and just between us two, gave me some nugget of information favorable to the magazine or to his own image. He must have known at the time (although it was still a secret) that he would be replaced as editor in a few weeks by Alan Coren, his deputy, but he gave no hint of it, talking freely of future plans for the magazine.

The incongruity of having a German at the head of a National Institution did not escape the comic and satirical British press, which had a good deal of fun at Davis's expense. Traditional English xenophobia, though somewhat diminished by the 1960s, had produced a certain grumbling antagonism toward him. Davis, who has no German accent and looks less Teutonic than the prime minister, managed to overcome this handicap with the full support of the proprietors of *Punch* and to remain editor for nearly ten years. Regarded by some as a genius (and by others as a piranha), his tenure as editor can be called a success.

"I don't see my job as editor as reading other people's work and making little pencil marks on it," he said, throwing open a liquor cabinet and indicating with a gesture that I was to help myself. "When I assign an article to a writer, I expect that that article will be perfect. Ready to go to the printer." He paused and looked me full in the eyes. "*Otherwise we never use that writer again.*"

What would the *New Yorker* say about that, I wondered, thinking about the writer-to-printer concept and remembering dreadful mutilations suffered at the hands of magazine editors in America.

It suddenly became apparent to me that a large group of people was

"THE MAHOGANY TREE."

The dinner celebrating Punch's *fiftieth anniversary. Standing left is the editor, Sir Francis C. Burnand. Around the table to his left are Thomas A. Guthrie ("F. Anstey"), Henry Lucy, E. T. Reed, G. A. à Beckett, E. J. Milliken, Sir William Agnew, W. H. Bradbury, George du Maurier, Harry Furniss, R. C. Lehmann, Arthur à Beckett, Linley Sambourne, and Sir John Tenniel. From left to right the portraits are Mark Lemon, Gilbert à Beckett, Douglas Jerrold, Shirley Brooks, Tom Taylor, and Charles Keene. The busts represent William Makepeace Thackeray, Richard Doyle, Thomas Hood, and John Leech. (Linley Sambourne, 1891)*

waiting outside the office door to see him. He looked at his watch. I put away my notebook and stood up. Paying no attention to me, the others began to drift in, mixing themselves drinks, and chatting with one another.

"We're going to have our weekly editorial lunch in a few minutes," Davis said. "Would you like to join us?"

Would I like to join them?

The editor's invitation was a very special honor indeed. Whereas the chairman had very kindly stood me a meal "on the firm" at a local restaurant, Davis was proposing that I sit at the famous *Punch* Table to participate in a ceremony that went back to the early days of the reign of Queen Victoria. The dinners (they did not become lunches until 1925) began 138 years ago, at first in taverns and then in the offices of the proprietors, the printers Bradbury and Evans, at 11 and later at 10 Bouverie Street. There the Parliament of Wits and Conclave of Humorists, who were *Punch*, deliberated on the "big cut," the political cartoon around which the jokes and articles that made up each weekly issue were carefully arranged. The origins of the Table are vague, but at some time in the mid-1800s Bradbury (or Evans) purchased or acquired the celebrated piece of furniture and established it in the "banquet room" of their premises.

The dinners were hilarious; devoted to gourmandizing, hearty boozing, jokes, horseplay, gossip, obscene limericks, and finally, to work. To be a permanent staff member at *Punch* did not automatically mean Table membership, although that might come in time. Members were arbitrarily selected by the editor because they were convivial drinking companions as well as Punchites. On the other hand, once a man joined the Table, he was a member for life, even if he left *Punch* and moved on to other activities. Thackeray dined there long after he had resigned in protest against *Punch*'s politics.

To symbolize the permanence of the Table, members were (and are) invited to carve their initials on it. A. P. Herbert wrote that being called to the Table had more significance for him than being called to the Bar. A. A. Milne worked as an assistant editor at *Punch* for a long time before he was accorded the honor. "In 1910 I was allowed downstairs," Milne wrote. "Graves [C. L. Graves, deputy editor] presented me with a knife with which to leave my mark on the Table, and I achieved a modest and monogrammatic A.A.M. which is already, I dare say, a hieroglyphic to him who sits in my place. Who was this, he wonders, and nobody now can tell him."

There are many legends about the Table. Malcolm Muggeridge, according to a present-day staffer, made such a botch of his initials that a

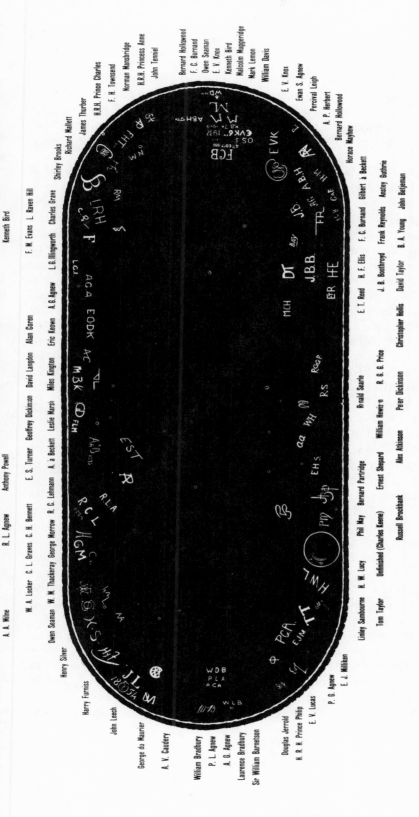

The Table, at which weekly editorial meals have been eaten for 138 years, is now at 23 Tudor Street. The staff meets here each Wednesday to discuss the forthcoming issue. This drawing shows the locations of the members' initials.

part of the Table had to be sent away for repair. Phil May, the cartoonist, is said to have been such a hearty drinker that he carved his initials under the Table instead of on its surface (this is apocryphal—I looked). May hated the dinners and would attend for only a few minutes at a time, keeping a hansom cab waiting outside to take him to some more congenial place.

In July 1907 Mark Twain came to dinner. Little Joy Agnew, the nine-year-old daughter of one of the proprietors, was costumed as an angel and concealed in a cupboard. She popped out on cue and made a charming little speech to the great man, after which she presented him with a cartoon by Sir Bernard Partridge in which Twain was represented. Twain was invited to inscribe his initials but politely declined, saying that he would be quite satisfied to share the last two initials carved by William Makepeace Thackeray. At a later date, James Thurber, less humble than Twain, did carve his, thus becoming the only American to be so honored.

As an illustration of the exclusiveness of the membership, at my visit there were only seventy-nine sets of initials on the Table although the custom dates back nearly a century and a half. There would have been even fewer, but while Davis was editor he decided for some reason to include the Royal Family, a breach of tradition that never would have been tolerated a hundred years ago when *Punch* devoted itself to ridiculing the Royals. Prince Philip carved a neat Greek *P* and Prince Charles did a little crown with his hereditary three feathers growing out of it, surrounded by a large *C*. He had some trouble doing the ostrich feathers, and so his monogram looks a little like the war bonnet of an impoverished Sioux chieftain. Princess Anne is there too, but the Queen has never been so honored, or perhaps she declined the invitation.

According to G. S. Layard, in his biography of *Punch* artist Charles Keene, ''No stranger was ever admitted to the Table on any pretext whatsoever.'' Layard seems to have been wrong. Even in the earliest days there were guests. Dickens sometimes joined the dinners although he never wrote for *Punch*. So did Thomas Hood, Sir John Millais, and Gladstone. Sir Joseph Paxton, who designed the Crystal Palace while doodling on a pad at a railway board of directors meeting, was also frequently present, although he was almost certainly a *Punch* financial backer.

One privilege that does accrue to members and has from the beginning (perhaps the explanation for their small number) is the right not to be edited. The elimination of the traditional blue pencil was a matter of choice with William Davis, but a matter of inalienable right with Table members. Their copy went directly to the printer, unchanged. In the early days the reason for this was apparently to keep the magazine from following too strict a political party line controlled by the editors and proprietors. Through the years the membership has been made up of flaming radicals and staunch conservatives who attacked each other furiously at the dinners and said what they pleased in print. A long-standing battle of opinion between Sir Owen Seaman and Milne ended by Milne's departure from *Punch* after World War I to Seaman's great relief, but Milne's articles were never censored.

A striking example of this forbearance is described by Milne in his *Autobiography*:

> When the slogan of the day was 'We want eight [battleships] and we won't wait' and Navy Leaguers were crying for Three and Four Power Standards without which we were at the mercy of our enemies, I suggested to Rudie Lehmann that he should rewrite the *Ballad of the Revenge* on the assumption that Sir Richard Grenville had refused to put to sea until he had a 53-power standard. . . . When the pages came up on Friday, Owen [Seaman] was more slow, more thoughtful over them than he had ever been. At last he said in his most cold voice: 'Have you seen Rudie's verses?' Naturally I said that though I hadn't seen them I knew what they were about as I had given him the idea. 'Then,' said the cold voice, 'you have done *Punch* and your country a great disservice.'

Seaman, who stood somewhat to the right of Kipling in his views on military and Empire matters, considered Milne and Lehmann guilty of treason, but there was no thought of not printing the poem.

Thackeray immortalized the Table and its members in his poem ''The Mahogany Tree,'' which appeared in 1847 and which celebrated the cheery conviviality of the merry crew of members. The menu usually consisted (in those days) of five courses and champagne, provided by Bradbury and Evans, who published *Punch* after buying up the magazine's debts in 1842. The dinners and the antics and conversations that went on at them were described in detail by Table member Henry Silver in his diary. *''Mock turtle, red mullet, turbot, saddle of mutton, boiled fowl, kidneys, ptarmigan, brown flesh. 'Deuced good'. Champagne and all this after reading of the Homes of the Poor in today's* Times*!''*

If the food was always ''deuced good'' at the Table, the conversation was better. Over the years the membership has included a surprisingly large number of men who were successful in other fields as well as in *Punch*. In contrast with the Algonquin round table people, very few of whom were able to produce any lasting work of literary value, and many of whom conducted themselves in a tragically unsuitable fashion outside their literary activities, the Punchites were exemplary citizens. A great

THE MAHOGANY TREE.

CHRISTMAS is here ;
Winds whistle shrill,
Icy and chill :
Little care we.
Little we fear
Weather without,
Sheltered about
The Mahogany Tree.

Commoner greens,
Ivy and oaks,
Poets, in jokes,
Sing, do ye see :
Good fellows' shins
Here, boys, are found,
Twisting around
The Mahogany Tree.

Once on the boughs,
Birds of rare plume
Sang, in its bloom ;
Night-birds are we :
Here we carouse,
Singing, like them,
Perched round the stem
Of the jolly old tree.

Here let us sport,
Boys, as we sit ;
Laughter and wit
Flashing so free.
Life is but short—
When we are gone,
Let them sing on,
Round the old tree.

Evenings we knew,
Happy as this ;
Faces we miss,
Pleasant to see.
Kind hearts and true,
Gentle and just,
Peace to your dust !
We sing round the tree.

Care, like a dun,
Lurks at the gate ;
Let the dog wait ;
Happy we'll be !
Drink every one ;
Pile up the coals,
Fill the red bowls,
Round the old tree !

Drain we the cup.—
Friend, art afraid ?
Spirits are laid
In the Red Sea.
Mantle it up ;
Empty it yet ;
Let us forget,
Round the old tree.

Sorrows, begone !
Life and its ills,
Duns and their bills,
Bid we to flee.
Come with the dawn,
Blue-devil sprite,
Leave us to night,
Round the old tree.

The Table was first called The Mahogany Tree in this poem. The figures in the drawing are Lord Brougham toasting Mr. Punch, the Duke of Wellington and Sir Robert Peel on the floor, and Lord John Russell asleep on the Table. (Drawing by Richard Doyle, poem by William Makepeace Thackeray, 1847)

many of them were members of Parliament. Some were magistrates and members of royal commissions. A. P. Herbert was personal private secretary to the attorney general as well as an M.P. There were lawyers, doctors, professors, economists, and successful playwrights. Tom Taylor, who edited *Punch* from 1874 to 1880, was also art critic of the *Times*. They were nearly all great boozers, and many of them shortened their lives with debauchery, but they kept the drinking in its place and worked hard when hard work was needed.

Let us have a look at the first appearance at the Table of young Henry Silver, law student and sometime guinea-a-column *Punch* contributor. After a period as a general-purpose writer and play reviewer, he was asked by Mark Lemon, the editor, to "keep yourself disengaged on Wednesdays, please.'' A new member was needed to replace the recently deceased writer Douglas Jerrold, and Silver was the lucky selectee. Arriving at his inaugural dinner, Silver found the senior proprietor, William Bradbury, in the chair, flanked by Sir Joseph Paxton and Peter Rackham, another outsider friend of the firm.* Around the Table were F. M. ''Pater'' Evans, Bradbury's partner; Tom Taylor, a future *Punch* editor; the cartoonist John Tenniel; Shirley Brooks, another future editor; Horace ''Ponny'' Mayhew; and Mark Lemon. The three other regulars, Thackeray, John Leech, and writer Percival Leigh, were all out of town.

''I recollect,'' says Silver in his diary, ''that when dessert was on the table 'Pater' achieved the perilous feat of bowling a big pineapple at his partner who had asked him for a slice of it. And I feel pretty sure that not a single wine glass was broken in the transit. Shirley made pretence of a debate on the cartoon 'just to give the new fellow some notion of how we do it.' Proposed a parody of Millais' picture which appeared next Wednesday ('The British Lion's Vengeance on the Bengal Tiger,' August 22, 1857).''

It was not until the following year that Silver's membership was confirmed and then most informally. ''Am to dine regularly now I suppose,'' he wrote on December 29, 1858. ''If I've not raised my standing I've at least secured my sitting.''

Fortunately for future historians, the shy Silver, who prided himself on ''keeping his eyes open and his mouth shut,'' missed very little of the conversations of his idols around the Mahogany Tree and carefully recorded every word. When the proprietors were not bowling pineapples and Leigh was not startling the others with his whoopee cushion (''a gutta-percha bladder that squeaked like a baby''), the conversational ball caromed madly about.

On post office prepayment (imagine having to pay for your stamp before the letter is even delivered!) Ponny Mayhew sourly predicts that ''the poor will suffer.'' ''The poor don't *want* to write letters'' says John Leech. The talk switches to Lord Palmerston's love life and the fact that he felt that ''no Gentleman ought to remain a half-hour in a lady's company without trying to seduce her.'' Leigh moves into the area of phrenology. No one, he believes, should hire a servant with a badly shaped head, because a good head betokens a good brain and a misshapen head, a bad one. (Leigh, called the ''Professor'' by the others because of his fluency in Latin and Greek, was a practicing physician.)

---

*Rackham was a friend of Dickens and Thackeray, both of whom inscribed presentation copies of their books to him. He was also a financial backer of the *Daily News*, a Bradbury and Evans enterprise. He died in 1859.

THE BRITISH LION'S VENGEANCE ON THE BENGAL TIGER.

The most famous of Tenniel's "Cawnpore Cartoons." It celebrates the capture of Bethan by General Havelock and the burning of the Mahratta Palace in retaliation for the massacre at Cawnpore. Its appearance in Punch *aroused strong emotions in the British public and helped to thwart Lord Canning's appeals for humane treatment for the Sepoy rebels. It also doubled* Punch's *circulation. (John Tenniel, 1857)*

Shirley Brooks interrupts to ask what planet you would see if you bent down and put your head between your legs. "*Uranus!*" he shouts, to the general hilarity. Everyone teases Silver for being "spoony" around Valentine's Day. Brooks pockets the leftover dessert for his children, explaining that Bradbury and Evans must pay for it whether it is eaten or not, so why let it go to waste? Silver, seeing his idol so occupied, surreptitiously pinches a few cigars, noting that as a writer-of-all-work he should have the same perquisites as a maid-of-all-work.

Leigh discourses on Mormonism and thinks plurality of wives not a bad idea, to much ribald comment from the group. "Aha!" says Thackeray, "I can tell your horrid thoughts!"

The new income tax infuriates all. The tax collectors have had the infernal gall to demand that Bradbury and Evans supply the names of the *Punch* writers, who enjoyed considerable freedom of expression since all of the articles in the magazine were printed unsigned. "We're not your *servants*!" says Tom Taylor, "nor are we in your *employ*!"

Down with the income tax, cries everyone. Brooks suggests that the proprietors place a large box of money in the office, from which the Punchites may draw when they need it, thus avoiding the tax. He points out that Palmerston, Brougham, Peel, and company appear in the magazine so frequently that they too can be considered as "working for *Punch*" and should be taxed for it. And how about those perennial writers to the editor of the *Times* who call themselves "Vindex" or "Constant Reader"? Will the *Times* have to tell the tax man their real names and addresses too? To add insult to injury, the Bouverie Street tax collector is a greengrocer! "Beast!" says Brooks.

Bradbury tells of the young Quakeress, forced to sit on a gentleman's knee in a crowded omnibus. "Friend, I fear I've given thee a stiff member!" Loud laughter. Taylor attacks Lemon for saying that under certain conditions working men should have the right to unite. Bradbury falls asleep on the table. Mayhew and Brooks, drunk, fall down the stairs. They struggle to their feet and gravely shake hands.

There is much amusement at the news that the actor, Macready, who is in his sixties, has taken a twenty-three-year-old wife.* "Ode to St. Cecilia—ascend ye nine times," says Brooks. "Once more into the breach!" Evans and Silver shout in unison. Lemon, imitating Macready's nasal voice and florid acting style, mouths a passionate love speech. Thackeray announces that he plans to run over to Paris when he finishes his current book** to "take a tour of the *in*continent," he says. There is a certain ex-governess over there. Brooks chimes in with his Vienna experiences and tells of how the waiter suggested that he and his lady friend dine in a private room where they will be "more comfortable."

The company agree that they all find *The Mill on the Floss* dreary and immoral. Scott is a different story. "Like a trumpet call," says Brooks, "stirs the blood." "But I don't *want* my blood stirred," says Thackeray.

Lemon tells of the man who dreamt he saw the letters *S* and *D* tattooed on his wife's buttocks. He buys a lottery ticket with *SD* on it but loses because he forgot the *O* in the middle.

Leigh says it's best to marry a rich woman who brings with her "something more than an aperture in her person." Lemon tells of a man offering a toast "to the place from which we came—and here's the messenger who would fetch us there," exposing himself.

Evans is reminded of a woman who had her bladder removed and Thackeray quickly improvises:

*William Charles Macready (1793–1873) was famous for Shakespearean roles. He managed the Covent Garden Theatre from 1837 to 1839 and the Drury Lane from 1841 to 1843. Tennyson wrote a sonnet on his retirement from the stage in 1851.

**This must have been either *The Virginians* or *Philip*.

19

There was a poor lady grown sadder,
By having disease of the bladder,
They put her to bed
And sewed it with thread,
And then the chirurgeon had her!

All laugh except Silver, who finds "hardly funny the brutal chirurgeon taking a mean advantage of her helplessness."

Charles Keene tells a long, involved joke that ends in a catch line that is not funny at all, and the others laugh politely. George du Maurier wants less serious talk and more about good-looking women. Brooks quotes an article in *Blackwood's* which says that Ruskin would make a safe tutor in a school for young ladies. Silver says it isn't fair, hitting a man in his privates, a foul blow. Du Maurier tells of Ruskin lashing his penis to a toothbrush. Everyone jokes about Ruskin's impotence. "Prix Fixe," says Brooks.

Jokes over and conversation stops. It is time to decide on the big cut. Tenniel, who will have to execute it (du Maurier does only the "socials"), pricks up his ears. Du Maurier settles back with a handkerchief over his face. Keene looks morosely into his glass. It is the writers' moment. The artists rarely contribute ideas or captions. The whole group is indignant over the *Trent* affair.* There is talk of war. Leigh is against it, but Lemon and Thackeray maintain that British ships are British soil. "If we submit," says Thackeray, "the Yankees will get the notion that British bottoms are made to be kicked."

Lemon suggests a new "Battle of Bull Run," showing a Yankee running away from John Bull, who is preparing to gore him. Leigh is against a cartoon that is an incitement. Thackeray thinks the nation's attitude is admirably calm after having had its arse kicked. He said so to a cabinet minister on Monday. ("Did you say 'arse kicked' to the Minister?" asks Keene.) Lemon suggests "Waiting the Answer" with a firm but not angrily belligerent John Bull. There is general applause and unanimous approval. Silver notes in his diary that fighting cuts always seem to raise circulation. The following week, "Waiting the Answer" will push sales two thousand above usual.

In excerpting the above bits and pieces, I have made it seem that the conversation took place at a single sitting. In fact, the quotations are from many sessions, a string of similar dinners covering a great many years.

*During the American Civil War, Union sailors had forcibly boarded the British ship *Trent* and arrested two Confederate commissioners.

20

Leech was dead when du Maurier became a regular Table member. I have tried to show the spirit of the Table talk rather than its actual content, which rarely varied. There was the eternal quarrel between the right- and left-wing factions of the staff, the rude jokes, the bad puns, the antics of the prima donnas, the sniggering, the wonderful high comedy, and the serious devotion to the big political cut. The discussion ranged from Swedenborgianism to spiritualism, from Dickens to Ibsen, from the Puseyites to the socialists, and always back to wine, women, and good times.

This was the Table to which Davis so casually invited me to lunch, to join the heirs of the Parliament of Wits and Conclave of Humorists. Meeting for drinks in the editor's office was traditional too, a libation before lunch to lubricate the discussion. I had had two during my interview, Davis seeing to it that my glass was always full. I now found myself balancing a third and remembering Brooks and Ponny Mayhew falling down the stairs. Richard Price, sensing that I felt very much a stranger, stationed himself near my left elbow and made sure that I met everybody and was included in the conversation. At last Davis called the group to attention and herded us down the corridor and into the dining area.

The banquet hall in the *Punch* office is not as distinguished as the one in the old Bradbury and Evans premises at 11 Bouverie Street. The portraits and marble and plaster busts of former *Punch* editors and notables have been replaced by photographs and a few outstanding cartoons. The portrait of Sir John Tenniel is now in the entry hall of the *Punch* offices. Sir Owen Seaman is in the corridor. Ponny Mayhew and Sir Francis Burnand are in the editor's office. The only vestige of past grandeur left in the dining room is the portrait of Mark Lemon, done by his friend Fred Chester, which hangs at the head of the Table.

I had half expected the Table to be a magnificent museum piece, but I was to be disappointed. The historic board was simply an inexpensive but sturdily built item of Victorian office furniture in ordinary deal, not mahogany, not an antique nor even of artistic design. The first proprietors were not extravagant with office furnishings, although they did not stint when it came to food and wine. The members' initials looked surprisingly fresh and new, probably the result of frequent cleaning and waxing. The successors of Lemon, Brooks, and Thackeray trooped in and headed for their usual places as waiters bustled about filling glasses.

Davis handed me into the seat at his right, and we sat down to the first of the traditional five courses, a pâté accompanied by liberal pourings of white wine. I picked up my napkin and saw that the placemat under my dish was also a printed chart of the Table, matching the carved initials

AUTHORS' MISERIES. No. VI.

Old Gentleman. Miss Wiggets. Two Authors.

Old Gentleman. "I AM SORRY TO SEE YOU OCCUPIED, MY DEAR MISS WIGGETS, WITH THAT TRIVIAL PAPER 'PUNCH.' A RAILWAY IS NOT A PLACE, IN MY OPINION, FOR JOKES. I NEVER JOKE—NEVER."

Miss W. "SO I SHOULD THINK, SIR."

Old Gentleman. "AND BESIDES, ARE YOU AWARE WHO ARE THE CONDUCTORS OF THAT PAPER, AND THAT THEY ARE CHARTISTS, DEISTS, ATHEISTS, ANARCHISTS, AND SOCIALISTS, TO A MAN! I HAVE IT FROM THE BEST AUTHORITY, THAT THEY MEET TOGETHER ONCE A WEEK IN A TAVERN IN SAINT GILES'S, WHERE THEY CONCOCT THEIR INFAMOUS PRINT. THE CHIEF PART OF THEIR INCOME IS DERIVED FROM THREATENING LETTERS WHICH THEY SEND TO THE NOBILITY AND GENTRY. THE PRINCIPAL WRITER IS A RETURNED CONVICT. TWO HAVE BEEN TRIED AT THE OLD BAILEY; AND THEIR ARTIST—AS FOR THEIR ARTIST . . . .

Guard. "SWIN-DUN! STA-TION!" [*Exeunt two Authors.*

The Punch artists loved to tease their friends by using them for cartoon models. Above, the tall gentleman reading the Sunday Times is Thackeray. His small companion is Douglas Jerrold. Below, the whiskered swell trying to undertip the waiter is Punch's drama critic, Henry Silver. (Above, John Leech, 1848; below, Charles Keene, 1859)

SCARCELY A DELICATE WAY OF PUTTING IT.

Swell Bagman. "*Now, what's the smallest sum I can give you without being considered mean!*"

with their famous owners. Lifting a corner of my mat, I saw Sir John Tenniel's hieroglyphic, and near it, to my surprise, a small neat AP, my own initials.

"There's a good omen," I said to Basil Boothroyd, my right-hand neighbor. "Whose are they?"

Boothroyd, a slim, white-haired man with a Ronald Colman moustache, looked down at the initials. "Anthony Powell," he said. "He used to do our book page. Have you heard of him? I don't know how well known he is in America."

I assured him that Powell·was very well known there and that I had read and enjoyed all of his novels.

"It's fucking well not!" said Davis behind my left ear, his voice quivering with outrage. "It's Princess Anne!"

"Nonsense!" Boothroyd said haughtily, his eyebrows going up and his expression indicating that he, Boothroyd, had been writing high comedy for *Punch* while the editor was scrambling around the streets of Hanover cadging chocolate bars. "It is Powell."

I shrank helplessly in my chair. On my left Davis was frowning, disgusted that he, the first editor in the magazine's history to lure a royal princess to the Table, was surrounded by people so obtuse that they didn't know or care where she had sat. On my right, Boothroyd, a distinguished writer, was aware that at this Table, at least, an author of Powell's stripe was, in order of precedence, considerably higher than an equestrienne princess. On the other hand, he was handicapped, by having collaborated on a book with Prince Philip, and, unlike Davis, by being a frequent visitor to Buckingham Palace. He could not say anything even mildly sarcastic about the Royal Family's presence at the *Punch* lunches.

Between them, I, the American, heartily wished I hadn't brought it up. A glance at the placemat had shown me that Davis was right and Boothroyd wrong. Fortunately, the ever-vigilant Price, who had shared the book page with Powell in the fifties, pointed this out, and the bitter quarrel instantly subsided as though it had never begun. Boothroyd and Davis began to chat amiably across me. Apparently this sort of violent controversy is usual at the Table, and grudges are never borne.

In the respite that followed, the Punchites devoted themselves to their soup and I had an opportunity to examine the Table members. The editor sat at the head and Mr. Caudery at the foot, a symbolic arrangement followed since the 1880s to show that during the editorial meal the creative head was in full charge, the businessmen taking a subordinate role, although at all other times they were the masters. On Davis's left sat Alan Coren, his deputy. In the remaining places were Michael Heath, the cartoonist; Sally Vincent, a frequent *Punch* contributor but a guest, not a

Table member; and Michael ffolkes. Next to ffolkes was Sheridan Morley, drama critic, who also hosts a television talk show and reviews plays for the *Times*. Morley is a large, robust man and the son of the actor Robert Morley, who contributes restaurant articles and reminiscences to *Punch*. It is a *Punch* family joke to pretend that Sheridan has a loud, booming voice that can be heard for miles, although, in fact, like most big-chested men he rumbles sonorously but does not bellow. There is much good-natured banter about Morley's voice around the Table. ''See if you can break this!'' Coren shouts, holding up his wine glass and shaking with laughter. Coren, a comparatively small man, is actually noisier than Morley, but everyone ignores this because the joke is a favorite one.

Beyond Morley is Miles Kington, assistant editor, jazz critic, and musician; William Hewison and Geoffrey Dickinson, art editors; Norman Mansbridge; David Langdon; Ian Lloyd; and R. G. G. Price. Facing me was Barry Took, a BBC writer-producer formerly associated with the Monte Python programs, who was present at the Table that afternoon because Davis had decided to hire him as permanent film and television critic.

With the arrival of a saddle of lamb and numerous bottles of claret, the Table settled down to its normal weekly procedure, a pitched battle between editor and staff, punctuated by side skirmishes between small groups of members and contributors. Davis, in his capacity as idea man, tendered proposal after proposal for future issues, each of which was angrily shouted down by his colleagues. Counterproposals flew up the Table, which Davis put down with lordly disdain.

''They'll stick in his mind,'' Price told me later. ''In two weeks' time he'll propose an idea that someone else proposed today, and he'll never realize it isn't his own. It will be accepted and he'll go to press thinking he was the originator of it and wondering why he doesn't get more help from his staff.''

''They all complain about him bitterly,'' another staffer said. ''In the office no one has a good word to say for him, but let anyone outside of *Punch* criticize him and they jump to his defense and say he's the best editor we've ever had.''

By the time the main course was cleared away and replaced by a dessert, cheese, and yet another wine, the intensity of the discussion had reached an almost unbelievable high. Davis suggested an issue on and by exiles: Britons who had left home to live in Ireland, the United States, or elsewhere to avoid taxes or for other reasons. They would explain why they had left and how they felt about it afterward. The idea was given lukewarm acceptance and earmarked for a future issue. (It appeared two months later as a double page of exile cartoons by David Langdon.)

AFTERNOON TEA.

STUDY OF A BASHFUL MAN, WHO HAS PRIVATELY TOLD AN AMUSING STORY TO THE HOST, AND HAS BEEN REQUESTED BY HIM TO REPEAT IT ALOUD FOR THE BENEFIT OF THE COMPANY. WE HAVE TRIED TO DEPICT THE WRETCHED INDIVIDUAL AT THE PRECISE MOMENT WHEN, HAVING MANAGED TO STAMMER THROUGH TWO-THIRDS OF HIS ANECDOTE (WHICH IS RATHER LONG), HE BECOMES CONSCIOUS, ALL OF A SUDDEN, THAT HE HAS COMPLETELY FORGOTTEN THE POINT.

George du Maurier, 1873

Davis, true to his reputation as icon smasher, suddenly changed the subject with a question. ''What would everyone think about changing the magazine's name? After all, *Punch* has Victorian connotations.'' There was a shocked silence, then a chorus of angry voices. It seemed to me, as an outsider, that he had no intention of doing anything of the kind. I felt that he was only trying to shake up the others, perhaps point out that he was, in fact, the boss; that in spite of his permitting absolute freedom of dissent, the last word was unquestionably his. Then suddenly, with another of his lightning about-faces, the editor turned to me and asked me to say a few words about my project.

It was like some sort of nightmare. I had not expected to be invited to lunch, much less to make a speech, and a speech, moreover, to an audience which only seconds before had been whipped to a fever pitch of outrage by my introducer. My mind was a total blank. As I struggled to my feet I became painfully aware that although it was early afternoon I had ingested an unaccustomed whiskey, two glasses of sherry, two of hock, three of claret, a sauterne, and two small brandies.

I thought of what a perfect situation it was for George du Maurier and how he would have immortalized it, portraying me as a wretched, unhappy-looking little man, like the bashful unfortunate in ''Afternoon

Tea,'' and the Punchites regarding me with polite loathing across the splendid napery.

AUTHOR, WHOSE PREVIOUS EFFORTS HAVE FAILED TO REVOLUTIONIZE THE LITERARY WORLD, AND WHO HAS HAD THE MISFORTUNE TO TAKE A GLASS OF BRANDY TOO MANY, HAS BEEN ASKED TO ADDRESS A DISTINGUISHED COMPANY MUCH AKIN TO A ROYAL ACADEMY OF SUCCESSFUL HUMORISTS AND FINDS THAT HE CANNOT THINK OF ANYTHING TO SAY.

A perfect subject for the "Authors' Miseries" series. I looked unhappily around the Table.

"How much was your advance?" Alan Coren yelled at the top of his lungs.

The atmosphere cleared. Mr. Caudery and Price smiled at me. They were, after all, responsible for my being there. The fog left my brain and I knew exactly what to say to the Parliament of Wits. I thanked them for their kindness, mentioned my book, and got off stage as quickly as possible. Price and Caudery nodded in approval. Ten seconds after I had resumed my seat the staff was happily engaged in a brand new all-out attack on the editor.

The lunch ended at four. I lurched, bleary eyed, back to the library, where a sympathetic Susan Jeffreys, who had seen it all before, brought me some Nescafé in a chipped mug. I scribbled furiously for an hour and a half so I wouldn't forget a single word.

In time I became a fixture in the library, which also serves as a kind of social center for blocked writers and cartoonists. The Punchites, now accustomed to my silent presence, surrounded by ancient books and documents, ignored me except when I had a question. Then they treated me with courtesy and interest, involving themselves in the quality of my project, which would, after all, reflect on them. Susan, the librarian, who resembles one of those dark-haired, long-limbed beauties painted by and married to the Pre-Raphaelites, rushed back and forth, waving away my requests for standard works and bringing out long-forgotten clippings and photographs, venerable cartoons, and rarities of all kinds.

The following Wednesday, Davis popped into the library in his usual headlong fashion and said that since I would only be at *Punch* for two more weeks why didn't I come and eat with them again. Susan's eyes widened. She stared at me in awe.

"Nobody has ever been invited *twice* before," she said in a hushed voice.

"Yes," said Price, who had been sipping a library Nescafé while waiting for the summons to drinks on the editor. "Yes, someone has. The Prime Minister."

"But not twice *running*," Susan said. "Not twice *concurrently*."

I, the scholar, did not see fit to remind them of Sir Joseph Paxton and walked down the corridor with Price. This time, no longer a stranger, I was seated down the Table equidistant from the editor and the chairman. Davis, with his brusque manner and his air of never really having enough time to bother with minor matters, had gone to a great deal of trouble to make me feel at home and to ease my way toward completion of my research. The Punchites had been kind, but he had set the standard. It was easy to make fun of him, but suddenly I was very grateful to him. He seemed to go out of his way to set himself up as a target, but like the Punchites, I felt that outside the office I would defend him against criticism. Except, of course, my own.

The guest of honor this time was Lord Mancroft, a former chairman of the Cunard Lines and a legislator who won fame for putting across one of those peculiarly British bills, impossible to explain to people born anywhere else in the world, giving a man permission to marry his sister-in-law if he chooses to do so. It took centuries to win the right to marry the sister of one's *deceased* wife. Now, thanks to Mancroft, any Briton may marry the sister of his living but divorced ex-wife. Americans and Europeans may consider this a storm in a teacup, but to the English it was a signal breakthrough. The other guests were art critic and *Harpers-Queen* stalwart Bevis Hillier and *Private Eye* staffer Barry Fantoni, a favorite Alan Coren target ("Barry Fantoni looks like a *muppet*!").

This time, like any good Punchite, I was able to control my alcohol intake since I knew exactly what to expect. When I got back to the library, Susan was proud of me, and Albert Barnes was waiting patiently for my return.

After half a century as a *Punch* employee, Albert Barnes probably knows more about the magazine than any other living person, with the exception of his old supervisor Maurice Grodin, who is retired and lives in Hertfordshire. Albert's function is loosely summed up as "maintenance."

"You should see his 'surgery'," Susan said. Albert holds a morning clinic to which the girls can bring their ailing lamps, toasters, phonographs, electric curlers, or whatever, for his diagnosis. The proprietors would never dream of interfering with this small side business on company time. After all, Albert is *von und zu Punch*. Nothing more need be said.

In 1929 sixteen-year-old Albert was hired as tea boy. He also did odd jobs, as required, and carried messages. The messages were important, because they brought with them an important source of supplementary income—tips. The canny Albert avoided routine messages, holding out for the big ones, and in time, using the lever of seniority, he was awarded the prize. He was assigned to deliver proofs for correction to the editor, Sir Owen Seaman, and to A. P. Herbert and E. V. Knox (''Evoe''). Proofs were delivered Sunday and their delivery was a double job because the messenger had to go back on Monday to pick up the corrected copy and take it to the printers.

Rain, snow, hail, or sleet, Albert pedaled off to Whitehall Court to Sir Owen's, then to Herbert's houseboat in the Thames, and then off to make the long trek to Hampstead to Knox. The Seaman cook had standing orders to bring him into the kitchen and fortify him with a nice hot cup of tea. Welcome as that may have been, there was never any cash to supplement it, although Seaman always descended to the kitchen to thank Albert in person. The kindly Knox was good for a shilling, and Herbert for a sixpence.

''Those were the days,'' Albert said to me, sighing. In time he was promoted from the tea wagon to an apprenticeship in the composing room. There a boy could swell his pay packet with ''pars,'' or paragraphs. These were the small items used as fillers when a column was too short or had to be made to fit a page with an advertisement on it. The apprentices collected misspellings, funny newsbreaks, and spoonerisms, some from other papers and some submitted by readers. If a par was used, the finder got five shillings.

''Nowadays isn't like the old days,'' Albert said. ''It was changing the cover that did it.'' He nodded sadly. ''Everyone used to get a free copy. We'd keep them until we had a volume, and then we'd get a half-price discount at the binders. Can't do it now. The paper's printed at Bletchley. Sir Owen was the best editor I ever saw. A real gentleman. Meticulous about the quality of the paper. Muggeridge, now, I didn't see it myself, but they say he got in at nine and was gone by five minutes after, off to do some television program.''

A splendid tribute for Seaman, taking into account that Albert has worked in close proximity with seven of the magazine's eleven editors. A stern indictment of Muggeridge who was, after all, the culprit who changed the covers.

''And what do you think of the present editor?'' I asked. Susan frowned at me behind Albert's back. It was an unfair question. He looked at me shrewdly and lowered his voice as though to tell a secret.

''Watch out on make-up day,'' he said. ''Corridor's a dangerous madhouse. Man can be run down, what with doors flying open and people charging in and out.''

Harold Pinter could not have phrased it better. It was obvious that the interview was at an end. We shook hands and Albert gravely refused the Havana cigar that I had brought with me from the Table, in the manner of

Henry Silver, to help me concentrate. Urging me to call his old friend and chief Maurice Grodin for earlier memories, Albert returned to his "surgery."

Since I had already broken some sort of record by lunching at the Table twice in a row, I determined to refuse a third invitation. After all, traditions are traditions. I need not have worried. I was not invited a third time. Instead, I offered to take Susan to lunch because she had been so helpful.

"Well," she said, "*We* were going to ask *you*."

"Who is we?"

"The Alternate *Punch* Table."

"What is the Alternate *Punch* Table?"

If I had thought being asked to the Table was an honor, I had no idea of the quality of the Alternate, a club far more exclusive and considerably more discriminating than even the venerable original.

Founded about two years ago by the girls of *Punch*, the Alternate is their reply in kind to their employers, who snobbishly exclude them from the Wednesday lunches. In any event, there is very little for them to do on Wednesdays, since the editorial meal lasts from noon until four. They have selected a table in the secretaries' room, put their initials on it in Lettrapress, and enjoy their own conviviality over sandwiches and Algerian plonk.

Membership in the Alternate is restricted to three categories: first, any employee, regardless of sex, who is excluded by reason of rank or inexperience from the Table; second, any employee fired by William Davis; third, anyone else they feel like inviting. Guests are rare. Somehow the girls' sympathy had been aroused when the secret *Punch* grapevine, mysterious as jungle drums, had informed them that I would not be invited to an unprecedented third editorial luncheon. This perfectly natural exclusion had made me eligible for the Alternate.

The day was a special one, and it turned out that we were not to eat at the Alternate Table after all but at the King's Head, a pub near Camden Passage. The members of the Alternate were turning out in a show of loyalty to Jeremy Kingston, novelist and playwright, who had been fired by Davis after ten years as *Punch* drama critic. The King's Head was a lunchtime theater pub, and a Kingston one-actor, *Oedipus at the Crossroads*, was being shown there for the first time.

As soon as the editors were safely tucked away behind the closed doors of the banquet room, our group—Caroline Cook, Davis's secretary; Olivia Grogono, Coren's secretary; Susan; Philip Hood, illustrator and layout artist; and Jonathan Sale, Davis's assistant—piled into a taxi and headed north.

29

The Punchites at play. The wicketkeeper is, of course, Mr. Punch. Thackeray is the batter and Percival Leigh the bowler. Mark Lemon and Gilbert à Beckett are playing battledore and shuttle-cock. Shirley Brooks, Ponny Mayhew, and Tom Taylor are playing leapfrog. Tenniel is in the background drawing Mr. Punch in armor. Douglas Jerrold is playing skittles, the pins being the tsar of Russia and other European political figures. John Leech is riding a hobbyhorse. In front of the tent, beaming proudly at their crew of geniuses, are the proprietors, William Bradbury in a black top hat and the rotund "Pater" Evans. (John Tenniel, 1854)

Our support was not needed, for the play was admirably written and acted. We ate hamburgers washed down with brown ale, served by intense young women in black sweaters, boots, and long cotton skirts. I had a marvelous time.

On the way back in the taxi there was much laughter and gossip about the enormities perpetrated by Davis who, they said, had once fired a secretary on a railway platform en route to an office outing. ("I don't think he really meant it," Susan said, "but she took him seriously and never came back.") A great deal of advice was offered about where I might buy gifts cheaply to take home to America. Everyone was aware that my *Punch* days were numbered, and *Punch* people are always saddened by change of any kind. It didn't matter to them whether my departure was of my own choosing or whether I was fired by Davis. They had gotten used to me.

Richard Price, who usually works at home in the country, came up to London my last week to have a farewell lunch with me at the Cheshire Cheese. We talked about Davis. "I knew him the minute I saw him," he said. "I was a schoolmaster, you know. He's the boy who always puts his hand up to answer the question before he knows what the question is. He has to be there ahead of everyone else. He was very kind to me, you know. When my wife died he asked me to take on a full-time job on the paper, not because *Punch* had any special need for more of my services, but because he thought it might help me to keep busy." He paused and thought for a moment. "He makes mistakes," he said, "but he is the only *Punch* editor I have ever known who was able to admit that he was wrong about anything."

On my last morning, Mr. Caudery came into the library. He glanced at me and cleared his throat. "I wonder if you would like to have one of these," he said, looking at me nervously as though he feared some embarrassing demonstration of effusive gratitude on my part. He was holding a leather-bound *Punch* desk diary for 1978.

"It's my own project," he said. The diary, which featured two cartoons to each page, was a creative editorial effort on his part, a once-a-year departure from balance sheets and budgets. "See what they've done," he continued. "I didn't have the time to supervise them properly this year, and it slipped through." He indicated with his finger a line on a page headed "International Public Holidays 1978." It showed different holidays in some months for the United Kingdom and for Scotland.

He looked at me anxiously, to see if I saw the full enormity of the error, which at first I did not. And then it came to me. Of course, Scotland is *part* of the United Kingdom. It should have said England and Wales, or something else, but not United Kingdom. He raised an eyebrow to indicate that we two, men of the world, knew what a state things had come to. An imperfection in a *Punch* publication! Probably the first in his three decades of association with the paper.

"Maybe there's a Scottish Nationalist in the composing room," I said.

"Very possibly." He looked pleased.

I thanked him for the book, pointing out that in my great grandchildren's time it would undoubtedly be a great rarity because of its flaw. We shook hands and said good-bye. In a few months he would be retiring, after first representing *Punch* at a convention in Canada, but he would still have the right to lunch at the Table every Wednesday as long as he lived.

I packed my briefcase and left Tudor Street for the Chancery Lane tube station. The following day, Sunday October 2, a stewardess on my British Airways flight to New York brought me a London *Times*. I read that Davis had been replaced by Alan Coren and moved to another editorial post in the United Newspapers conglomerate.

Susan Hood wrote in October:

> I am sorry I couldn't tell you before you left. The news was to have been kept quiet for a while longer but on Friday at about 5:30 it was decided that the world was ready. We are all very pleased. I think it will make a great deal of difference to *Punch*. Alan, as well as being a very funny writer, has a grasp of the problems of type setting, printing, etc. He is also well informed on the history of *Punch* without being overwhelmed by it. He likes to have things planned in advance and done well. The art department will have longer to prepare rag pages and parodies and the writers won't have to produce stuff at the last minute as work will be commissioned in advance. Bill was under the illusion that the readers wanted the magazine to be topical. Alan realizes that they want it to be funny. It is a great shame that you are not here at the moment as everyone is feeling quite excited at the prospect of having an editor who is actually in the same country as his staff.
>
> I think that brings you up to date with recent events. I will let you know if there are any other changes, palace plots, massacres, etc., but we oracles have our work cut out for us at the moment and the library is knee-deep in entrails.

Which is a good time to leave it and start on Mark Lemon.

The origin of *Punch* is shrouded in mystery. The founding Punchites were artists and craftsmen, consequently their records-keeping was primitive at best. Business organization and office procedures were practically nonexistent until Bradbury and Evans came into the picture in 1843. A great many memoirs and chronicles have been written about the paper's beginnings and its eccentric star performers, but nobody seems to be quite sure about the person responsible for getting the project under way.

On the other hand, everyone, however remotely concerned, has been willing to offer an opinion and grab for a little of the credit. To add to the confusion, as soon as the paper became an established success, the founders' children got into the act, publishing furiously, each insisting that his own father was the man-with-a-dream who first said, ''Let's start a new comic weekly and call it *Punch*.''

Historians can only try to gather together the few known facts, place them in the context of the period, and try to arrive at a rational supposition. Taking into account the journalistic climate of the times, it is logical to assume that the idea of starting *Punch* may have occurred to a number of serious writers and editors simultaneously, a concept that seems to have escaped some *Punch* chroniclers and the descendents of the first proprietors.

One thing is certain: The subtitle *The London Charivari* admits unashamedly that *Punch* was modeled on the successful and respected Paris paper of that name. Charles Philipon's *La Charivari* stood alone in a vast swampland of scurrilous, semipornographic, crudely drawn and badly written periodicals. It proved that a paper could exist without ribaldry. It maintained a high standard of clever and devastating political satire. It was also funny without having to rely on the vulgarity that characterized so much of the so-called humor of the period.

Philipon was a brilliant, fiercely Republican editor whose journals were much applauded on both sides of the Channel. In 1830 he had founded *La Caricature*, a weekly paper featuring full-page engravings that lampooned social foibles and the misconduct of public figures. In those days political criticism was a dangerous sport in France. Almost from the day his first issue appeared, Philipon was in trouble, hauled endlessly in and out of court. The most famous lawsuit against him was the result of a series of drawings showing the bulbous King Louis Philippe gradually turning into a huge pear, a play on the French word *poire*, which also means an imbecile. *La Caricature* was finally suspended from publication for portraying His Majesty as Gargantua. Philipon was sentenced to six months in prison. He had already begun a new paper, *La Charivari*, which embodied all the features of *La Caricature* on a daily rather than a weekly basis. At the time he was twenty-four years old.

Philipon's persecutions were followed sympathetically by his English counterparts, who could and did print anything they pleased with little fear of reprisal. Prince Albert would probably have welcomed Philipon's *poire* metaphor over some of the liberties that were taken with him in *Punch*'s early years. It is interesting to note that in the 1840s and 1850s two of the political figures most cruelly ridiculed in John Leech's cartoons were Benjamin Disraeli and Lord John Russell, whose policies *Punch* frequently disapproved of. Yet both men, instead of seeking the revenge that power assured them, treated Leech with great kindness. Russell helped him get his son into Charterhouse, and Disraeli secured a pension for his widow after his death. No Punchite, however outspoken, ever faced the remotest danger of prison, except for debt. Even the famous British sense of fair play boggled at that.

Philipon was a hero to British journalists. He was also fortunate in his ability to attract talented help. Much of the success of his papers was due to the work of two brilliant artists, Honoré Daumier and Gustave Doré. It is not surprising that London editors dreamed of founding a paper like *La Charivari*. The difficulty for historians is not in finding a man who said, "Let's start a London *Charivari*," but in finding one who didn't.

The founders of *Punch* were aware of the esteem in which *La Charivari* was held when they decided to model their paper after it, even to the extent of borrowing its name as a subtitle. They were respectable men. They were not *Bohemian*, a term that at that time had not yet achieved the panache it was later to enjoy. *Bohemian* was a denigratory term

"WELL, JACK! HERE'S GOOD NEWS FROM HOME. WE'RE TO HAVE A MEDAL."
"THAT'S VERY KIND. MAYBE ONE OF THESE DAYS WE'LL HAVE A COAT TO STICK IT ON?"

Punch was opposed to the Crimean War and gave only grudging approval to the Light Brigade, possibly because Tennyson's poem was published in another paper. The Punchites preferred to dwell on the appalling mismanagement and the command ineptitude that characterized the war. (John Leech, 1855)

applied to literary and artistic riffraff. True, Ebenezer Landells, the engraver, and Joseph Last, the printer, had been associated with the *Town*, a ribald comic paper, but that was a part of the past, and one of which neither was proud.

The early Punchites prided themselves on the fact that their paper was run by gentlemen who sat their horses well, who belonged to clubs and hunted foxes and would not have been out of place in any drawing room in England. When they weren't snubbing outsiders (or deploring other people's snobbery), they snubbed each other. Henry Mayhew and Gilbert à Beckett, who had been at Westminster, looked down their noses at Leech and Thackeray, who had gone to Charterhouse. They, in turn, felt superior to Mark Lemon, who had studied at Cheam. In Silver's diary Thackeray claimed that Douglas Jerrold, who had not attended a public school, ''ate peas with his knife.'' When F. C. Burnand, an Etonian, joined the staff, he was regarded with suspicion at first by one and all. It was arrant snobbery, yet it may have been this snobbery that kept *Punch*'s standards high for such a long time.

The earliest reliable documentary evidence of *Punch*'s beginnings consists of two instruments: its prospectus, written in Mark Lemon's distinctive handwriting; and its articles of agreement drawn up by the lawyers, Mayhew, Johnston, and Mayhew of Carey Street. The elder Mayhew was the father of Henry Mayhew, at that time already a well-known comic writer and contributor to numerous periodicals, who had once tried unsuccessfully to start a *Charivari* imitation to be called *Cupid*.

The agreement, which still exists in the *Punch* archives, is signed by Mark Lemon, Henry Mayhew, Joseph Last, Joseph Stirling Coyne, and Ebenezer Landells, who thus became the first owners and operators of *Punch*. It divided the ownership of *Punch* into three parts. A third went to Last, who was to supply all printing services. A third went to Landells, who was responsible for engraving and also served as art editor and who contributed twenty-five pounds to the enterprise. The final third went jointly to Mark Lemon, Stirling Coyne, and Henry Mayhew, who were to be coeditors.

What coordinating force brought these men to the offices of Messrs. Mayhew and Company to sign the agreement is a mystery as yet unsolved. There are two perfectly plausible stories, and partisans have been quarreling about them for 138 years. In the first explanation, Last calls on his lawyers to ask if they know the address of young Henry Mayhew and whether or not he is available for employment. Receiving favorable replies to both questions, Last goes to see Mayhew and proposes a London *Charivari*. Mayhew is delighted and sends a note round to Mark Lemon advising him that he is bringing Last to Lemon's Newcastle Street house to discuss the project. The three draw up preliminary plans for *Punch*. At some time during the discussion, Last suggests that his good friend and colleague Ebenezer Landells be called in to take over the engraving chores.

The second story is very much like the first, except that it is Landells who thinks up the idea and brings it to Last, after which the two call on Mayhew and Lemon in turn. A great many words have been published supporting one or the other of these stories or any number of variations of them. M. H. Spielmann, in his *History of Punch* (1895), leans toward Landells as the founder. R. G. G. Price, the present *Punch* historian, does not take sides. The Last family and Sidney Blanchard are for Last. Joseph Hatton, a journalist friend of Lemon's, says the idea originated jointly with Lemon and Henry Mayhew. The Mayhew family says the idea originated with Mayhew who brought it to Last and Landells. The Jerrold family gives it all to Douglas Jerrold; the à Beckett family says the credit is Gilbert à Beckett's; and the Coyne family maintains that Stirling Coyne not only originated the magazine but also was responsible for suggesting the name *Punch*.

Everyone, however, agrees that a meeting did take place some time in early June 1841, at Mark Lemon's house on Newcastle Street, and that Lemon, Mayhew, and Last were present and Landells may or may not have been there. Other meetings were held at the house of the artist Joseph Allen and at a tavern in the Strand called the Edinburgh Castle. At the meetings were Lemon, Landells, Last, and Mayhew, the artists William Newman and Archibald Henning, Stirling Coyne, Douglas Jerrold, and others. Gilbert à Beckett, H. P. Grattan, and W. H. Wills were invited but were unable to attend. A list of potential contributors was drawn up at the meetings, and the prospectus was read aloud and some changes were proposed.

At one of the meetings, probably at Allen's house, the name *The Funny Dog* was chosen for the new paper, because "funny dogs have comic tails (tales)." Then, legend has it, someone made a jocular reference to Lemon's name, saying that *Punch* might be a good title for the magazine because "you can't have a good punch without lemon." This was universally applauded, and another member (Mayhew, according to his son Athol; or Coyne, according to *his* son) said, "A capital idea. We'll call it *Punch*."

Someone pointed out that a paper called *Penny Punch* had been published in the recent past, as well as a *Punchinello*, *Punch in Cambridge*, and *Punch in London* (edited by Douglas Jerrold). It was decided that the existence of these defunct periodicals did not bar the use of *Punch* as a title, and it was duly approved. Lemon had already begun to write "The Funny Dog" in the prospectus, getting as far as "The Fun—" which he now scratched out, substituting the new name. The funny dogs joke, a favorite of Lemon's (or possibly Mayhew's) was incorporated into the prospectus later in the form of a comic drawing of dogs dressed in bizarre costumes.

Thus the new venture was launched. Birket Foster, the landscape artist and water colorist, who was Landells's apprentice at the time, recalls the engraver striding into his workshop and saying, "Well, boys, the title for the new work is to be *Punch*." When he was gone, the apprentices decided that the title was a very stupid one, "little thinking what a great thing it was to become."

Up to this point in the narrative, I have bombarded the reader with a great many names, familiar to Victorians but long since forgotten. This is an excellent place to pause for a closer look at the men who brought *Punch* into existence.

Joseph William Last, friend and colleague of Ebenezer Landells, was one of the best-known printers in London. He was an experienced proprietor of periodical papers. He had been associated with Landells on the *Town*, and the two were working on a proposal for a new paper to be called *Cosmorama* when the idea of *Punch* came up. Last would later make a fortune by joining with Herbert Ingram in the production of the *Illustrated London News*. He seems to me to be the most logical candidate for *Punch* originator, being the only businessman in the group. He was probably the coordinating spirit who brought all the dreamers together and got the lawyers to prepare the agreement.

Last was one of the pioneers of the cylinder press, an innovation which reproduced woodcuts with greater fidelity than the older-style presses and which is credited with some of *Punch*'s success. His office, at which *Punch* was first printed, was located at 3 Crane Court. Last shared these premises with Ingram, who also launched his famous patent medicine, Parr's Life Pills, from that address. Ingram, who became a Member of Parliament, employed most of the Punchites on his papers at one time or another and later published the *Man in the Moon*, a *Punch* arch-rival. For a short period Mark Lemon was Ingram's secretary.

It was Last who bore the brunt of *Punch*'s early financial losses. He is said to have sunk as much as six hundred pounds into the project before he finally decided that the paper was a hopeless proposition. He sold his share to Landells, who thus became the majority proprietor.

Ebenezer Landells was a tall, handsome man who looked, according to existing portraits, like the late Errol Flynn. He had a strong North-umbrian accent that delighted his apprentices, who imitated him when he was away from the studio. Old Tooch-it-Oop was a favorite nickname his students had for him when he was out of earshot.

Landells had been a favorite pupil of the famous wood engraver Thomas Bewick and had enjoyed considerable success in London both as an engraver and as a newspaper proprietor. He was not as astute an investor as Last and was more inclined to speculate on projects that were risky, such as the London *Charivari*. It was characteristic of him that when Last pulled out of *Punch*, instead of following suit, Landells doubled his investment.

Landells had a small, volatile, highly talkative wife who was never backward about offering her opinions on any and all subjects. She called him Daddy, and it was as Daddy Landells or sometimes Daddy Long-Legs that he was known to his friends. Mrs. Landells was a source of great amusement to Douglas Jerrold, who later used her as the model for his highly successful "Mrs. Caudle" comic series in *Punch*.

Landells was a man of great energy, hardworking and artistically demanding. He had no patience with second-rate material. From the beginning it was he who insisted that *Punch* maintain high quality standards, while Last would have been happy to compromise in return for

"I BEG YOUR PARDON, MA'AM, BUT I THINK YOU DROPPED THIS?"

Initial-letter drawings were an important source of extra income for Punch's underpaid artists. The H above is a typical piece of Leech snobbery. Du Maurier has put his friend and art school classmate James McNeill Whistler in the Q. The A shows du Maurier and Charles Keene sketching each other. (Top, John Leech, 1855; middle, George du Maurier, 1860; bottom, George du Maurier, 1861)

higher profits. Mayhew might have sacrificed some literary quality in return for a strongly radical political stand, but Landells cared less for politics than he did for art.

At the time *Punch* was started, the position of the engraver was one of importance. Artists drew their illustrations directly on blocks of wood, which were then sent to the engraver, who engraved them to the best of his ability. Obviously, an artist's work, no matter how skillful, could be ruined by a clumsy engraver. A comparison of the preliminary sketches of Charles Keene and John Leech with the finished illustrations that appeared in *Punch* shows that in some cases small lines were lost entirely because the engravers simply could not reproduce them. The wood-block process began to die in 1892 and was replaced by the halftone process, which gave faster, better-quality reproduction.

Although Landells was one of the more respected members of his craft, Bradbury and Evans eased him out of *Punch* when they took over in 1842. This came as a surprise to Landells, who had been under the impression that the agreement of sale included the proviso that he would continue to do the engraving. With some bitterness, and perhaps with some justification, Landells always felt that the new proprietors had taken advantage of his inexperience in commercial matters. Bradbury and Evans further aggravated the situation by allowing a rumor to spread that the reason for Landells's departure was the inferior quality of his work. Mark Lemon, in his speech at *Punch*'s coming-of-age dinner in 1862, went out of his way to make a snide attack on Landells, claiming that the third issue of the paper was delayed, causing a circulation drop, because the engraver was late in carrying out his duties. Even if this were true, the accusation had no place at a festive occasion. In fact the delay was caused by John Leech, who had not sent in his drawing on time. Leech, who was present at the dinner (Landells was not), did not take the trouble to correct Lemon on this point.

When the paper's fortunes took an upturn after Bradbury and Evans took over its management, Jerrold was heard to remark that this was due to the departure of "that engraving Jonah." But his opinion did not prevent him from working for Landells again on the *Illuminated Magazine*, another Herbert Ingram enterprise. The disappointed engraver finally got his revenge by doing the artwork on *A Word with Punch*, a fierce and successful attack on the magazine and its people.*

A Word with Punch was a one-time *Punch* parody put out by Alfred Bunn (a theatrical and operatic manager who had been the butt of *Punch* jokes for six years) with the help of George Augustus Sala and Albert Smith. It made fun of all the principal Punchites. *Punch* did not reply and left Bunn alone thereafter—the only defeat of its kind in the magazine's history.

When Landells or Last or both of them sought out Henry Mayhew to draw up a list of contributors for their new paper, the choice was not a random one. Mayhew was famous in London as a brilliant writer of humor. He was a cheery, lovable man with (as his son Athol remembers) "an extraordinary mop of hair that badly wanted trimming." He had many friends and interests. When he was not writing, he dabbled in electricity, carrying out endless experiments in the hope that he would find the secret of producing artificial diamonds. He was constantly brimming with new ideas and projects. Unfortunately, he was painfully lazy about putting them down on paper or bringing them to any kind of fruition. Writing was drudgery for him, a problem that he solved by dictating to his patient wife Jane, who was Douglas Jerrold's daughter.

When he was only a boy, Mayhew ran away to sea as a midshipman on a tea clipper bound for India. With his friend and Westminster schoolmate Gilbert à Beckett, he had started a comic paper, *Cerberus*, paying a London printer three pounds to set it. À Beckett's father, like Mayhew's, was a solicitor. He read the paper and told the boys he had discovered more than forty actionable libels on the first page. The boys were unconcerned, but the printer was appalled. He pied the type and refused to put the paper out. The boys ran away and walked all the way from London to Edinburgh, where they hoped to join a theater company as resident playwright-actors. They were not hired, and returned home again as steerage passengers on a Scottish fishing boat.

After these adventures, Mayhew made an attempt to settle down and study law in his father's office, but he had neither the patience nor the ambition to succeed in the legal profession. In 1831, still only nineteen years of age, he joined up with à Beckett again on the weekly paper *Figaro in London*. He wrote several farces, one of which, *The Wandering Minstrel*, was a London hit in 1834.

He wrote his most important work, *London Labour and the London Poor*, in the period between 1851 and 1864. It was the first time any writer had attempted to show the miseries of slum dwellers in a realistic rather than fictionalized manner. Mayhew wandered around London collecting human flotsam: a blind bootlace seller, orphaned flower girls, a "cheap-John" (beggar), a pickpocket, crossing sweepers, a cesspool sewerman, and many more. He brought them to his house, where they were made to tell their stories in their own words to his wife and his brothers Augustus and Horace, who carefully took it all down. "If his lines had been cast in more serious places," Spielmann wrote in his *History of Punch*, "he might have been a sociologist, the equal of John Stuart Mill or Herbert Spencer."

When *Punch* was projected, Mayhew had already agreed to write for

Cosmorama, but he was so fired with enthusiasm for the London *Charivari* that he advised Last and Landells to drop the earlier project and concentrate all their resources on *Punch*. In the beginning, he was the paper's guiding spirit.

> Mayhew [made] his personality felt, for the character of the paper, instead of partaking of the acidulated, sardonic satire which was distinctive of Philipon's journal . . . took its tone from Mayhew's genial temperament and from the first became, or aimed at becoming, a budget of wit, fun and kindly humour, and of honest opposition based on fairness and justice.

It was Mayhew who recruited à Beckett, Jerrold, Lemon, Coyne, and the rest. It was he who suggested many of the original ideas for funny series and cartoons. Leech called him the "broad grin provider." In the first issue of *Punch* Mayhew contributed "A Conversation Between Two Hackney-Coach Horses," "On the Introduction of Pantomime into the English Language," and collaborated with F. G. Tomlins on "A Synopsis of Voting, Arranged According to the Categories of 'Cant'."

Mayhew suggested *Punch*'s first big money-maker, the 1841 Almanack, which was published at the end of that year. It was a collection of jokes and comic drawings, mostly the work of the artists H. G. Hine and Hablôt Browne (Dickens's illustrator, "Phiz"). The Almanack was enormously popular and raised circulation from somewhere between five and six thousand to ninety thousand for the week.

Mayhew wrote the Almanack with "H. P. Grattan" (Henry Plunkett). Some difficulty was experienced in the project because Grattan was serving a brief term in the Fleet Prison ("Her Majesty's Fleet") for debt. Debtors' prisons were considerably more comfortable than the other kind. The Fleet featured tennis courts and outside catering services for the gently born inmates. In order to work with Grattan, Mayhew, without asking permission of the authorities, simply moved into the prison and stayed there a week. They wrote thirty-five jokes a day, relaxing between work sessions by playing tennis.

Among the inmates of the Fleet was the gentle and beloved Dr. William Maginn, who contributed occasionally to *Punch* and *Blackwood's Magazine* (using the pseudonym "Ensign O'Doherty"). Maginn was Thackeray's model for Captain Shandon in *Pendennis*. He had founded *Fraser's Magazine* with Thomas Carlyle and Samuel Taylor Coleridge. Although he was in poor health, he helped Mayhew and Grattan with the Almanack to the best of his ability. He died the following year of consumption.

Another inmate was also helpful in a different way. Frederick Villebois was a reckless young spendthrift who had managed to run up two

The first page of the 1845 Almanack. The center drawing shows Daniel O'Connell toadying to the Roman Catholic hierarchy. In the lower right-hand corner is what is probably the most famous joke ever printed in the English language: "WORTHY OF ATTENTION. ADVICE TO PERSONS ABOUT TO MARRY,—Don't." Nobody knows why this joke was so loved by Victorians. It is still quoted by Englishmen today. (H. G. Hine, Kenny Meadows, and John Leech, 1845)

thousand pounds in debts. His angry father had put him away in the Fleet to cool his ardor and teach him a lesson in economy. However, Villebois was a gentleman and his father was not so furious as to require that his son live on prison rations. Huge hampers arrived daily, generously packed with dainty foods and fine wines, which Villebois shared with his hard-working literary friends.

Mayhew remained with *Punch* after Bradbury and Evans took over until 1845. He was cruelly disappointed when the new owners demoted him and relieved him of his coeditorship, creating for him the title of suggestor-in-chief, for which he was actually much better suited. He attributed his downgrading to a sellout by Lemon, who, according to him, had given over the paper's early political principles in an attempt to placate the upper middle class. The bitterness between the two men was exacerbated when Mayhew (who was always in debt although he made plenty of money) heard that Bradbury and Agnew were paying Lemon one thousand pounds a year, the highest salary of any editor in London. Reminiscing about *Punch*, Mayhew wrote:

> To me *Punch* was always a labour of love and certainly never proved a source of profit; for, after planning and arranging the entire work, selecting the whole of the old staff of contributors, and having edited it for the first six months of its career without having received a single farthing for my pains, it so happened when those who started it were obliged to sell their bantling to Bradbury & Evans, that on the payment of all the debts connected with the production of the work there remained a clear surplus of seven-and-sixpence to be divided among the three original proprietors of which the munificent sum of half a crown fell to my share.

In 1864, Mayhew tried to launch a paper in competition with *Punch*. Henry Silver wrote, ''M. L. has seen a prospectus of H. M.'s opposition *Punch*, *Joke Co. Ltd*. Vulgar and abusive.'' The venture was not a success. The improvident Mayhew was later to testify in bankruptcy court that he could have paid his debts if Lemon had honored an agreement with him to share the proceeds of jointly written plays.* Lemon did not comment on this. In the drawing by Linley Sambourne of the founding and current Punchites in the 1891 Jubilee issue, Mayhew and Stirling Coyne are pointedly omitted. Mayhew died in 1887 at the age of seventy-five.

*The plays were *The Ladies Club*, *Grandfather Whitehead*, and *Gwynneth Vaughan*. There is no evidence that Mayhew actually collaborated with Lemon on them. Another Lemon play, *The Gentleman in Black*, was adapted from a Mayhew story, ''Mr. Peter Punctilio.''

Joseph Stirling Coyne was a man of some importance in London journalism when he was offered the coeditorship of *Punch*. He was twenty-eight at the time of the meeting at the Edinburgh Castle and had been a successful playwright and founder of the Dramatic Authors' Society, in which he served as secretary. When he accepted the *Punch* job, he was drama editor of the *Sunday Times*. He was originally recruited by Mayhew, who had a great deal of respect for Coyne's abilities. The author of more than fifty plays, including the popular *Did You Ever Send Your Wife to Camberwell?* he was well able to support himself as a dramatist and editor, but the extra money from *Punch* was irresistible.

Coyne was a large, untidy man (Jerrold always called him "Filthy Lucre") and a hearty drinker, roaring with loud Irish humor. His appearance was imposing. His hair was prematurely gray (it later turned pure white) in contrast to a fierce black moustache. From the very first he was not a success at *Punch*. He wrote very little. Sir William Hardman said of him in his memoirs that "he had little to say, and what he said he said badly." He knew he was not liked by the other Punchites and that he was not pulling his weight as coeditor, but he still disliked being forced out when the magazine was sold. He stayed on as a contributor, but Lemon (who had no use for him and always referred to him as "Paddy") accused him of plagiarizing one of his "Puff Papers" from a Dublin periodical. Whether this accusation was true or not, Coyne promptly resigned from *Punch*, which, as Spielmann pointed out, "had brought him neither reputation nor pleasure, and only a hundred pounds in cash."

The fifth and last of the original signers of the *Punch* agreement was Mark Lemon, "Uncle Mark" to the other Punchites (he was thirty-one). The Dickens's children, with their hereditary flair for the descriptive phrase, called him "Uncle Porpoise." He was a huge, stout, shambling, bushy bearded man who looked like Sir John Falstaff and who had, indeed, had a moderate success touring England in that role in a version written by himself. Lemon was a notable child-pleaser, boisterous and bubbling over with avuncular fun. He was a member of the Dickens's set (though he was probably not, as Henry Silver suggested, "Dickens' oldest friend"). He frequently accompanied Dickens on his "London rambles," long walks through the poor districts of London, in search of usable local dialogue or color. They shared a passion for amateur theatricals, and he dramatized the Christmas story *The Haunted Man* at Dickens's request.

The two men quarreled when Lemon refused to publish a letter in which Dickens sought, for some reason, to explain to the world his own version of his tangled marital problems. In time he forgave Lemon, and

45

the two became friends again. Joseph Hatton, a journalist of the period, has described a typical party of Punchites at which Lemon played his usual role of jolly uncle.

> The crowning effort . . . was a general attempt to go heels over head upon haycocks in the orchard—a feat which vanquished the skill of the laughing host [Jerrold] and left a very stout and very responsible editor, upon his head, without power to retrieve his natural position. Again . . . the hearty host, including Mr. Charles Dickens, Mr. Maclise, Mr. Macready, and Mr. John Forster, indulged in a most active game of leap-frog, the backs being requested to turn in any obtrusive twopenny with the real zest of fourteen.

The stout editor upside down in the haycock was, of course, Mark Lemon.

R. G. G. Price says that Lemon was Jewish, and Spielmann refers to his "Jewish heritage." Nevertheless, there is no evidence to this effect. Testifying in court under oath, Lemon was asked by a cross-examiner if he was a Jew and replied that he was not. Parish records exist showing that both his parents and his grandparents were married in St. Marylebone's Church. Lemon himself was married at Holy Trinity in 1839 and his son Mark was christened at St. Paul's, Covent Garden. If there was a Jewish heritage, or if a conversion had taken place, it would have to have been a century or more before his association with *Punch*.

In Victorian days the implication of Jewishness was a denigratory one, meaning greed, sharp business practices, and tightfistedness, and Lemon's reluctance to turn loose any of *Punch*'s profits was proverbial among his colleagues. "I smell lots of tin thereabouts," Mayhew wrote, "but our Lemon requires a great deal of squeezing." In the 1840s, before the passage of the Jewish Relief Act, which gave Jews equal rights with other British subjects, *Jew* was a term of contempt. Even the liberal *Punch* (under Lemon's editorship) printed anti-Semitic articles and cartoons, although these were more in the spirit of tasteless racial humor than of race hatred.

Lemon's supposed Jewishness was used by *Punch*'s enemies to ridicule him and the magazine in the eyes of the public. In 1849 some verses appeared in *Chat* to the effect that "in hall the world [Lemon] looked unkimmon like a Jew" and

> His 'air 'ung in corkscrew curls,
> He had a heager look;
> His chin it vos a double vun,
> His nose it vos a hook.

" HA! CHRISTMAS!" shouted MR. PUNCH, upspringing from his nap. "Jolly Old CHRISTMAS, crowned with holly, and bearing the wassail bowl. Show him in. Show him in."

Keene liked to portray the stout, bearded Mark Lemon as Father Christmas and, sometimes, as John Bull. This drawing appeared in Punch *not long after Lemon's death, and served as a kind of memorial to him. (Charles Keene, 1871)*

The editor of *Chat* (and the probable author of the verses) was an old *Punch* antagonist, George Augustus Sala, who later became special correspondent to the *Telegraph* during the American Civil War. Lemon, who called him a ''graceless young whelp,'' had turned down some of Sala's work as being not good enough for *Punch*. ''Pater'' Evans said at a dinner that Sala would have had a seat at the Table ''if he had been a gentleman.'' Oddly enough, the *Jewish Chronicle*, writing about Lemon, said that he did not look Jewish at all.

Lemon had been at Cheam, which, at that time, was near the bottom of the school barrel. (A century and a half later Cheam would number among its old boys the Prince of Wales, Prince Philip, Lord Louis Mountbatten, and Randolph Churchill.) His cherished dream was to write for the stage, but like most young men without incomes who had families to support, he had to take any employment that was offered. For a while he contributed short pieces to *Bentley's Miscellany* using the name ''Tom Moody,'' but necessity forced him to become a clerk in a Kentish Town brewery. He stayed in that job for three years until the brewery went out of business in 1840.

Lemon then took over the management of his mother's hotel, the Shakespeare's Head in Wych Street, a favorite haunt of writers and artists. With his genial, coarse-grained wit he quickly made friends. Unfortunately, the tavern went bankrupt, too, and he was forced to turn to his pen again, writing farces, and not doing too badly at it. In the summer of 1841, he received a fateful message from one of the tavern habitués, his friend Henry Mayhew. Duly recorded in Henry Silver's diary, it read, "Come to town—here's a man with a notion for a comic paper and he has £2000 to lose!" The man was apparently Last, or possibly Landells (whose gamble was twenty-five pounds, not two thousand). The famous visit to Lemon at his Newcastle Street quarters followed soon after.

What happened next is another unsolved *Punch* mystery. Lemon was a literary dabbler, a hack playwright, a brewer's clerk, and a failed tavern-keeper. He was a stranger to Last and Landells. To Mayhew he was a public-house acquaintance. His management abilities were questionable. He was the son of people in the licensed victualing trade and thus, in spite of Cheam, not quite a gentleman in the sense that Mayhew, à Beckett, Thackeray, Bradbury, and Evans were gentlemen. Yet the original proprietors and the later buyers placed him in a responsible editorial post on a paper they hoped would be the equal of the celebrated *La Charivari*. A considerable amount of money was at stake. Landells was a perfectionist and Last was a smart businessman. Why Lemon? It was as though Harold Ross had decided to start the *New Yorker* and asked the bartender at the Algonquin Hotel to share the editorial duties with him.

Spielmann says that it was "his sound business capacity and character, in addition to his literary aptitude that induced Henry Mayhew and Landells to nominate him," which seems unlikely since his literary ability had not yet emerged and his business capacity had not saved the Shakespeare's Head. He was a convivial man, a kind soul, a good friend, and a hearty, Rabelaisian wit, but was that enough? Last and Landells, the financial team, must certainly have demanded something more than good-fellowship.

Either the force of his personality must have been more powerful than is indicated by historians, or his relatives were secret financial backers. The latter theory holds water in the light of subsequent events, when the new owners retained the services of the "pot-boy editor" and placed him in full charge at an astronomical salary. It is a known fact that when the paper was in its darkest days Lemon supported it with the proceeds of his farces. Although there is no record of it, there may have been earlier Lemon money in *Punch* as well as Landells and Last backing.

Whatever the reason for the choice of Lemon to run the magazine, it turned out to be a lucky one. Lemon was a natural editor. Although he had his bad qualities (one journalist called him a "mealy-mouthed sycophant" and another "one of the most accomplished humbugs of his time"), he had the knack of keeping his temperamental crew in order and extracting their best work from them. Jerrold called him the spoon with which the volatile ingredients that made up *Punch* were stirred into a smooth emulsion. He was a brilliant organizer with a flair for selecting just the right material for *Punch*.

Lemon knew he was a third-rate writer and wrote little. His comic verses, "Songs for the Sentimental," are not bad, but certainly not brilliant humor. They consisted of ordinary little poems with a supposed snapper in the last line. This one celebrates a young man declining to dance the polka.

> It may not be—at least not yet;
>   'Tis no slight cause that bids me own it;
> Think not my promise I'd forget,
>   But for a while I must postpone it.
>
> Think not I've ceased to love the whirl
>   Of giddy waltz or polka mazy;
> Nor that thy hair is out of curl
>   Nor that thy Edwin's getting lazy.
>
> Think not 'tis through some jealous qualms
>   That thus I'd have thee disappointed;
> Nor that a prettier rival's charms
>   Thy nasal organ have disjointed.
>
> Nay, teach not those sweet lips to pout,
>   Nor at my pleading make wry faces;
> Canst still thy faithful Edwin doubt?
>   Know then the truth: I've broke my braces!

Mark Lemon's Jest Book, written in 1864, was one of the unfunniest joke books ever written. He had more success with children's literature: His most popular book for the young, *The Enchanted Doll*, overmoralizes about the sickness of selfishness, although it was well-received by Victorian children. *Tinykins Transformations*, dedicated to his six grandchildren the year before he died, describes a series of possession trances, and presents the fairy Titania as an odd mixture of motherliness and sensuality.

Lemon's farces are, for the most part, unreadable today. Nevertheless, if it were not for them, *Punch* would probably not have survived its lean

THE SONG OF THE SHIRT.

WITH fingers weary and worn,
  With eyelids heavy and red,
A Woman sat, in unwomanly rags,
  Plying her needle and thread—
    Stitch ! stitch ! stitch !
In poverty, hunger, and dirt,
  And still with a voice of dolorous pitch
She sang the " Song of the Shirt ! "

  " Work ! work ! work !
While the cock is crowing aloof !
  And work—work—work,
Till the stars shine through the roof !
It 's O ! to be a slave
  Along with the barbarous Turk,
Where woman has never a soul to save,
  If this is Christian work !

  " Work—work—work
Till the brain begins to swim ;
  Work—work—work
Till the eyes are heavy and dim !
Seam, and gusset, and band,
  Band, and gusset, and seam,
    Till over the buttons I fall asleep,
  And sew them on in a dream !

" O ! Men, with Sisters dear !
  O ! Men ! with Mothers and Wives !
It is not linen you 're wearing out,
  But human creatures' lives !
    Stitch—stitch—stitch,
In poverty, hunger, and dirt,
Sewing at once, with a double thread,
  A Shroud as well as a Shirt.

" But why do I talk of Death !
  That Phantom of grisly bone,
I hardly fear his terrible shape,
  It seems so like my own—
  It seems so like my own,
Because of the fasts I keep,
Oh ! God ! that bread should be so dear,
  And flesh and blood so cheap !

" Work—work—work !
  My labour never flags ;
And what are its wages ! A bed of straw,
  A crust of bread—and rags.

That shatter'd roof—and this naked floor—
  A table—a broken chair—
And a wall so blank, my shadow I thank
  For sometimes falling there !

  " Work—work—work !
From weary chime to chime,
  Work—work—work—
As prisoners work for crime !
  Band, and gusset, and seam,
  Seam, and gusset, and band,
Till the heart is sick, and the brain benumb'd,
  As well as the weary hand.

  " Work—work—work,
In the dull December light,
  And work—work—work,
When the weather is warm and bright—
While underneath the eaves
  The brooding swallows cling
As if to show me their sunny backs
  And twit me with the spring.

  " Oh ! but to breathe the breath
Of the cowslip and primrose sweet—
  With the sky above my head,
And the grass beneath my feet,
For only one short hour
  To feel as I used to feel,
Before I knew the woes of want
  And the walk that costs a meal !

  " Oh but for one short hour !
  A respite however brief !
No blessed leisure for Love or Hope,
  But only time for Grief !
A little weeping would ease my heart,
  But in their briny bed
My tears must stop, for every drop
  Hinders needle and thread ! "

With fingers weary and worn,
  With eyelids heavy and red,
A Woman sate in unwomanly rags,
  Plying her needle and thread—
    Stitch ! stitch ! stitch !
In poverty, hunger, and dirt,
And still with a voice of dolorous pitch,
Would that its tone could reach the Rich !
  She sang this "Song of the Shirt ! "

Hood's poem was inspired by the plight of female factory workers. It had been turned down by three other editors before Lemon bought it. It was an instant success. Every newspaper reprinted it. Henry Tully set it to music, and Lemon dramatized it in a play entitled The Sempstress. *Since it was printed anonymously, a number of literary pirates claimed its authorship, and Hood was hard pressed to prove that he had actually written it. (Drawings by Richard Doyle, poem by Thomas Hood, 1843)*

years. The third issue might not have gone to press had Lemon not sold a two-act play, *The Silver Thimble*, for thirty pounds and turned the money over to Bryant, the publisher of *Punch*. He later wrote another farce called *Punch* (revised as *The Star of the Streets*), and used the proceeds to keep the magazine alive.

His series in *Punch* "The Heir of Applebite" was mildly amusing but nothing special compared with the writings of à Beckett, Mayhew, Jerrold, and the other stars of the paper. It was overwritten and the jokes were very broad. Nevertheless, he knew good writing from bad when it was done by other people, and he was willing to gamble on what he believed in. It was Lemon who decided to publish Thomas Hood's controversial poem "The Song of the Shirt" after it had been refused by a number of other papers. The poem, a stirring denunciation of the plight of women garment workers, seemed out of place in the 1843 Christmas issue, with its hearty plum-pudding and mistletoe jokes, but Lemon could not let it get away. It raised the circulation sharply, was widely reprinted, and eventually was set to music by Henry Tully. Lemon himself dramatized it as *The Sempstress*.

Lemon had a natural ability for recognizing talent. Although he had nothing but contempt for Sala, another *Punch* antagonist, Shirley Brooks, caught his eye when he wrote anti-*Punch* verses in *The Man in the Moon*. Lemon insisted on hiring Brooks, who became a staunch Table member and eventually *Punch*'s second editor.

It was Lemon who later recognized George du Maurier's genius and hired him over the objections of some of the other Table members who found him brash and arrogant. He wisely forced du Maurier to stick to the "socials" and leave the political cartoons to John Tenniel. It was a brilliant stroke; du Maurier's drawings carried *Punch* for years.

Lemon wrote the new paper's first article, "The Moral of Punch," in 1841. It outlined rather limply the paper's philosophy and its undying opposition to debtors' prisons, capital punishment, and other abuses. The article was supposed to have been written by Douglas Jerrold, but he was in France hiding from his creditors and Lemon had to take over.

THE MORAL OF PUNCH

As we hope, gentle public, to pass many happy hours in your society, we think it right that you should know something of our character and intentions. Our title, at a first glance, may have misled you into a belief that we have no other intention than the amusement of a thoughtless crowd, and the collection of pence. We have a higher object. Few of the admirers of our prototype, merry Master Punch, have looked upon his vagaries but as the practical outpourings of a rude and boisterous mirth. We have considered

51

him as a teacher of no mean pretensions, and have, therefore, adopted him as the sponsor for our weekly sheet of pleasant instruction. When we have seen him parading in the glories of his motley, flourishing his baton (like our friend Jullien at Drury-lane) in time with his own unrivalled discord, by which he seeks to win the attention and admiration of the crowd, what visions of graver puppetry have passed before our eyes! Golden circlets, with their adornments of coloured and lustrous gems, have bound the brow of infamy as well as that of honour—a mockery to both; as though virtue required a reward beyond the fulfilment of its own high purposes, or that infamy could be cheated into the forgetfulness of its vileness, by the weight around its temples. Gilded coaches have glided before us, in which sat men who thought the buzz and shouts of crowds a guerdon for the toils, the anxieties, and, too often, the peculations of a life. Our ears have rung with the noisy frothiness of those who have bought their fellow-men as beasts in the market-place, and found their reward in the sycophancy of a degraded constituency, or the patronage of a venal ministry—no matter of what creed, for party *must* destroy patriotism.

The noble in his robes and coronet—the beadle in his gaudy livery of scarlet, and purple, and gold—the dignitary in the fulness of his pomp—the demagogue in the triumph of his hollowness—these and other visual and oral cheats by which mankind are cajoled, have passed in review before us, conjured up by the magic wand of PUNCH.

How we envy his philosophy, when SHALLA-BA-LA, that demon with the bell, besets him at every turn, almost teazing the sap out of him! The moment that his tormentor quits the scene, PUNCH seems to forget the existence of his annoyance, and, carolling the mellifluous numbers of *Jim Crow,* or some other strain of equal beauty, makes the most of the present, regardless of the past or future; and when SHALLA-BA-LA renews his persecutions, PUNCH boldly faces his enemy, and ultimately becomes the victor. All have a SHALLA-BA-LA in some shape of other; but few, how few, the philosophy of PUNCH!

We are afraid our prototype is no favourite with the ladies. PUNCH is (and we reluctantly admit the fact) a Malthusian in principle, and somewhat of a domestic tyrant; for his conduct is at times harsh and ungentlemanly to Mrs. P.

Eve of a land that still is Paradise,
Italian beauty!''

But as we never look for perfection in human nature, it is too much to expect it in wood. We wish to be understood that we repudiate such principles and conduct. We have a Judy of our own, and a little Punchininny that commits innumerable improprieties; but we fearlessly aver that we never threw him out of window, nor belaboured the lady with a stick—even of the size allowed by law.

There is one portion of the drama we wish was omitted, for it always saddens us—we allude to the prison scene. PUNCH, it is true, sings in durance, but we hear the ring of the bars mingling with the song. We are advocates for the *correction* of offenders; but how many generous and kindly beings are there pining within the walls of a prison, whose only crimes are poverty and misfortune! They, too sing and laugh, and appear jocund, but the *heart* can ever hear the ring of the bars.

We never looked upon a lark in a cage, and heard him trilling out his music as he sprung upwards to the roof of his prison, but we felt sickened with the sight and sound, as contrasting, in our thought, the free minstrel of the morning, bounding as it were into the blue caverns of the heavens, with the bird to whom the world was circumscribed. May the time soon arrive, when every prison shall be a palace of the mind—when we shall seek to instruct and cease to punish. PUNCH has already advocated education by example. Look at his dog Toby! The instinct of the brute has almost germinated into reason. Man *has* reason, why not give him intelligence?

We now come to the last great lesson of our motley teacher—the gallows! that accursed tree, which has its *root* in injuries. How clearly PUNCH exposes the fallacy of that dreadful law which authorises the destruction of life! PUNCH sometimes destroys the hangman: and why not? Where is the divine injunction against the shedder of man's blood to rest? None *can* answer! To us there is but one disposer of life. At other times PUNCH hangs the devil: this is as it should be. Destroy the principle of evil by increasing the means of cultivating the good, and the gallows will then become as much a wonder as it is now a jest.

We shall always play PUNCH, for we consider it best to be merry and wise—

> "And laugh at all things, for we wish to know,
> What, after all, are all things but a show!"—*Byron*.

As on the stage of Punch's theatre, many characters appear to fill up the interstices of the more important story, so our pages will be interspersed with trifles that have no other object than the moment's approbation—an end which will never be sought for at the expense of others, beyond the evanescent smile of a harmless satire.

Lemon kept his good nature at all times, accepting calmly the brickbats, the snubs, the fits of pique, the sulks, and the blockages of his crew of geniuses. The Punchites, who would not accept criticism from anybody else, accepted his meekly. He would assign an article to a writer and then would drop in unannounced at the writer's house to see if he was working and how he was making out.

Punch became Lemon's whole existence: "I was made for *Punch* and *Punch* for me," he said. "I could not have succeeded any other way." The paper's welfare came first, even if it meant alienating old friends. He turned down a lucrative lecture tour in America because he could not bear to think of anyone else running his beloved magazine for so long a time.

His obsession with the theater never left him, and he continued to write plays and act. He did his best to combine his two passions by setting up *Punch*-connected amateur productions into which his staff and contributors were shanghaied whether they liked it or not. It was considered part of the job.

A notable gap in his flair for attracting the best to *Punch* was his rejection of W. S. Gilbert, who had submitted some of his *Bab Ballads* to him. Lemon recognized the quality of the poems but refused to take them unless Gilbert would agree not to write for other publications. Gilbert pointed out sensibly that he could not guarantee this unless *Punch* assured him a steady salary, but Lemon refused to hire him. Gilbert took his poems elsewhere.

One of Lemon's sincerest admirers was Henry Silver, who appointed himself his editor's unofficial Boswell. "Glorious imitator and jolly," he writes in 1859, describing one of Lemon's comical impersonations. Referring to Lemon's defense of Silver as a drama critic, Silver quotes him as saying, "I don't agree with Shirley that *Punch* should be all pitch and no praise." On his editorial philosophy, Silver notes: "His place as Editor has always been to avoid dictation, reserving merely the power of correction—thereby has the benefit of a variety of minds unfettered by his own," which places Lemon in direct contradiction with the principle of William Davis a century later.

At an exceptionally convivial dinner, reports Silver, when reminiscences were flying thick and fast, Lemon convulsed his young friend by describing the night when the stage parrot in his farce *Star of the Streets* died. An assistant rushed out and borrowed an understudy parrot from a local brothel. The bird caused consternation on and off stage by shouting "Show us your cock" at embarrassingly inconvenient times in the play.

Lemon's health began to fail in the late 1860s. Time and again Silver reports him absent from the dinners or drinking plain water instead of champagne because of his doctor's orders. His eyes troubled him, his stomach gave him difficulties, but still he steered his beloved magazine

X. 42. "DID YOU CALL THE POLICE, SIR?"

Swell (who would perish rather than disturb his shirt-collar). "YA—AS, A—I'VE HAD THE MISFORTUNE TO DWOP MY UMBRELLAW, AND THERE ISN'T A BOY WITHIN A MILE TO PICK IT UP—A—WILL YOU HAVE THE GOODNESS?"

Among Punch's *favorite targets were drawling swells and effusive lady novelists. (Above, George du Maurier, 1891; below, John Leech, 1853)*

THE SECRETS OF LITERARY COMPOSITION.

The Fair Authoress of "Passionate Pauline," gazing fondly at her own reflection, writes as follows:—

" I look into the glass, Reader. What do I see?

" I see a pair of laughing, *espiègle,* forget-me-not blue eyes, saucy and defiant ; a *mutine* little rose-bud of a mouth, with its ever-mocking *moue* ; a tiny shell-like ear, trying to play hide-and-seek in a tangled maze of rebellious russet gold ; while, from underneath the satin folds of a *rose-thé* dressing-gown, a dainty foot peeps coyly forth in its exquisitely-pointed gold morocco slipper," &c., &c.

(Vide " Passionate Pauline," by Parbleu.)

and its unruly crew on to new successes. He died in 1870, at the age of sixty, within a few weeks of the death of his old friend Charles Dickens.

When Henry Mayhew was asked to draw up a list of possible writers and artists for *Punch*, he went directly to the two finest writers of political satire and sophisticated whimsy in London. One was his old schoolfellow and partner in juvenile adventure, Gilbert Abbott à Beckett. The other was Douglas Jerrold.

Jerrold was a tiny, caustic, bad-tempered homunculus known to his friends as the "Little Wasp." His specialty was the scathing insult. No one was spared the acid of his stinging wit. Because of this quality, a great many orphaned barbs were fathered on him, just as a century later numerous gratuitous insults never uttered by Dorothy Parker were credited to her for want of anyone else to blame. Jerrold was guilty of hundreds of painful attacks on people who probably did not deserve them but who had somehow incurred his displeasure.

Jerrold was a bad drunk. Sober, he could be warm, funny, tender, the best of companions. Tipsy and spurred on by a crushing inferiority complex born of his small size and lowly background, he grew belligerent. It is said that after boozy evenings he would tie around his neck a label inscribed with his name and address so that passersby could steer him in the direction of home.

His appearance was striking. He had a massive, handsome head with a thick mane of swept-back hair and piercing blue eyes, sometimes twinkling with humor, sometimes icy cold. His small, ugly body seemed charged with electricity. Leech and Thackeray disliked him because of his savage radicalism and what they felt was his lack of breeding. Lemon defended him because of his kindness, especially toward aspiring young writers, to whom he was always willing to lend a helping hand. Dickens considered him a close and valued friend and served as one of his pallbearers when he died.

Thackeray, who contemptuously referred to him as "Master Douglas," said that his table manners made him unfit company. Thackeray's animosity, like that displayed in his quarrel with Dickens, was probably due to the fact that Jerrold (like Dickens) was better known than he was in the 1840s and enjoyed a success that Thackeray had not yet achieved. Jerrold's "Mrs. Caudle" series and his "Story of a Feather" in *Punch* had had a great vogue and raised the paper's circulation. Thackeray's "Snob Papers" and his "Miss Tickletoby" series were met with only a lukewarm response, and the latter was discontinued by the editors.

Later, when Thackeray had scored as a novelist and Jerrold was sliding downhill after several failures, they became guardedly friendly again. But

Jerrold was never one to let well enough alone. When Thackeray gave his first public reading, he nervously asked Jerrold how it had gone over. Jerrold gave him a long, cool look. Then he muttered, ''Wants a piano.''

In spite of this and similar incidents, Thackeray made a long journey up to London especially to support Jerrold's bid for membership in the Reform Club. When he was elected, Thackeray was heard to cry out joyfully, ''We've got the little man in!'' He later pointed out to a mutual friend, ''What's the use of quarreling with a man if you have to meet him every Wednesday at dinner?''

Nevertheless, he changed his seat at the *Punch* Table, something rarely done, in order to sit further away from Jerrold. Lemon kept a close watch on them at the dinners and managed to quash any incipient hostilities, always steering the conversation back to safe ground.

Jerrold's background was one of struggle, poverty, and disappointment. His father was a sometime theatrical printer and small-time actor-manager, constantly on the brink of bankruptcy. In 1807, Jerrold, Sr., leased the Sheerness Theatre and cast his family as often as possible to save actors' salaries. Little Douglas, then four years old, scored a notable success as the child in Kotzebue's *The Stranger*, a famous tearjerker of the period. His stage success caused his education to be sadly neglected, and he was almost entirely self-taught.

Through what was either an astonishing piece of good luck or a family-solicited bit of political preference, the boy took a social step upward when, at the age of ten, he was appointed a midshipman in the navy. He never received a commission. The end of the Napoleonic Wars and subsequent military cutbacks put an end to his career.

Back down the social scale again, Jerrold became a printer's apprentice and later, at the age of sixteen, a compositor on the *Sunday Monitor*. As the story goes, one morning he dropped an unsolicited review of *Der Freischütz* in his editor's morning mail. It was accepted. Soon he was drama critic of the *Monitor* and a contributor to such prestigious journals as *Blackwood's* and the *Athenaeum*. He also wrote plays. In 1821, when he was eighteen, his comedy *More Frightened Than Hurt* appeared at the Sadler's Wells Theatre and earned him a job as resident writer at the Coburg Theatre for a few pounds a week.

In 1829, R. W. Elliston of the Surrey Theatre produced Jerrold's seafaring melodrama, *Black-eyed Susan: or All in the Downs*. Its success was enormous. It had a record run of four hundred performances at six different theaters in its first year. Elliston made a five-figure profit from it, and T. P. Cooke, the leading actor, made his reputation. The impoverished Jerrold, who had signed away most of his rights, made about sixty pounds. Elliston hired him as resident playwright at five pounds a week.

He followed *Susan* with *The Bride of Ludgate*, produced at the Drury Lane in 1831, and was manager of the Strand Theatre for a while. He acted (unsuccessfully) in one of his own plays. All the while he continued to contribute to the better journals. When he joined *Punch* in 1841 he was considered the best humor writer in England.

Jerrold's political opinions were hazy and indefinite. He loved freedom-fighters such as Mazzini, Kossuth, and Louis Blanc. He hated war, luxury-loving bishops, and oppression. He was never really sure about what political philosophy he favored but he knew what he was against. He hated the Tories, the idle-rich aristocracy, and the tyrannical branches of European royalty. He was a champion of the working poor, having been one of them himself, unlike the other Punchites who saw the poor as a wonderful source of jokes.

His attacks in *Punch* on what he believed to be social injustice were savage and ruthless. It was Jerrold's political commentary that gave *Punch* its early crusading image and kept it from becoming just one more Victorian joke book. Although *Punch*'s articles were anonymous, after the first few issues Jerrold began to sign his with the initial *Q*. His first "Q paper," entitled "Peel Regularly Called In," appeared in 1841 and contained some characteristic slashing prose.

> Whilst there's life there's profit— is the philosophy of the Tory College; hence poor Mr. John Bull, though shrunk, attentuated,—with a blister on his head, and cataplasms at his soles—has been kept just alive enough to pay. And then his patience under Tory treatment—the obedience of his swallow! "Admirable! Excellent!" cried a certain Doctor (we will not swear that his name was not PEEL), when his patient pointed to a dozen empty phials. "Taken them all, eh? Delightful! My dear sir, you are *worthy* to be ill." JOHN BULL, having again called in the Tories, is "worthy to be ill;" and very ill he will be. . . .
>
> Now, however, there are no Tories. Oh no! SIR ROBERT PEEL is a Conservative.—LYNDHURST is a Conservative—all are Conservatives. Toyrism has sloughed its old skin and rejoices in a new coat of many colours; but the sting remains—the venom is the same: the reptile that would have struck to the heart the freedom of Europe elaborates the self-same poison, is endowed with the same subtlety, the same grovelling tortuous action. It still creeps upon its belly, and wriggles to its purpose. When adders shall become eels, then will we believe that Conservatives cannot be Tories.

When he was not occupied in flaying the rich or the Tories, Jerrold wrote wonderful high comedy. His series, "Punch's Letters to His Son,"

THE RECENT HIDEOUS CASE OF HYDROPHOBIA.

(Vide Letter in the Times of 6th July.)

" SIR,—At half-past six o'clock this morning I was fishing in the Hampstead ponds, near the Vale of Health. A well-fed smooth black and tan terrier came behind me and shook the leg of my trowsers.

" The terrier led me on for some hundred yards to a pit with high banks, where I discovered a puppy, to which the dog (not its mother) had brought me, and which unfortunate little animal I extricated as quickly as possible.

" Thinking it not quite safe, after your late police dog-reports, I gave it a kick.

" The dog and puppy followed me some distance, but I purposely evaded them.

" I am, Sir, &c. &c."

" Again, however, it returned, and from its movements I could evidently see it wanted to draw my attention to something amiss.

"The Recent Hideous Case of Hydrophobia" was one of Gilbert's few Punch contributions. After it appeared, he quarreled with Lemon and refused to write for Punch again, even after Lemon's death. (William Schwenk Gilbert, 1865)

MRS. CAUDLE'S CURTAIN LECTURES.

LECTURE VIII.

CAUDLE HAS BEEN MADE A MASON.—MRS. CAUDLE INDIGNANT AND CURIOUS.

The drawing for the Mrs. Caudle series was used again and again in Punch, *once as a political cartoon with Lord Brougham and the Duke of Wellington as the Caudles.* (John Leech, 1845)

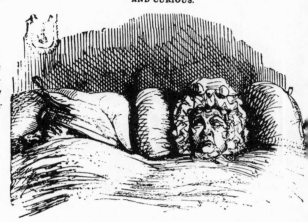

was gentle and philosophical. He revealed a Dickensian style in "The Story of a Feather" with the power to evoke both laughter and tears. But he is best remembered today for "Mrs. Caudle's Curtain Lectures," begun on November 8, 1945. Once again *Punch*'s circulation shot skyward and Caudle engravings and souvenirs (pirated) were sold on every street corner.

The series dealt with the miseries of the long-suffering Job Caudle, a lower-middle-class merchant who kept a toy shop. The "lectures" took place in bed, where poor Caudle was trying to get a little sleep while his termagant of a wife, who "like the owl, hooted only at night," took him to task for some recent misdemeanor. Caudle had lent five pounds to a friend and the family would certainly end up in the workhouse. He had stopped at a tavern with his acquaintances, and whiskey would certainly be the end of them all. He joined a club; he lent someone the family umbrella; he "ventured a remonstrance on the day's dinner"; he was unenthusiastic when Mrs. Caudle suggested that her mother come to live with them. While walking with Mrs. Caudle, he was greeted by a pretty young woman. It was pure comic-strip stuff, and it would be repeated again and again in the following century in such vehicles as "Bringing up Father" or "Blondie." Nevertheless, all England adored it. A typical "lecture" rattled on as follows:

CAUDLE HAS BEEN MADE A MASON—
MRS. CAUDLE INDIGNANT AND CURIOUS

"Now, Mr. Caudle—Mr. Caudle, I say: oh! you can't be asleep already, I know—Now, what I mean to say is this; there's no use, none at all, in our having any disturbance about the matter; but, at last my mind's made up, Mr. Caudle; I shall leave you. Either I know all you've been doing to-night, or to-morrow morning I quit the house. No, no; there's an end of the marriage-state, I think—an end of all confidence between man and wife—if a husband's to have secrets and keep 'em all to himself. Pretty secrets they must be, when his own wife can't know 'em. Not fit for any decent person to know, I'm sure, if that's the case. Now, Caudle, don't let us quarrel; there's a good soul, tell me what's it all about? A pack of nonsense, I dare say; still—not that I care much about it—still, I *should* like to know. There's a dear. Eh? Oh, don't tell me there's nothing in it; I know better. I'm not a fool, Mr. Caudle; I know there's a good deal in it. Now, Caudle; just tell me a little bit of it. I'm sure I'd tell you anything. You know I would. Well?

"Caudle, you're enough to vex a saint! Now, don't you think you're going to sleep; because you're not. Do you suppose I'd ever suffered you to go and be made a mason, if I didn't suppose I was to know the secret, too? Not that it's anything to know, I dare say; and that's why I'm determined to know it.

"But I know what it is; oh yes, there can be no doubt. The secret is, to ill-use poor women; to tyrannise over 'em; to make 'em your slaves; especially your wives. It must be something of the sort, or you wouldn't be ashamed to have it known. What's right and proper never need be done in secret. It's an insult to a woman for a man to be a free-mason, and let his wife know nothing of it. But, poor soul! she's sure to know it somehow—for nice husbands they all make. Yes, yes; a part of the secret is to think better of all the world than their own wives and families. I'm sure men have quite enough to care for—that is, if they act properly—to care for them they have at home. They can't have much care to spare for the world besides.

"And I suppose they call you Brother Caudle? A pretty brother, indeed! Going and dressing yourself up in an apron like a turnpike man—for that's what you look like. And I should like to know what the apron's for? There must be something in it not very respectable, I'm sure. Well, I only wish I was Queen for a day or two. I'd put an end to free-masonry, and all such trumpery, I know.

"Now, come, Caudle; don't let's quarrel. Eh! You're not in pain, dear? What's it all about? What are you lying laughing there at? But I'm a fool to trouble my head about you.

"And you're not going to let me know the secret, eh? You mean to say,—you're not? Now, CAUDLE, you know it's a hard matter to put me in a passion—not that I care about the secret itself: no, I wouldn't give a button to know it, for it's all nonsense I'm sure. It isn't the secret I care about: it's the slight, MR. CAUDLE; it's the studied insult that a man pays to his wife, when he thinks of going through the world keeping something to himself which he won't let her know. Man and wife one, indeed! I should like to know how that can be when a man's a mason—when he keeps a secret that sets him and his wife apart? Ha, you men make the laws, and so you take good care to have all the best of 'em to yourselves: otherwise a woman ought to be allowed a divorce when a man becomes a mason. When he's got a sort of corner-cupboard in his heart—a secret place in his mind—that his poor wife isn't allowed to rummage!

"CAUDLE, you shan't close your eyes for a week—no, you shan't—unless you tell me some of it. Come, there's a good creature; there's a love. I'm sure, CAUDLE, I wouldn't refuse you anything—and you know it, or ought to know it by this time. I only wish I had a secret! To whom should I think of confiding it, but to my dear husband? I should be miserable to keep it to myself, and you know it. Now, CAUDLE?

"Was there ever such a man! A man, indeed! A brute!—yes, MR. CAUDLE, an unfeeling, brutal creature, when you might oblige me, and you won't. I'm sure I don't object to your being a mason; not at all, CAUDLE, I dare say it's a very good thing; I dare say it is—it's only your making a secret of it that vexes me. But you'll tell me—you'll tell your own MARGARET? You won't! You're a wretch, MR. CAUDLE.

"But I know why: oh, yes, I can tell. The fact is, you're ashamed to let me know what a fool they've been making of you. That's it. You, at your time of life—the father of a family. I should be ashamed of myself, CAUDLE.

"And I suppose you'll be going to what you call your Lodge every night, now. Lodge, indeed! Pretty place it must be, where they don't admit women. Nice goings on, I dare say. Then you call one another brethren. Brethren! I'm sure you'd relations enough, you didn't want any more.

"But I know what all this masonry's about. It's only an excuse to get away from your wives and families, that you may feast and drink together, that's all. That's the secret. And to abuse women,—as if they were inferior animals, and not to be trusted. That's the secret; and nothing else.

"Now, CAUDLE, don't let us quarrel. Yes, I know you're in pain. Still CAUDLE, my love; CAUDLE! Dearest, I say! CAUDLE! CAUD—"

"I recollect nothing more," says CAUDLE, "for here, thank Providence! I fell asleep."

Jerrold was not at all pleased that his fame in London was based on *Black-eyed Susan* and Mrs. Caudle. He would have preferred a reputation founded on higher things. When Ebenezer Landells congratulated him on the Caudle success, he replied testily, ''It just shows what stuff people will swallow.'' In due course he allowed Mrs. Caudle to die, as she had always predicted she would (''The Tragedy of Thin Shoes''). Such was the popular demand that he had to let Caudle remarry, after a decent period of mourning. This time, surprisingly enough, it was Caudle who did the nagging and the new wife who was the patient martyr. The new series was not a success.

Jerrold was not above using the pages of *Punch* for his own personal vendettas. He attacked the luckless Alfred Bunn, manager of the Drury Lane Theatre (''the Poet Bunn'') again and again, apparently for no reason. He launched repeated assaults on the actor Charles Kean, son of the tragedian Edmund Kean, in retaliation for a quarrel that predated *Punch*. He wrote:

> Oh Mr. Punch! What glorious times
> Are these, for humbly gifted mimes;
>   When spite of each detractor,
> Paternal name and filial love,
> Assisted by ''the powers above''
>   Have made C – – – – – s K – – n an actor!

Jerrold received three hundred pounds a year from *Punch*, plus an additional thirty shillings a week for the Caudle series. He continued to contribute to other papers and to write and produce his plays. Between 1842 and 1850, he edited the *Illuminated Magazine* for Ingram and also *Douglas Jerrold's Weekly Newspaper* and *Douglas Jerrold's Shilling Magazine*. In 1852, he became editor of *Lloyd's Weekly Newspaper* at one thousand pounds a year.

In 1853, his comedy *St. Cupid* was given a command performance at Windsor Castle. Jerrold was deliberately omitted from the invitation, snubbed by Queen Victoria for the treatment he had accorded the royal family in *Punch*. It was the greatest tribute she could have paid him. He was delighted.

He died in 1857 at the age of fifty-four of what the Victorians called ''burning out the lamp.'' Too much good living had done its work on a body that was not too robust in the first place. Even his enemies, who, after all, respected his talents, gathered at his funeral to do him honor. Thackeray was a pallbearer. Albert Smith, to whom he had always been unnecessarily cruel, organized a benefit to raise a fund for his family.

It is strange that Jerrold, in his lifetime the equal of Dickens and Thackeray, whose writing is still (unlike that of many other Punchites) delightfully readable, should be forgotten. An inch or two in the

Britannica, a mention in the *Oxford Companion to English Literature*, and nothing at all in *Bartlett's* about the man who said, "Religion's in the heart, not in the knees," and "Love's like the measles—all the worse when it comes late in life"; who coined the phrase "peace at any price" and the name "Crystal Palace" for Sir Joseph Paxton's masterpiece. His books are long out of print. He exists only in old copies of *Punch*.

Jerrold's colleague and opposite number on the paper, Gilbert à Beckett, had a background that could not have differed more widely from that of the Little Wasp. The son and grandson of gentlemen, he was educated at Westminster and was called to the Bar at Gray's Inn. We have already heard of his boyhood escapades with Henry Mayhew and of the ill-fated *Cerberus*, stifled at birth by its panicky printer. He never practiced law, but in 1849 he was appointed a metropolitan police magistrate, to the amusement of his *Punch* colleagues, over the strenuous objections of Lord Selborne, who insisted that "no person connected with the press nor any gentleman in the wine trade" should be accorded the honor of the Bench.

He was the first editor of *Figaro in London*, and, according to Spielmann, was "always ready in a humorous bombastic sort of spirit, to smash the aristocracy, to chaff Alfred Bunn, to abuse low-class Jews, and to discuss the theatre." Henry Silver writes of à Beckett's being locked in a room with a pen, ink, and a bottle of gin when *Figaro* needed copy. He was also, at the same time, leader writer for the *Illustrated London News*, the *Times*, and the *Morning Herald*. In his spare time, he wrote fifty plays.

After *Figaro* died, à Beckett was associated with a number of inconsequential comic papers—the *Evangelical Penny Magazine*, the *Terrific Penny Magazine*, the *Gallery of Terrors*, and others which Spielmann calls his "journalistic wild oats."

He was best known for his *Comic History of England*, his *Comic History of Rome*, his *Comic Blackstone*, and similar volumes which Agnes Repplier described as being "so congested with puns that only the flawless fun of John Leech's pictures can carry the reader over them." Indeed, they make very heavy reading today. Thomas Hood's puns carry over from century to century as delightfully as W. S. Gilbert's; à Beckett's do not. The comic histories eventually reached a point where the dyspeptic Jerrold was moved to grumble in a letter to Dickens, "Some men, would, I believe, write a Comic Sermon on the Mount." Dickens agreed heartily.

À Beckett was *Punch*'s most prolific contributor. His first article, "Commercial Intelligence," appeared in the paper's first issue, and his last article appeared on the day of his death. He was a true professional and could always be counted on to fill empty space and to produce completed copy on time, unlike the other Punchites who tended to vanish at critical moments. He contributed an average of one hundred columns per volume. Nevertheless, his role at *Punch* was only that of a capable and versatile supporting player. He never became a star.

His best-known work in *Punch* was his series on the adventures of the pompous, down-at-the-heel ''Mr. Briefless,'' the clientless lawyer. It was a sophisticated and whimsical series about a gentleman (*Punch*'s other butts, like the Caudles, were lower class).

À Beckett left *Punch* abruptly when Bradbury and Evans took over and demoted his friend Mayhew. He attributed this to the machinations of Lemon, and because of it there was a marked coolness between them. He went off to edit the *Squib*, a *Punch*-like comic paper owned by Joseph Last. The *Squib* fizzled out, and seven months after his departure à Beckett was back at *Punch*, once again on cordial terms with Lemon.

Silver reminisces about him some years after his death. At a dinner in 1863 there was ''talk of G. à B. as a quiet, pleasant talker—answering D. J[errold]'s fulminations with a pithy, pregnant joke.''

The even-tempered à Beckett died suddenly of typhus in 1856, during a holiday trip to Boulogne. He was forty-five years old. His death was a shock to the Punchites, who had assumed that he would outlive them all. Since his old schoolmate, Henry Mayhew, was no longer there to celebrate him in print, Jerrold was assigned to write his obituary in *Punch*. À Beckett was probably the only colleague who had been spared the irritations of the Little Wasp's stinging invective. Jerrold loved him as much as it was possible for him to love another writer who approached him in ability. He was so affected by à Beckett's sudden departure from the Table festivities that he was never able to return to Boulogne again, although the city had formerly been his favorite continental watering place.

Why is a loud laugh in the House of Commons like
Napoleon Buonaparte?

Because it's an *M.P. roar*. (Emperor)
                                        —Punch (*1841*)

he first issue of *Punch*
appeared on July 17, 1841. It sold two editions of five thousand each,
barely enough to cover production costs. The newborn London *Charivari*
did not make a great impression on the general reading public. In the
opinion of readers and booksellers it was an interesting and amusing
experiment but not one destined to last for more than a few months.

The press reviewed it in generally favorable terms. Some papers, such
as the *Morning Advertiser*, gushed so effusively over its ''exquisite woodcuts,'' which were not exquisite, and its ''hearty laughs,'' which were
not all that hearty, that it seemed certain Lemon and his crew had
somehow gotten to the critics, calling in old debts from former Fleet
Street comrades. The *Sunday Times* and a number of provincial papers
commented on *Punch*'s lack of grossness and profanity and assured the
world that the new journal ''would not call a blush to the most delicate
cheek.'' This was an important point. There were very few humorous
papers at the time that could be brought home by Victorian gentlemen
and left where they could be read by wives and daughters.

The cover of the first issue was drawn by *Punch*'s principal artist,
Archibald Henning, an amiable but not too talented craftsman who left
Punch in 1842. Henning also did a large cut—engraved by Landells who
took the opportunity, since he owned a third of the magazine, to sign his
name in letters as large as the artist's. Smaller cuts and illustrations were
done by Newman and Brine.

As I have noted earlier, the leading article, ''The Moral of Punch,''
was written by Lemon, who also contributed a short poem. The other ma-

Punch *came out strongly against dueling. The Punchites were outraged when Lord Cardigan wounded a gentleman who had had the misfortune to disagree with him. In this cartoon, Cardigan is shown as a fool in cap and bells waiting to kill another fool similarly attired. Death waits in a newly dug grave. (John Leech, 1843)*

jor articles were by à Beckett, H. P. Grattan (temporarily out of debtors' prison) and Henry Mayhew. The other short articles and pars were done by Stirling Coyne, W. H. Wills, Frederick Guest, Joseph Allen, and F. G. Tomlins.

A short piece entitled "Lessons in Punmanship," suggesting that Thomas Hood was setting up a school to teach the "dull and witless" how to contrive elegant puns, was read with great displeasure by Hood and very nearly lost the paper his friendship and his future services. Like most really good humorists, Hood had very little sense of humor when it came to jokes on himself.

A little verse on page eleven, "To the Black-Balled of the United Service," was a direct attack on Lord Cardigan, who had insulted an officer under his command for having a "black bottle" of Moselle on the mess table instead of a decanter, and who had ordered a soldier flogged on a Sunday, causing great public outrage. In the summer of 1841, Cardigan was probably the most unpopular man in England; he was repeatedly hissed out of his box at the theater.

The general format of the magazine was a jovial communication between Mr. Punch himself and the readers, a device that had been used earlier by Jerrold in *Punch in London*. The little puppet, or his dog Toby, was the supposed author of most of the articles, except those specifically signed with a hieroglyphic such as Jerrold's *Q* or Grattan's *Fusbos*. The promise that the magazine would be a refuge for "destitute wit" and "orphan jokes" or "perishing puns" was kept with a vengeance. In the early volumes the spaces at the end of each major article were filled with dreadful conundrums, even by Victorian standards.

> How many young ladies will it take to reach from London to Brighton?
> Fifty-two; because a MISS is as good as a mile.

> When does a man have a vegetable time-piece?
> When he gets a potato clock. [Gets up-at-eight-o'clock.]

Most of these appeared in "Sibthorpe's Corner," a feature created to tease Colonel Sibthorpe, the jovial but not-too-bright member of Parliament from Lincoln, who accepted *Punch*'s raillery with good nature and not a little pride.

The illustrations and initial letter drawings, except for those which were explanatory of specific articles, were usually little visual puns. "War with China" is the caption of a sketch showing two grotesque women hitting each other with china plates, while "Drawn from Life" labels a picture of three disembodied teeth.

Enraged by the fawning society columns in such papers as the *Morning Post*, Jerrold treated the reading public to a withering parody called "*Punch*'s Fashionable Movements." The social lions celebrated in his gazette were people named Smith and Jones and the ridiculous Baron Nathan, a well-known Kensington dancing master with delusions of grandeur. (Baron was his first name, and he invited his friends to stop calling him *Mr.* Baron Nathan in order to give the impression of titled aristocracy.) The Punchites devoted acres of space to him.

Typical of Jerrold's "fashionable movements" are these:

> Mr. Llewellyn Price of Llanfairpwlllgwynglet passed his examination at the Apothecaries' Hall on Thursday evening last and was licensed to sell pepper and vinegar accordingly.

> The driver of Street-Sweeping Machine No. 2, attended by a numerous suite of little boys on Friday last, promenaded up and down Regent Street several times during the day.

Jerrold's fierce loathing for the bootlicking of *Punch*'s journalistic contemporaries was responsible for the creation of one of his best-loved fictional characters, the servile and toadying "Jenkins of the *Morning Post*." Whenever a particularly fulsome paragraph of idolatry of the upper classes appeared (anonymously, as most newspaper articles did in those days), *Punch* insisted that it had been written by Jenkins. With the help of Thackeray, and later à Beckett, Jerrold made a star of Jenkins. Although he was entirely fictional, many London journalists claimed him, each seeing in him a personal libel.

He first appeared in an article entitled "The *Post* at the Opera" after a March 13, 1843, review in that journal had brought the dyspeptic Jerrold to the boiling point. Jerrold quoted from the article, including the *Post*'s own lavish italics, as an example of Jenkins's writing. ("Writing, do we call it? Inspiration we should say!") According to him, Jenkins, who had the "true aristocratic ichor in his veins," had written:

> Ever since the Italian lyrical drama crossed the Alps in the suite of the tasteful Medicis, its *vogue* has daily increased, it has become a ruling passion—it is the *quintessence of all civilized pleasures* and *wherever* its principal *virtuosi hoist their standards, there for the time* is the CAPITAL OF EUROPE where the most illustrious, noble, elegant and tasteful members of Society *assemble*.

The *Post* went on to describe these "*ornaments of Society*," magnificently condescending in their gorgeous clothes, sitting in their boxes; people whom we "*respect, esteem*, or *love*," as opposed to the "*objectionable spectators*" in the cheap seats with their "*frowsy dames*," who were, fortunately, so magnetized by the spectacle that they remained "nailed to the benches as not to offend the eye."

Mr. Punch earnestly implored the opera stars not to carry their artistry to Sydney, Adelaide, or Macquarrie Harbour, any of which would thus instantly become the "capital of Europe" and draw the illustrious, noble, and elegant away from London.

Jerrold, Thackeray, and à Beckett carried Jenkins on for a long time, in spite of the angry complaints of some competitors and the imitations of others. At one point he was allowed to die but was later resurrected for a few ghostly postmortem appearances. He was placed in line for a mythical earldom, nominated for the Laureateship, awarded the Légion d'Honneur, and finally allowed to accept a dukedom especially created for him by the Comte de Chambord. For this final honor, a special ducal hat was designed for him by no less a personage than Prince Albert himself. The

Russian Intelligence.

The public functionaries of the Russian provinces have just been forbidden to wear either beard or moustachioes. The prohibition of moustachioes seems rather unreasonable, but we think it quite right that the authorities should not continue to be in the slightest degree bearded. What is to become of the home trade in Russian bear's grease?

CUTTING AND CURLING.

THE CIVIC PRETENDERS.

Considerable excitement has been occasioned in the City by a sort of Legitimist movement in favour of Alderman Thomas Wood, who by right of succession is entitled to the Civic Sovereignty. It is true that circumstances conspired to seat Magnay on the Mayoral throne, but several of the old cockney noblesse insist on the claims of the pretender Wood, being paramount. By many, the present monarch of the City is openly denounced as Magnay the Usurper—and it is declared by several, that Wood is *de jure* king of the City, while Magnay is *de facto* king of the citizens. Encouraged by the example of the Duke of Bordeaux, the city pretender—Wood—is trying to rally round him as many as possible of the civic Legitimists, and he holds a levee every morning at his office. A good deal of the *jure divino* feeling exists in the Poultry, which is to the City what La Vendée was to France in the days of the Revolution.

THE DUCAL HAT FOR JENKINS.

We hasten to lay before our readers the following ill-spelt and worse-conceived communication. It came to us by our usual express, through Lord Lowther's office in St. Martin's-le-Grand. It was sealed with a large, we may say an enormous, circular seal, on which are emblazoned the royal arms of England, and in all respects similar to that with-some-people-very-uncommon-coin the half-crown. But though the appearance of the seal may have deceived the young gentleman in our office (who, from taking several hundred thousand half-crowns for "Punch's Pocket-Book," ought to have known the coin better), to *our* more acute eyes the flimsy deceit was at once apparent.

We unhesitatingly pronounce the letter an audacious forgery; and, in the words of the great bard, "would whip the rascal with his clothes off through the world"—or at least down the Strand as far as Charing Cross—did we know him, and were he inclined to submit to the punishment. As, however, he would probably resist, and as we are not acquainted with him, we leave him *to the pangs of his own conscience* and the opprobrium of an indignant public.

Ed.*

---

* It has been said that *Punch* has not been grave enough on all occasions in the conduct of this miscellany, and therefore, ever anxious to please the public, Mr. *Punch* has engaged, at an immense expense, a moral young man of great parts and eloquence, and who has been, according to his own statement, connected with the *Observer* and the *Morning Herald* newspapers. He will be employed to write upon all great public questions ana is, in fact, the author of the letter signed Philodicky, which appeared in our last.

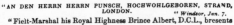

"Fielt-Marshal his Royal Highness Brince Albert, D.C.L., bresents his gomblimends to Mr. Punch.

"Having heard of the bromotion of Mr. Jenkins by H.R.H. the Comte de Chambord, the Fielt-Marshal has retired to his study and gombosed for the use of Herzog Jenkins and the other dukes who have been greated by the D. of Bordeaux, a ducal hat, of which the following is an aggurate design.

"The dugal goronet, it vill be obserfed, will surmounts de hat, vich may be a livery hat, a beafer hat, or vat you call a four-and-nine, at bleasure.

"De gockade vill be vite (emblematic of videlity, burity, and de house of Bourbon). A bouquet of lilies may be vorn in de goat, and de rest of de gostume vil be left to de taste of de vearer, or of de nobel and disdingirshed bersonages vid whom Duke Jenkins may dvell.

"Ven de hat grow old (or vat you call zeedy), Brinz Albert has arranged so dat it vil make a beawdiful and ornamendal flower-bot for a drawing-room vindow. Dis vas also de indention of de military hat vich has obdained so much bobularity in de army.

"B.S. Venever I invend any more hats, I vill send dem to you, mein dear *Bunch*.

"B.S. I bercief dat Herr Grunt, de zelebrated liderary man, has been greated Ritter of de Order of de Big (pig) and Vistle. I ave no vistles, but I can subbly him from my farm vid some bigs very fine.

"A."

Punch *teasing Prince Albert. The letter supposedly from the Prince, written in comic German dialect, is by Thackeray, who would later chide his editor about the magazine's disrespect for His Royal Highness. (Drawings by Richard Doyle, 1844)* design was accompanied by a letter explaining how the hat was to be worn, written in low-comedy music-hall German dialect and supposedly signed by the Prince himself. ("AN AUDACIOUS FORGERY," cried Mr. Punch.) The author of the letter, who (Mr. Punch said) must be "left to the pangs of his own conscience," was Thackeray.

The *Post* eventually found a way of revenging itself on the Punchites. When Thackeray's novels made him a celebrity and he began to dine frequently at aristocratic houses, his name was always omitted from the lists of "among those present" published in that paper. This was an annoyance to the author of *The Book of Snobs*, who became something of a snob himself as he grew richer and more famous.

Jokes about Prince Albert and hats were enormously popular with the *Punch* staff. The Prince had earned their derision, through no fault of his own, when the Duke of Wellington created him a field marshal, after which *Punch* never failed to refer to him as "F. M. H. R. H. Prince Albert." The unlucky prince had designed a disastrous hat for the army, which was soon discarded after strenuous objections from the ranks. *Punch* never forgot it or let the Prince forget it. The following notice was printed:

THE NEW REGULATION HAT

Considerable sensation has been excited in military circles, and particularly among the heads of the Army, by the announcement of an intent to bonnet the whole infantry with a sort of pantomimic head-gear, such as is generally worn by the Demon of Revenge in the Cave of Despair, just before the scene changes to the abode of blue fire and blissfulness. This extraordinary castor is due to the inventive power of Prince Albert.

The paper went on to say that the hat, which resembled a "cross between a muff, a coal scuttle, and a slop-pail," had been withdrawn but that those already made were enjoying notable success on scarecrows.

The Prince was distressed at the liberties that *Punch* took with him and with other high officials. He felt that France, Germany, and the other European powers believed that *Punch* was a reflection of British public opinion and government policy. Nevertheless, he secretly collected the cartoons in which he appeared, especially those done by Leech, whom he adored. He was fond of saying that history would best judge a man by the caricatures that were drawn of him.

At this point it might be useful to survey the events that were taking place in the world outside the narrow confines of Whitefriars, in order to

THE NEW REGULATION HAT.

CONSIDERABLE sensation has been excited in military circles, and particularly among the heads of the army, by the announcement of an intention to bonnet the whole infantry with a sort of pantomimic head-gear, such as is generally worn by the Demon of Revenge in the Cave of Despair, just before the scene changes to the abode of blue fire and blissfulness. This extraordinary castor is due to the inventive power of Prince Albert, who, with a spirit of pure philanthropy, has endeavoured to devise a hat which may spare the effusion of blood, by substituting the terrors of the *sombrero* for the horrors of the musket. It is expected that when an opposing rank catches a glimpse of the frightful old files, that the veterans of the British army will be converted into by these monstrosities, they will instantly take to their heels. We should earnestly recommend that if the pensioners lately hunted out from the Hospital at Chelsea, are to be thrown again into arms—some of them, alas! have long ceased to know the solace and convenience of legs—we should suggest, we say, that these veterans should be provided with these hats, and thus rendered serviceable in the only way in which they can be expected to become so—as scarecrows to a rebellious and unarmed populace. It is true that to a mob a soldier is formidable in any guise, but we doubt if much terror will be inspired by such Guys, as the Regulation Hat will render the ignoble and degraded successor of the Saxon warrior.

We have been at an enormous expense to get a drawing of this hat, and the only merit we claim for our sketch is its being wholly unlike the unsightly original. Our artist has flattered the hat, with considerable tastiness.

H. G. Hine, 1843

THE NEW POLICE HAT.

THIS ingenious invention bids fair to rival the celebrated ALBERT Hat in popularity. The moment HIS ROYAL HIGHNESS OF GOTHA became acquainted with the fact that the Police were to wear a ventilating hat, he declared his gracious intention to devote his head to it, for the purpose of suggesting further improvements. The Prince at length succeeded in concocting the very elaborate head-gear, of which our engraving furnishes a fac-simile. The original design was very meagre, consisting of the insertion of a common ventilator in the front of an ordinary hat ; but the sagacity of the Prince immediately saw that the ventilator could not be always kept going without the aid of a windmill, which was consequently added. In order, however, to counterbalance the weight of the windmill, it was thought desirable to add something to the other side of the hat ; and the Prince, after much patient reflection, at length hit upon a weathercock, because the duty of a policeman is to know what is in the wind—a knowledge he is sure to acquire with such aids as a ventilator, a windmill, and a weathercock. It is also evident that the hat, as altered by his Royal Highness, must keep the police constantly alive to any breeze that may be springing up ; and the points of the compass being indicated on the weathercock, will enable them to steer their course in the right direction.

H. G. Hine, 1844

place the origins and early volumes of *Punch* in their proper perspective.

Queen Victoria was an attractive young woman of twenty-two when *Punch* first saw the light of day. She had been married to Prince Albert for about a year, and the honeymoon was definitely not over. In spite of the irreverent view of him taken by *Punch*, the Prince was extremely popular with the general public. The happy, young couple were a welcome change from the profligate George IV and his cronies and the weak and unpopular William IV.

William Lamb Melbourne was prime minister, but not for long. In 1841, his attempt to adjust the sugar bounties (and incidentally the Corn Laws) was taken as encouragement for the production of sugar in Cuba and other slave states at the expense of British colonies, which had abolished slavery. Antislavery Whigs joined with Sir Robert Peel's Tories to topple the Melbourne government by a majority of only thirty-six votes. Melbourne's ministers refused to resign, but Peel called for a vote of no confidence and soon replaced Melbourne as prime minister.

The death of Beau Brummel in 1840 put an end to the Georgian era forever. Dr. Livingstone was in Africa, preaching the gospel to the Hottentots. The adhesive postage stamp made its triumphant appearance in England, starting a new custom of collecting stamps and putting them in albums. Telegraph wires were strung from London all the way to Glasgow.

The Opium War was going very well for the British in China, in contrast with the war in Afghanistan which was going very badly indeed. *Punch* devoted little space to the hostilities in Hong Kong and in the Khyber Pass, except for an occasional notice and a famous joke—a pun on the message supposedly sent to his superiors by Sir Charles Napier when he occupied the fortress of Scinde. Napier (according to *Punch*) had sent the single word *Peccavi*, ''I have sinned'' (Scinde). The joke was repeated everywhere.

The major topics of the day were free trade, the Chartists, and a proposed new reform bill based on household suffrage. There was widespread anti-Catholic prejudice (shared heartily by the Punchites), and popular indignation was inflamed when the government announced that it would assist schools that used the Douay Version, or Roman Catholic Testament, in their religious services. An attempt to reform Irish registration threatened to increase the number of Catholics in Parliament. Worst of all, according to the general public (and to *Punch*), was the ''Papal Aggression,'' an attempt by the Vatican to give its clergy in Great Britain geographical names; for example, Archbishop of London or Manchester instead of Cardinal Smith or Jones. For some reason, the furious British public viewed this as the beginning of an all-out invasion that would culminate in the conversion of British women and children to Catholicism.

The Jewish Disabilities Relief Bill, which would have simply given British subjects of the Jewish faith the same rights as other Englishmen, including the right to stand for Parliament, won a resounding victory in the House of Commons only to be crushed by the traditionally anti-Semitic lords. It would pass eventually but not until 1858. At first *Punch* took the aristocratic view and strongly opposed the "Jew Bill," publishing a devastating cartoon by Leech depicting Baron Rothschild trying to insert his nose ("the thin end of the wedge") into the doors of Parliament.* In time, however, the Punchites eased their opposition and published the arguments of those who favored the bill ("If we obey your Government, shall we not have a hand in it?"). At the same time, the paper reserved the right to ridicule Jews and their customs in cartoons and jokes.

Henry Silver records in his diary a brief Table exchange on the subject of Jews in February 1859, when Austria was seeking a British loan.

> The Jews govern the world. J. L[eech] thinks we don't half pitch into the Jews. "Then," says H. S[ilver], "Let's turn over a new leaf." J. L. then recollects that he has an invitation to a Jew's place to hunt. Says S. B[rooks] private arrangements must not interfere with public duties. Men who sit down at this Table must not remember they have friends.

The Punchites used Jews as a constant source of denigratory humor, usually depicting them as greasy individuals with large noses wearing three or four hats like secondhand clothes peddlers. Nevertheless, when the chips were down, the paper usually came through on the side of tolerance. In due course *Punch* would get itself banned from Russia for a cartoon protesting Jewish persecution in Russia and representing Tsar Alexander III as the "New Pharaoh." For this stand, Mr. Punch received a citation from the head of the Jewish community in London for his "great service in the cause of freedom and humanity."

In *Punch*'s first years the duke of Wellington, then in his seventies, was a cabinet minister without portfolio and a field marshal in full control of army policy. Napoleon III was an exile, living in London. The pretensions of Mehemet Ali of Egypt against Turkey were the major international concerns of the European nations.

In the literary world Bulwer-Lytton was at the peak of his popularity,

---

* Rothschild had been elected to Parliament but was not allowed to take his seat because he was a Jew.

THE JEW BAILIFF'S COMPLAINT.

"MR. DISRAELI did not vote in favour of the proposition of LORD JOHN RUSSELL for the removal of Jewish Disabilities."—*Evening Paper.*

FORCED from writs and all their pleasures,
  Fetter Lane I've left forlorn;
Men no more, t' increase our treasures,
  Are to spunging-houses borne.
Men in Parliament have sold us,
  Altering laws that gave us gold;
But we had doubted, had they told us,
  We by DIZZY should be sold.

Since you thought our race so clever,
  What's your motive, may I ask,
From the "peoplesh" cause to sever,
  When to aid us was your task?
Curly locks and dark complexion
  Cannot alter nature's claim;
Though you cut us, your connexion
  Is apparent all the same.

Why did you, in novels flashy,
  For our elevation toil?
Promises are poor and trashy,
  From us if your acts recoil.
Think, young master, iron'd-shirted,
  Publishing your books in boards,
'Tis by deeds that you have hurted,
  While your kindness was but wor...

"AM I NOT A MAN AND A BROTHER?"

The Jewish Disabilities Relief Bill would have given Jews the same rights as other Englishmen, including the right to stand for Parliament. English Jews were appalled when Disraeli, whose father was a converted Jew, voted against the bill and helped to defeat it. Punch *loved to make fun of Disraeli's foppish dress and frizzy hair. (Above, drawing by John Leech, poem by Percival Leigh, 1849; facing page, John Leech, 1849)*

"HAVE YOU GOT SUCH A THING AS A TURNED
COAT FOR SALE?"

soon to become a perennial *Punch* butt and the target of a vicious attack
in the paper by Tennyson. Lytton wrote a poem denouncing Tennyson as

> A quaint Farrago of absurd conceits,
> Out-babying Wordsworth and out-glittering Keats.

Tennyson was furious and replied with this severe attack on Lytton,
signed, ''Alcibiades.''

THE NEW TIMON, AND THE POETS.

We know him, out of SHAKSPEARE'S art,
    And those fine curses which he spoke;
The old TIMON, with his noble heart,
    That, strongly loathing, greatly broke.

So died the Old: here comes the New.
    Regard him: a familiar face:
I *thought* we knew him: What, it's you,
    The padded man—that wears the stays—

Who kill'd the girls and thrill'd the boys,
    With dandy pathos when you wrote,
A Lion, you, that made a noise,
    And shook a mane en papillotes.

And once you tried the Muses too;
    You fail'd, Sir: therefore now you turn,
You fall on those who are to you,
    As Captain is to Subaltern.

But men of long-enduring hopes,
    And careless what this hour may bring,
Can pardon little would-be POPES
    And BRUMMELS, when they try to sting.

An artist, Sir, should rest in Art,
    And waive a little of his claim;
To have the deep Poetic heart
    Is more than all poetic fame.

But you, Sir, you are hard to please;
    You never look but half content:
Nor like a gentleman at ease,
    With moral breadth of temperament.

And what with spies and what with fears,
　　You cannot let a body be:
It's always ringing in your ears,
　　"They call this man as good as *me*."

What profits now to understand
　　The merits of a spotless shirt—
A dapper boot—a little hand—
　　If half the little soul is dirt?

You talk of tinsel! why we see
　　The old mark of rouge upon your cheeks.
You prate of Nature! you are he
　　That spilt his life about the cliques.

A Timon you! Nay, nay, for shame:
　　It looks too arrogant a jest—
The fierce old man—to take *his* name
　　You bandbox. Off, and let him rest.

Appalled at the effect his poem had, he later denied sending it to *Punch*. "Wretched work," he wrote, "*Odium literarium*. I never sent my lines to *Punch*. John Forster [editor of the *Examiner*] did. They were too bitter. I do not think I should have published them."

Punch's early troubles were aggravated by the fact that the paper first appeared during a period of financial depression. There were numerous "taxes on knowledge," on paper, and on advertisements. A stamp duty was levied on newspapers. Postal fees were high. *Punch*'s price of three pence, though cheap for what the buyer was getting (most good writing was limited to half-crown monthly magazines), placed it beyond the reach of many poor but educated British readers. There were plenty of competing papers that could be bought for a penny.

The new little paper floundered helplessly in a morass of money problems. Its owners held firmly to the misconception that the public would beat a path to their door if they produced a quality product rather than a cheaper, lesser one. With bankruptcy looming ahead, it became apparent to the proprietors that the paper's only chance for survival was a fresh infusion of cash—in short, a purchaser. After a long and acrimonious (on the part of the suspicious Landells) negotiation, the printing firm of Bradbury and Evans agreed to take *Punch* over for the amount of its debts, a sum in the neighborhood of £300. They also assumed the printing responsibilities relinquished by Joseph Last. The transfer, more the result of Mark Lemon's persuasive powers than the magazine's financial potential, took place at Christmas time in 1842.

As we have seen, at the transfer of ownership, Jerrold, Lemon, à Beckett, Mayhew, and a few others stayed on. After a short period, Coyne and Grattan departed. Wills resigned to become subeditor (with Dickens) of *Household Words* and *All the Year Round*, and later of the *Daily News*. Henning accepted a job in New York. Newman joined the ill-fated *Squib*. Mayhew left in 1845, closely followed by his old classmate, à Beckett. The latter returned a few months later and remained a Punchite until his death eleven years later in 1856.

Mayhew's demotion, his departure, and his subsequent bitterness toward Mark Lemon and *Punch* did not deter his brother Horace "Ponny" Mayhew from joining the staff and the Table in 1845. He was hired as subeditor but did not have the force to handle the paper's prima donnas. It was decided at last that Lemon would handle all the editorial work himself. Ponny became a kind of staff-writer-of-all-work, suggesting ideas to the others and contributing charming but ineffectual little pieces better suited for filling odd lots of empty space than for making his reputation in the literary world. He wrote a series called "Model Men, Women and Children," which had a moderate success. Later, when he had inherited a small income and was no longer dependent on wages, he stopped writing altogether but remained a member of the staff and the Table for the companionship he found there.

Because of his charm and his value as a drinking companion, Lemon, Brooks, and the others found things for him to do. Everyone loved Ponny. On his fiftieth birthday the Punchites feted him at the Table, and Shirley Brooks wrote a long poem in his praise, which he sang to the delighted Ponny.

> No; black are our bosoms and red are our hands,
>   But a model of virtue our Ponniboy stands;
> And his basest detractors can only say this,
>   He's fond of the cup, and the card, and the kiss.

Ponny was, in fact, a colossal boozer; a cheerful, good-natured dandy reputed to be a great womanizer, for which du Maurier teased him unmercifully. Unlike his brother, he was delighted to be relieved of his editorial duties. He was lazy and not ashamed to admit it. Thackeray, on seeing him one evening, said, "Here comes Colonel Newcome," a compliment that Ponny treasured ever after.* He did at last achieve an eternal

---

*In his book *The Newcomes* Thackeray portrayed Colonel Newcome as a model of many virtues.

celebrity, exceeding in luster even that of Thackeray himself, but it was not through his own efforts. His friend and drinking companion John Tenniel used Ponny as his model for the White Knight in Lewis Carroll's *Through the Looking-Glass*. Today Ponny Mayhew is probably the only Punchite whose features would be instantly recognizable to literate people.

Punch's steady climb to success meant success for the firm of Bradbury and Evans, too. The delighted printers moved more and more into the publishing world. In time they would publish both Dickens and Thackeray and a number of important periodicals, including the *Field*, the *Daily News*, the *Countryman*, the *Army and Navy Gazette*, the *Family Herald*, the *London Journal*, and their own *English Encyclopedia*.

The senior partner, William Bradbury, was succeeded in the firm after his death in 1869 by his son William Hardwick Bradbury. Pater Evans died a year later. His son, William F. M. Evans, left the firm in the 1870s. By this time young Bradbury had married a daughter of the art dealer Thomas Agnew, and eventually he brought his in-laws into the business, changing the company name to Bradbury and Agnew, and later to Bradbury, Agnew, & Co. E. V. Lucas, writing of his *Punch* days, notes the death of Sir William Agnew in 1911 by the following epithet: "a very kindly entertainer and admirable mixer of salads." Apparently the Agnews were the equal of the Evanses as Table hosts and companions.

A Bradbury (Lord Amulree) still sits on the board of directors of *Punch* today, although the company is now a wholly owned subsidiary of United Newspapers. So does an Agnew. Peter Graeme Agnew, sixth generation of *Punch* proprietors, began work as a student printer in 1935, working his way up to managing director, with a break to serve in World War II as an RAF wing commander.

In the first few months of *Punch*'s existence, before the Bradbury and Evans takeover, Henry Mayhew was charged with the responsibility of gathering together London's finest writers and artists for the new paper. As we have seen, it was he who recruited Lemon, à Beckett, Coyne, and the rest. During his quest, he had become interested in a writer named "Paul Prendergast" who recently had published a popular best-seller called *The Comic Latin Grammar*. Tracked to his lair, "Prendergast" turned out to be a successful London physician with a literary flair, one Percival Leigh. Mayhew invited him to write for *Punch*, but the cautious doctor dragged his feet for a few issues to see what sort of paper it would turn out to be. He discussed the matter at length with his illustrator, John Leech, and the two decided that they could join *Punch* without loss of dignity.

Leigh was an intellectual and a highbrow. His humor consisted in large

July 17 1841
Designed by A. S. Henning

January 1842
Designed by Hablôt Knight Browne ("Phiz")

July 1842
Designed by William Harvey

January 1843
Designed by Sir John Gilbert

July 1843
Designed by Kenny Meadows

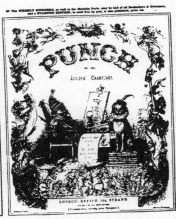

January 1844—January 1849
Richard Doyle's first design

The early covers of Punch

part of Latin and Greek puns, parodies or comic allusions to the classics, and dog-Latin poetry. Members of the table called him ''Professor.'' It was Leigh who raised the scholarship level of *Punch*'s output by demanding of his readers a certain amount of learning. A true *Punch* radical in his younger days, Leigh's poem ''The Pauper's Song'' attracted wide attention for its moving portrayal of a man who preferred prison food and shelter to London poverty.

Surprisingly enough, he had a large following, although his style would have ordinarily attracted a small, elite group. The readers loved him. His series, ''The Labours of Hercules,'' was a great success, and his ''Mr. Pipp's Diary'' accompanied Richard Doyle's drawings of ''Ye Manners and Customs of ye Englyshe.''

In his final years he was a Swedenborgian and a health-food fanatic. He could be found daily in Richmond Park grubbing about for edible herbs and roots, which he brought to his Spartan rooms to cook. The former dapper Professor who discoursed so pleasantly on wine and women at the Wednesday dinners resembled an ancient derelict.

Unlike his Table mates, Leigh outlived three *Punch* editors. As the solitary survivor of the original Punchites, he had a special position among the paper's contributors. He continued to work until his death. Unfortunately, his writing deteriorated as much as his appearance. In order not to hurt his feelings, Burnand or Arthur à Beckett (Gilbert's son) would rewrite his pieces for publication. At last it became apparent that his offerings were useless, but each week his copy was duly returned to him in the form of proofs for correction. The corrected copy never appeared in the magazine. No questions were asked. It was enough for the old Professor to feel needed until his death in 1889 at the age of seventy-eight. His appearance was so scruffy that when he died Bradbury brought his checkbook to Leigh's funeral, expecting to pay his debts and burial expenses. He discovered to his surprise that the Professor had left an estate of eleven thousand pounds.

It was John Leech who brought Albert Smith to *Punch*. Smith was an old medical school friend and roommate of Leech's who had set up practice as a dental surgeon in London without much success. He was one of the most versatile and dependable of the original Punchites. His copy was always clean, publishable, and on time. Last and Landells had asked him to write for the stillborn *Cosmorama*, so obviously he was not unknown in the journalistic world.

Unfortunately, Smith the man was not as presentable as Smith the writer. He was vulgar, aggressive, and self-serving. Much of his talent depended on clever imitations of the writing of other people, such as

Dickens and later Jerrold. He was one of those merely adequate writers who, for some reason, catch the public fancy and become immensely popular. His *Punch* comic series, "The Physiology of a London Medical Student," which celebrated the ups and downs of the hapless going men training for medical careers, was well received and called for sequels, the "physiologies" of London evening parties and of London idlers.

He was one of those literary workhorses who could have gone on forever turning out reams of funny, readable prose on demand, but as a Table companion Smith was impossible. Boorish, ill-mannered, and stingy, he was simply not a gentleman of the sort that Thackeray, Bradbury, Evans, and the rest cared to associate with. Thackeray and Jerrold detested him, Jerrold loudly and openly, and Thackeray in a more subdued manner. He got himself into trouble with the Punchites by publishing an unflattering parody of Jerrold's style, "The Adventures of Mrs. Ledbury," which drove the Little Wasp into a fury. *Punch* people only skewered outsiders. They never attacked each other—in public. Smith had broken the rules.

It was a custom among the Punchites that each man, on his birthday, would put up a guinea to stand the others a bowl of hot punch. Smith not only refused to pay for his bowl, he flatly refused even to tell the others the date of his birth. They found it out somehow, and when the day arrived, the Punchites each contributed a share of the sum for the purchase of the bowl and solemnly drank Smith's health. Smith participated cheerfully in the drinking. He was never shy about imbibing more than his share on the others' birthdays, why not on his own? When the party was over he looked about for his new cloak but it was gone. Henry Mayhew and Joseph Allen had stolen it and pawned it to pay for the birthday bowl. They presented the furious Smith with the pawn ticket.

It was characteristic of Smith that he took the joke badly. Instead of accepting the fact that it was his turn to pay for the drink and that he had been fairly tricked into doing so, he sent for the police and had the other Punchites arrested for theft. They were forced to post bail, and the incident ended with ill-feeling and bitterness instead of the expected laughter.

It was obvious to all that Smith had to go. In spite of his success as a circulation raiser, his faults as a Table companion forced his early exit. Lemon, who had rid himself of Coyne in the same way, accused him of plagiarizing some of his pieces from a foreign journal. Jerrold, still smarting about "Mrs. Ledbury," demanded his ouster. Smith left the Table and the paper, never to return.

After his departure, Smith scored an outstanding success as a lecturer and composer of "public entertainments" at the Egyptian Hall in Oxford

Street. His lecture "The Ascent of Mont Blanc" made him an instant London celebrity.* He also started his own paper, the *Man in the Moon*, which was dedicated almost entirely to humorous attacks on *Punch*. The paper was a success and a threat to its archenemy until Lemon deflated it by hiring away its star writer, Shirley Brooks.

Smith was an admirer of Dickens and dramatized his Christmas story *The Battle of Life* in 1846. He presented the novelist with a St. Bernard puppy, which Dickens christened Linda. When he was asked why he tolerated Smith, of whom he was fond and with whom he sometimes shared his Bohemian pleasures, Dickens shrugged his shoulders. "We all have our Smiths," he said wryly.

Affluence seems to have ennobled Smith in the end. When his enemy Jerrold died, he organized a benefit of one of his highly lucrative "entertainments" to raise a fund for Jerrold's family. Smith died at the relatively early age of forty-four, unmourned by his fellow journalists, of the common Victorian complaint, "ill-health due to an over-taxed constitution."

The first of *Punch*'s great superstars was John Leech. He was the son of an impecunious Ludgate Hill coffeehouse keeper. The charming but inadequate parent figure, reminiscent of Mr. Micawber, always out of pocket but always amusing, seems to reoccur frequently among the artists of the period. Dickens had one; so did Jerrold. They may have acted as a spur to achievement. Leech, Sr., was constantly in debt and would remain a thorn in his son's sensitive side for many years to come.

Somehow Leech, Sr., got his son into Charterhouse, not an easy thing to do for someone of his social level and his financial circumstances. Two things happened there to young Leech that affected his life: He became a gentleman and something of a snob; and he began a lifelong friendship with his schoolmate William Makepeace Thackeray. It was Leech who convinced Thackeray to join the *Punch* staff, after Edward Fitzgerald had advised him not to do so for fear of injuring his reputation.

The earliest recorded memory we have of the man who popularized the "social" cartoon is of "the little John Leech on first coming to Charterhouse . . . put upon a table in a blue jacket and high-buttoned trousers and made to sing to the other boys." He would sing again, nearly forty years later, on the sad Christmas Eve in 1863 when William Makepeace Thackeray died. The song was Barry Cornwall's "King Death," sung in chorus with the other Punchites, followed by Tully's version of "The Mahogany Tree."

* Smith had actually climbed Mount Blanc. The lecture included scenic diorama views, a piano, and a patter song entitled "Galignani's Messenger."

"GENERAL FÉVRIER" TURNED TRAITOR.

"RUSSIA HAS TWO GENERALS IN WHOM SHE CAN CONFIDE—GENERALS JANVIER AND FÉVRIER."—*Speech of the late Emperor of Russia.*

John Leech, 1855

After Charterhouse, Leech intended to study medicine, but halfway through his training his father went bankrupt. Leech's career as a doctor, like Jerrold's navy commission, vanished into thin air, and he was forced to earn his own living.

He worked briefly as an assistant to a physician and then decided to become an artist.

In 1835 Leech published a series of drawings of comic London street characters called *Etchings and Drawings by A. Pen, Esq.* It led to an assignment with *Bell's Life*, a harum-scarum journal that was a favorite with sporting university students. He collaborated with George Cruikshank on contributions to *Bentley's Miscellany*, and Cruikshank seems to have had a strong effect on Leech's early style.

He was a kind and generous man and a good friend, a trait which got him into trouble twice before he joined *Punch*. In each case he backed a bill for a friend who defaulted. He was sent to debtors' prison, an injustice which, according to Spielmann, may account for his dislike of Jews. This is probably untrue, since his prejudices also extended to Irishmen and Frenchmen, neither of whom in any way affected his life or were responsible for his incarceration.

Leech is said to have discovered the woman he would eventually marry while walking down a London street. He is supposed to have followed her home, found her name in the directory, and contrived an introduction, after which he devoted himself to wooing and wedding her. However he found her, it was apparent to everyone except himself that she was an unfortunate mistake. Du Maurier described her as "the silliest he had ever seen." Her absurd social pretenses kept Leech poor in spite of his considerable earning power. Nevertheless, he loved her and could see no flaw in her. She was the model for the "Leech girl" in *Punch*.

Leech's girls were prototypes of the Victorian young woman as she is known today. Small, curvaceous, with large innocent eyes, a soft round chin, and dimples, her hair in ringlets, she charmed one and all. In 1860, Shirley Brooks remarked to Henry Silver that he hoped Leech "won't get aristocratic in his girls' noses and give up drawing cuddleable girls." Keene was incapable of drawing a pretty woman, and du Maurier's tall, cool, drawing-room goddesses were hardly the cuddleable type. Leech's women, except when they were made ugly for a purpose, were adorable.

Leech joined *Punch* in 1841, contributing his first big cut in the fourth issue on August 7, 1841. It was called "Foreign Affairs" and illustrated an article of the same name by Percival Leigh. He soon surpassed the paper's big artistic guns, H. G. Hine, William Newman, Kenny Meadows, and Hablôt K. Browne ("Phiz"), in popularity. He preferred to portray "social miseries" rather than serious political subjects and was relieved when Tenniel took over the responsibility for the big cut in 1850, leaving him to devote himself to the socials with their humorous captions (called the "cackle"). However, he was perfectly capable of turning out superb political caricatures.

One of his most memorable engravings appeared on February 10, 1855. It was "General Février Turned Traitor." The cartoon, which was printed at the height of the Crimean War, marked the death of Tsar Nicholas I. The tsar, remarking on the inability of enemies of Russia to withstand the cruel Russian winters, had said, "Russia has two generals in whom she can confide—Generals Janvier and Février." He died on February 2nd. The drawing shows the tsar on his deathbed, clutching a paper announcing a Russian defeat. Death, in military uniform, stands beside him, one bony hand on his chest. William Powell Frith, the painter of *Derby Day*, wrote "Of all Leech's work, this seems to be the finest example. Think how savage Gillray or vulgar Rowlandson would have handled the theme! The Emperor would have been caricatured into a repulsive monster, and Death would have lost his terror."

During his twenty-three years with *Punch*, Leech contributed about three thousand drawings, of which about six hundred were full-page cuts. He loved comic scenes of low-life, valets who aped their masters, silly or presumptuous servant girls, drunken cabdrivers, and officious railway conductors. He pilloried arrogant swells and foolish young misses. He created and destroyed fads in men's and women's clothes. (It was probably thanks to Leech that the bloomer craze never caught on in England.) He hated crinolines, bizarre hats, moustaches (on anyone except officers of crack cavalry regiments), and middle-class burghers who got above themselves.

One of his best creations was the snug, comfortable, little Mr. Briggs, who, having amassed a small nest egg (probably as a shopkeeper in the genre of Mr. Caudle) and a certain amount of leisure, decided to try the hunting field. Leech was a passionate hunter and rarely let a week go by without riding to hounds, sometimes with Tenniel and often with Sir John Millais. For more than thirty years he filled the pages of *Punch* with hunting jokes: the man who fell off his horse, the man whose horse refused the fence, the man who got caught in driving rain or snow, ad infinitum. Briggs eventually branched out into salmon fishing and other pursuits to the chagrin of his disapproving wife and silly daughters.

Leech is sometimes credited with the invention of the term *cartoon* in its present-day meaning as a humorous drawing in a magazine. In fact, although he did not invent the term, a Leech drawing was the first in history to bear that designation. "Cartoon No. 1" appeared in *Punch* in 1843, as a drawing called "Substance and Shadow." A cartoon is (and

SUBSTANCE AND SHADOW.

This was the first magazine drawing ever to be called a cartoon. The designation caught on and has been used for political or humorous drawings ever since. (John Leech, 1843)

was), of course, a sketch or plan for a mural painting. An exhibition was being held of cartoons for the forthcoming redecoration of the Houses of Parliament. *Punch* countered with its own cartoons—six of them— commenting on various social evils: weaknesses in public education, the way Britons fawned on the hereditary aristocracy, the wide difference between the status of capital and the living conditions of labor, and the way the government danced attendance on the ancient Duke of Wellington.

Leech's Cartoon No. 1 showed a group of poverty-stricken Londoners at the exhibition, regarding with some bewilderment the portraits of gorgeously uniformed and decorated notables. "The poor ask for bread," Jerrold wrote in an accompanying paragraph, "and the philanthropy of the State accords—an exhibition." The sixth cartoon was an indictment of duelling. It showed Lord Cardigan, who had recently wounded a former officer of his regiment for disagreeing with him, wearing a foolscap and bells as he prepares to shoot another victim similarly attired. Death waits in a newly dug grave.

Leech's first big comic hit in *Punch* was the "Anti-Graham Envelope.'' The home secretary, Sir James Graham, had outraged England by opening mail sent to Giuseppe Mazzini and his supporters and informing the government of Naples of the contents. This was highly illegal. A parliamentary investigation was held in secret, and Graham was cleared in a general whitewash. *Punch* leaped to the attack with a deluge of Graham jokes. The most popular was Leech's drawing, a takeoff on the ''Mulready Envelope,'' designed by William Mulready, a genre painter who had created a postal envelope festooned with allegorical subjects, elephants and other foolery. Leech's parody showed Graham in the guise of a snake in the grass, and his agents nosing about peering at other people's letters. Mulready was furious at Leech, sensing in the drawing a personal affront rather than an attack on a larger political evil, but the two men later became friends.

Leech was the first artist to introduce a marginally sexual theme into a *Punch* drawing. In 1857, his cartoon ''The Great Social Evil'' pointed up London poverty by showing a ragged young woman saying to an old friend whom she has obviously not seen in a long time, ''Ah! Fanny! How long have you been gay?'' Seeing a girl of her own class in a pretty dress, bonnet, and crinoline, she assumes that her friend has become a prostitute, since there could have been no other avenue to affluence for her. It is obvious from the second girl's attitude (and a hastily fastened dress leaving one button unbuttoned) that she is right. The expression *gay* in Victorian times meant prostitution rather than homosexuality.

''The Great Social Evil'' was a variation of Leigh's poem indicating that gaol (jail) was preferable to London poverty. In this case the protagonist is female and has taken the obvious way to a better world. Whether or not this cartoon caused a blush to appear on the most delicate cheek is not recorded.

As an artist, Leech was somewhat less of a draughtsman than Charles Keene and perhaps a little less clever than du Maurier in his perceptions of humor in social situations. Nevertheless, in his time he was much discussed and much admired. After he joined *Punch*, on the strength of his illustrations for Leigh's *Comic Latin Grammar*, he continued to do illustrations, contributing four etchings to *A Christmas Carol* in 1844, drawings for Gilbert à Beckett's *Comic Histories*, and outdoor sporting scenes for novels by R. G. Surtees. John Ruskin, in an Oxford lecture in 1883, praised his ''natural simplicity and aerial space'' and called attention to his ''vivid genius capable in its brightness of finding pretty jest in everything, but capable in its tenderness also of rejoicing in the heart of everything.'' Frith called him the ''prime exponent of the action of wind on objects.'' The American artist John Sloan later said that Leech's drawings put him as a line draughtsman in the class of Rembrandt.

THE GREAT SOCIAL EVIL.

TIME:—Midnight. A Sketch not a Hundred Miles from the Haymarket.

Bella. "AH! FANNY! HOW LONG HAVE YOU BEEN *GAY?*"

John Leech, 1857

Surprisingly enough, Henry James said that Leech had "no great sense of beauty." In rebuttal, Dickens pointed out that:

> Leech was the very first Englishman who had made beauty a part of his art. . . . He turned caricature into character. In all his designs, whatever he designed to do, he did. . . . Will no Associate of the Royal Academy be found on its books one of these days, the labours of whose oil and brushes will have sunk into the profoundest obscurity when many pencil marks of John Leech will be still fresh in half the houses of the land?

No portrait of John Leech would be complete without mention of his pathological hatred of street noises, an obsession that many people (including Thomas Carlyle) felt contributed to his early death. Faced with an organ-grinder or a noisy workman, he went into a kind of nervous prostration. His house was soundproofed with double windows and heavy curtains, but it was no use. He fought a constant, bitter, crazy war with street musicians and loud carpenters and plasterers, who, knowing of his peculiarity, increased their din and then demanded bribes to keep quiet.

"J. L. still nervous about himself," Silver notes in his diary in June 1864. "Defied by two organ men yesterday, who called him 'you bloody shit' and 'you bloody bugger' etc., in the choicest Billingsgate. Said if he hadn't feared the excitement he would have knocked them down, the beasts, for he had his children with him."

Leech's improvident father dogged his days of success. It took the whole sum he received for his first hundred paintings, about three thousand pounds, to clear away the old man's debts. Unsatisfied, the senior Leech tried to borrow money from Mark Lemon against his son's future production, a request that the astute Lemon promptly refused. Leech was furious at his father's presumption. Lemon advised him that his duty was to work for his wife and children. "If buttoning up your pockets leads to a quarrel with your father, I should still advise you to button them up." Leech did thereafter.

Leech died suddenly in November 1864, of angina pectoris, at the age of forty-seven. Lemon called a meeting at the Bedford Hotel in Russell Square to arrange the funeral* and to decide on his successor as principal artist. After some argument du Maurier was proposed by Keene, Tenniel,

---

*It seemed curious to me that Lemon did this rather than Mrs. Leech. On further research, I found to my amazement that Victorian women were not permitted to make such serious arrangements or even to attend funerals without a husband's or other male relative's consent. It was feared they would behave in an embarrassingly overemotional fashion.

and Silver. In spite of opposition by Tom Taylor and lack of enthusiasm from Brooks, du Maurier was elected.

"If ever there was a square English hole and a square English peg to fit it," du Maurier said later, "that hole was *Punch* and that peg was John Leech. He was John Bull himself, but John Bull polite, modest, gentle—full of self-respect . . . and with all the bully softened out of him."

Describing Leech's funeral, du Maurier wrote:

> You never saw such an affecting sight as when they put him into his grave. Millais suddenly burst out crying convulsively, and several others sobbed out loud while the parson read in a trembly voice and could hardly help breaking down too. Poor old Mark Lemon as well; really it was quite awful and I was so demoralized that my nervous system is hardly steady yet.

Although in his last years he had been earning two thousand pounds a year, a magnificent sum for the period, Leech died penniless. Neither his closest friends nor his wife knew where the money had gone. Disraeli, long one of his favorite targets, saw to it that a Civil List pension was granted to his widow. His knighthood, of course, had flown out of the window with his first funny drawing of Prince Albert.

It was Leech who introduced to *Punch* the paper's first immortal, William Makepeace Thackeray. If *Punch* was made for Mark Lemon and he for *Punch*, the Table was made for Thackeray and vice versa. He was an immensely clubbable man, prone to fits of depression when he was alone, cheerful and secure when he was surrounded by his fellows in an atmosphere of good food, drink, and conversation. The Table meant a great deal to him, and as he grew richer from his novels he supported it along with Bradbury and Evans, supplying such delightful extras as oysters, turtle soup, and champagne. Even after he left *Punch*, he dined at the Table often, joking, drinking, and enjoying himself with the others.

On one sad occasion Thackeray was almost banished from his place at the Table. He had written an essay in which he praised Leech, saying that without his old friend *Punch* would be nothing. The other Punchites were up in arms at once. Sensitive egos had been trodden on. Harsh words were spoken, and a miserably contrite Thackeray wrote his Table mates a letter offering to stand them all a splendid dinner if he could be forgiven. His offer was taken in the spirit in which he intended it and all became friends again.

Thackeray had plenty to be depressed about. At the age of twenty-one he inherited a fortune and lost it through gambling and profligacy. His

HORRID TRAGEDY IN PRIVATE LIFE!

Punch's *mysterious cartoon. This cartoon appeared in the magazine in the form in which it appears here. Students of* Punch *humor have been trying for years to figure out what the joke was, and one historian offered a reward of five pounds to anyone who could explain it. Fifty years after Thackeray's death, a Punchite suggested that it represented Thackeray's two little daughters playing at Kings and Queens and that the taller girl has just sentenced her little sister to be beheaded in the Tower. A good explanation; no one will ever know for sure.* (William Makepeace Thackeray, 1847) young wife, whom he loved dearly, drifted into incurable insanity, leaving him with two small daughters to raise. He was intensely sensitive to criticism and suffered keenly from envy and disappointment when his friends Dickens and Jerrold became more successful than he. At the end of his life he was in poor health.

He was a tall (six feet, three inches) pink-cheeked, uncertain-mannered man, who peered nervously through round eyeglasses. In an early altercation at school his nose had been broken by a boy named Venables ("the boy who spoilt my profile"). He had a habit of tucking his thumbs and forefingers into his waistcoat pockets as he talked. Teasing was one of his favorite pastimes. He would address some unsuspecting young colleague, saying, "I've written a little poem today:

> The mouse lay cosy in her hole
> And nothing could be snugger . . . "

Then, with an expression of great perplexity, he would confess that for the life of him he was unable to find a rhyme. Falling all over himself in his anxiety to help the great man, his victim would blurt out "bugger!" Thackeray's eyebrows would go up. "Dear me!" he would say. "Yes, of course! I never thought of that." It would gradually dawn on his listener that he had been had.

An old Carthusian, like Leech and Silver, Thackeray had spent a year and a half at Trinity College, Cambridge. He solemnly informed Silver that his first instruction from the editor of *Punch* was, "Come and frig me. Curious how Charterhouse has eventuated in *Punch*."

When he came to *Punch* in 1842, he was already an established general-purpose writer-journalist, though unknown to the public due to his habit of writing under pseudonyms. In 1837 he had published a book of drawings as "Theophilus Wagstaff." In *Fraser's Magazine*, to which he contributed "The Yellowplush Papers," he was "Michael Angelo Titmarsh." He had been "George Savage Fitz-Boodle," "Major Goliah Gahagan," and others. It was as Fitz-Boodle that he wrote *Barry Lyndon* in 1844. At *Punch* he was "Mr. Punch," Hibernis Hibernior," "Our Fat Contributor," and many more. It was not until his novel *Vanity Fair* appeared in 1847 that he first used his own name. Meanwhile, to his distress, his friend Dickens, whose name always appeared on all his writings in large letters, was becoming famous.

After he left Cambridge, Thackeray traveled for a while and in 1831 entered the Middle Temple, where he shared rooms with Tom Taylor. He gave up the legal profession very shortly, and wrote and drew for the short-lived *National Standard*. This first experience as a contributing illustrator motivated him to move to Paris to study art. That, too, ceased to interest him, and he returned to join *Fraser's* and ended up at *Punch*.

Thackeray became a regular contributor in 1844, writing parodies, burlesques, satires, essays, jokes, and poems. At first he was unpopular, overshadowed by Jerrold, à Beckett, Mayhew, and the other stars, but soon he attracted a huge public. His contributions, according to Spielmann, ranged from short paragraphs of a line or two to major efforts of up to twenty-five hundred words, from couplets to poems and ballads of more than a hundred lines. Between 1844 and 1848 he wrote an average of a column and a half a week.

His first article in *Punch* was, Spielmann says, either "The Legend of Jawbrahim Heraudee," a mock-Oriental spoof of the literary celebrities of the day, in 1842 (Vol. II, p. 254) or the lampoon "Miss Tickletoby's Lectures on English History" in 1842 (Vol. III, p. 8).

Athol Mayhew says in his book about *Punch* that his father told him Thackeray's debut in the paper was in July 1841, with "A Fair Offer," a comic letter purporting to be from a scoundrelly petty criminal who wants a job as a *Punch* critic and who is promptly hired by Mr. Punch. The style is very like Thackeray's, but there is no evidence, except for Mayhew's memory of his deceased father's possible statement, to prove that he actually wrote it.

There is not much documentary proof to authenticate the history of Thackeray's days at *Punch*. Spielmann credits him with 428 contributions and has done enough research on the subject to write a book about it (*The Hitherto Unidentified Contributions of W. M. Thackeray to PUNCH*, 1896). He makes no mention of "A Fair Offer." Thackeray's daughter, Lady Ritchie, places her father's total contributions at only 380.

Whatever the exact number may have been, Thackeray's work included some of the finest writing to appear in *Punch*. He was responsible for much of "Jenkins." In "Jeames' Diary" he portrayed a semiliterate footman, describing the notable events of his life in service. It was "The Snob Papers" (by "One of Themselves") that first made him popular. They had a tremendous reception and raised the circulation of the paper, to Thackeray's delight. After the failure of "Miss Tickletoby's Lectures," aborted by the editor, he needed an ego boost badly. The "Snob" articles, which went on for fifty-one issues, made him a star on a level with Jerrold, who was already on the way down. They were compared widely with the Mrs. Caudle series and said to be better. "Punch's Prize Novels" raised his reputation even more. They were hilarious, sharply accurate parodies of the work of Charles Lever, Bulwer-Lytton, Alexandre Dumas, Fenimore Cooper, Disraeli, Marie Corelli, and others.

Many people are unaware that Thackeray was an artist as well as an author. He illustrated seventeen of his own books, including *Vanity Fair*, *Pendennis,* and *The Virginians.* He and Leech applied to illustrate *The Pickwick Papers* but were turned down (an event that Thackeray referred to afterwards as "Mr. Pickwick's Lucky Escape"). He usually signed his drawings with a little pair of spectacles.

His caricature of Louis Philippe, "A Case of Real Distress," which showed the king as a "*pauvre malheurex* [sic]," got *Punch* banned in France for some months.

The article "A Pretty Little Picture for Pretty Little Protestants" is a typical example of *Punch*-cum-Thackeray anti-Catholicism, warning that if a Roman Catholic hierarchy and cathedral were established in England, Catholic troops could not be far behind. In addition to the "Mahogany Tree," another of his best ballads appeared in *Punch*, "The Ballad of Bouillabaisse," celebrating the famous soup.

The lack of cultural eminence at Windsor was a longtime joke to the Punchites. The philistinism of the Royal Family was an endless source of fun, especially to Jerrold. When the news was released that the Queen and Prince Albert were to have Shakespearean plays presented at the palace in a form "a little compressed"—a kind of *Reader's Digest* condensed book production of the bard—the Punchites were ecstatic. Thackeray immediately wrote, the poem "Great News, Wonderful News" and illustrated it himself.

During his productive period at *Punch*, Thackeray was a man of tremendous energy. Within an eight-year period, he wrote his four best novels.* He visited America twice, stood for Parliament (unsuccessfully), and led an unusually full and demanding social life. He also wrote for *Punch* and established the *Cornhill Magazine*. His old Cambridge friend Edward Fitzgerald wrote, in a letter to Frederick Tennyson,

> Meanwhile old Thackeray laughs at all this . . . and goes on in his own way, writing hard for half a dozen reviews and newspapers all the morning; driving, drinking, talking of a night; managing to preserve a fresh colour and perpetual flow of spirits under a wear and tear of thinking and feeding that would have knocked up any other man I know two years ago at least.

Henry Silver confided to his diary that Thackeray "takes a brandy and soda before breakfast 'to give him an appetite' " and "talks of using that umbrella instrument for his erectile tissue—erectile disuse it has now

---

*Vanity Fair (1847), *Pendennis* (1850), *The History of Henry Esmond Esq.* (1852), *The Newcomes* (1855).

GREAT NEWS! WONDERFUL NEWS!

SHAKSPEARE COMPRESSED.

Punch wonbereth that Shakspeare hath at length appeared before ye Queene.

WHAT wonderful news from the Court,
Old Will's at the palace a guest,
The Queen and her Royal Consort
Have received him " a little compressed."

He saith her Grace will heare no more Italians nor Almagne fiddlers, but take ye right English waye.

Who'll venture to whisper henceforth
Her Grace loves the Opera best ?
Our QUEEN has acknowledged to the worth
Of SHAKSPEARE a little compress'd.

Neither will her Grace see Amburgh his beastes never no mo.

Who'll talk of VAN AMBURGH again !
No more are his beasts in request ;
They're good but for poor Drury Lane,
At home She has SHAKSPEARE compressed.

Nor ye littel Thumbe (a sillie vaine fellowe).

Away with the tiny TOM THUMB,
Like mighty NAPOLEON dress'd ;
For SHAKSPEARE a courting has come,
Like TOMMY " a little compressed."

Punch sees (in imaggnacion) the courte assemble, and Master Kemble the Player with his boke.

The Court in its splendour assembles,
(The play gives its dullness a zest),
And the last of the Royal old KEMBLES
Reads SHAKSPEARE a little compressed.

They forme round Master Kemble a ring royall, and ting, ding, ding ! ye Playe beginneth.

Behold them all diamonds and jewels,
Our QUEEN and our PRINCE, and the rest ;
As they sit upon gilded fauteuils,
And listen to SHAKSPEARE compress'd.

Ye firste Acte. (After this ye servants hand muffinncs aboute.)

ACT I.

Great CYMBELINE's Court 's in a gloom,
Rash POSTHUMUS' flame is confess'd ;
Poor IMOGEN 's locked in her room,
And her love is a little compressed.

Ye seconde Acte. After the which an Enterlude of Ginger-Beere.

ACT II.

Fair IMOGEN sleeps in her bed,
IACHIMO lurks in a chest ;
What, locked in a drunk ! the PRINCE said,
I think *he 's* a little gombress'd.

Ye thirde Acte. A straunge incident of Imogen. Flourish of Crumpets

ACT III.

Now IMOGEN, flying the Court,
Appears in boys' trousers and vest ;
O fie ! Mr. KEMBLE stops short,
And the act is a little compress'd.

Ye fourthe 'cte. Ye Queene's Grace weepeth for Imogen, poore maybe !

ACT IV.

When the QUEEN heard how IMOGEN died,
(Poor child ! like a dove in a nest),
She looked at the PRINCE at her side,
And her tears were a little compress'd.

Ye Queene's Grace rejoyceth that Imogen is not dedde.

ACT V.

But O ! how HER MAJESTY laughed,
When she found 'twasn't dying she saw,
But fainting, brought on by a draught
From IMOGEN's mother-in-law.

The Play draweth nigh to a close.
Virtue is rewarded.

And now come the Romans in force,
And POSTHUMUS comes in their train ;
With their foot, and their chariots, and horse,
They come over England to reign.

Britannia ruleth ye waytes.
Ye play endeth.

Impossible ! here says the QUEEN—
Our lady, with pride in her breast :
O bring me the lovers again,
And pray let the fight be compress'd.

Ye curtain falleth.

GRAND TABLEAU.

Master Kemble boweth.

The lovers are happy as just ;
The lecturer closes his book,
And bows from the presence august,
Well paid with a smile and a look.

Punch Moraliseth.

Great Lady ! the news of thy court Poor *Punch* has oft read as a pest ; But with this he inclines not to sport, As he solemnly here does attest. If it please you our bard to cut short, It doubtless is done for the best. Be pleased, too, we pray, to exhort SIR BOB with your royal behest	To shorten his speeches, and for 't Your Grace shall be heartily blest ; And fiercely I'll joke and retort On all who your peace would infest. And, though joking is known as my forte, I never will jibe or will jest. If you'll list to our Poet immort-AL, and love him complete or compress'd !

The Necessity of Duelling.

TO THE EDITOR OF " PUNCH."

HAPPEN lately, Sir, to have seen one or two numbers of your paper, which, I am sorry to find, is taken in by some who ought to know better. You have thought proper, I perceive, to make various ridiculous remarks upon the subject of duelling, which it is not possible that you should know anything about ; and by these, and by a series of impertinent caricatures, you have been striving to bring it into contempt.

I desire, Sir, that you will desist, for the future, from the absurd observations above alluded to, and turn your disrespectful pencil to some other purpose.

In the first place, let me request you to take notice that your object is perfectly understood. You wish to deprive the aristocracy of a privilege which they have enjoyed from time immemorial, and thus to efface one of the chief distinctions which separate them from shoemakers, tinkers, tailors, low writers, and that sort of people. If you expect to succeed, I assure you you are very much mistaken. Gentlemen, I can tell you, are not going to be laughed out of their principles and opinions by you.

Duelling does not concern the common people. A duel is an affair of honour ; and trades-persons, workmen, and so forth, have no honour to defend. It is of no consequence to them whether they are insulted or not ; and if they have disputes, these may be easily settled by their fists, or by going to law. Among them, therefore, duelling is unnecessary, and recourse to it would be a presumptuous imitation of their superiors ; on which account, so far as they are concerned, it unquestionably ought not to be suffered.

Honour is that quality in one gentleman which deters another from daring to breathe a syllable against his character ; and which, consequently, keeps that character unsullied. Honour, then, you will say, is ferocity. Do not be impertinent, Sir. It is proper that you should be made aware that the preservation of an unsullied character is incumbent upon every gentleman.

The imputation of falsehood or dishonesty to a gentleman always renders it imperative that he should send a challenge. I imagine I hear you ask whether a refutation of the charge would not do as well ? None of your vulgar sneering, Sir—No, it would not do as well. The gentleman owes it, as a duty, to the society to which he belongs, to go out and fight. In so doing, he asserts the principle that no gentleman can become the accuser of another, but at the risk of being shot. Whatever one gentleman may think of another, the institution of duelling tends to make him keep his thoughts to himself. In this manner are often prevented those painful exposures, which, when allowed to take place, are so highly prejudicial to the exclusive circles, and the general reputation of the world of Fashion is upheld. Again, I suppose you will have the audacity to demand whether the number of blacklegs, swindlers, seducers, and asserters of untruths, included in the Army and Navy and the ranks of the aristocracy in general, is really so alarmingly great as to render the protection of the duelling system indispensable to the existence of that august body. I will tell you what, Sir ; your plebeian insolence deserves a severe chastisement, and I have only to add that you may consider yourself horsewhipped by Your humble servant,

SABRETASH.

Horse Guards.

The Punchites had a great deal of fun with the Royal Family's lack of culture. When the news was released that Shakespeare's plays would be acted at Windsor Castle in a form "a little compressed," Thackeray couldn't wait to announce it in verse. (Drawings and poem by William Makepeace Thackeray, 1844) fallen into. 'Better abstain from drink,' says Pater Evans. 'But I *like* drink,' says T.''

His famous quarrels with Jerrold and Dickens were triggered by temperaments and the clashes of ego that so often occur among men of genius. In both cases friendship was restored by Thackeray making the first overtures. His defeat in 1857, when he stood for the constituency of Oxford for a seat in the House of Commons, was largely due to a gentlemanly reluctance to buy votes and an inescapable compulsion to speak his mind regardless of political expediency. He lost by a majority of only 67 votes, most of which his opponent bought very cheaply.

There are a number of stories surrounding Thackeray's departure from *Punch*. He seems to have resigned several times. His first departure was due to a scathing political article by Jerrold to which he objected. (''Upon my word, I don't think I ought to pull any longer in the same boat with such a savage little Robespierre.'') The proprietors refused to accept his resignation and withdrew the offending article. The second time, he was returning from a trip to Edinburgh and stopped to buy a *Punch* at a news dealer's. He was appalled to see a big cut of the Emperor Napoleon III as a ''Beggar on Horseback'' galloping to hell with a bloody sword in his hand. He had already differed with the *Punch* management on questions of disrespect to Prince Albert, although he was the author of the ''ducal hat'' letter mentiond earlier herein, and on the Crystal Palace. The attack on the emperor was too much. This time it was too late to withdraw the cartoon, and his resignation was accepted.

That is Thackeray's own version of the story. Lemon confided to Henry Silver that a salary dispute had caused him to leave. There was, in fact, a money quarrel between Thackeray and Bradbury and Evans, but he maintains that that was not the main cause of his leaving. His novels were making him rich and famous, and the need to turn out so many words per week for *Punch* was an onerous chore that kept him from devoting full time to his more important works. His departure was probably due to all three reasons—political incompatibility, money, and time. Whatever the cause, he remained a loyal and congenial Table member until his death.

Thackeray died of apoplexy on Christmas Eve 1863 at the age of fifty-two. For some time he had suffered from strictures and kidney disease. Sir William Hardman, in a letter to his friend E. D. Holroyd, comments on the death of Thackeray thus:

> And now for the gossip about poor old Thackeray. The papers say that it was a spasm of the *heart* which brought on vomiting and burst a blood vessel on the brain. Now I have it on good authority that of late years Thackeray has been what may be called a ''boozer'', that is, he never went to bed in a

strictly sober condition. He was subject to spasm of the *stomach* in consequence, accompanied by vomiting. The papers say he died peaceably and his corpse was calm. Poor fellow! I regret to contradict this on the authority of Leech . . . who, living near, was the first person sent for by the family. The features were much distorted and discoloured by the bursting of the blood-vessel, of course. Moreover, both arms were bent, the hands clutching at the collar of his night-shirt, and were so rigidly fixed that he was buried in that position.

Apparently death was not a surprise to him. For some months before he died, he had spoken of it to his daughter Anne and to a friend, Mr. Synge ("I want to tell you that I shall never see you again. I feel that I am doomed."). It was, however, a surprise and shock to his friends, many of whom had talked or dined with him and had seen no symptoms at all of anything more than his usual infirmities.

He [Mr. Punch] cracks his jokes still, for satire must live; but he is combed, washed, neatly clothed, and perfectly presentable. He goes into the very best company; he keeps a stud at Melton; he has a moor in Scotland; he rides in the Park; has his stall at the Opera; is constantly dining out at clubs and in private society; and goes every night in the season to balls and parties where you see the most beautiful women possible.

—W. M. Thackeray

y 1847 *Punch* had become a power in England. It was read in every vicarage and officers' mess, in country houses and gentlemen's clubs, in palaces and in universities. Its contributors were the leading wits and literary lions of the day. Its humor was by definition the most amusing anywhere. If it was in *Punch*, it was funny. If you didn't think it was funny, you had no sense of humor. The London *Charivari* had made its impression on the nation.

Mark Lemon's innovative practice of paying his staff a salary—not just a token stipend, but a real income that a gentleman could live on—relieved his artists and writers of the need to work elsewhere. Many of them wrote novels and plays and some contributed occasionally to other periodicals, but the fear of poverty was gone; they could depend on *Punch*. This system of putting together a permanent team, a kind of literary stock company, was followed a century later by Harold Ross at the *New Yorker*, with similar success. In return for their security, the writers gave the magazine their best efforts.

Stimulated by prosperity, the Punchites satirized everyone and everything in sight. The sycophantic relationship of the politically ambitious Lord Brougham with the Duke of Wellington was a favorite target. In a single year the two were represented as Robinson Crusoe and Friday; a circus ringmaster and clown; a king and his jester; political canvassers; a gentleman and a gillie at a shooting party; and a performer with a trained flea, among others.

Lord John Russell, Sir Robert Peel, Gladstone, Disraeli, Palmerston, and Daniel O'Connell were mercilessly pilloried. The *Post*, the *Morning*

A SCENE IN WESTMINSTER CIRCUS.

CLOWN TO THE RING *loq.*) —" Now, Mr. WELLINGTON, is there anything I can run for to fetch—for to come—for to go—for to carry—for to bring—for to take," &c. &c. &c.

The Duke of Wellington is shown as Mr. Widdicomb, the ringmaster of Astley's Circus and a great favorite of the Punchites. Lord Brougham is the clown. Sir Robert Peel is shown in the costume of Mercury as Astley the proprietor. (John Leech, 1843)

Herald, and the *Evening Standard*; Bulwer-Lytton, Sir Peter Laurie (who had promised to legislate suicide out of existence), Sir James Graham, and the lord mayor; greedy bishops, pretentious writers, bad actors, and haughty noblemen—all were relentlessly hounded by the Punchites and soundly drubbed with Mr. Punch's baton.

The Pope, Louis Philippe, Napoleon III (until he became a Crimean ally, at which time his caricatures suddenly got taller and handsomer), the tsar of Russia—none were spared. We have seen how Mr. Punch amused himself with Prince Albert. The paper was banned from Austria, Russia, and Germany, and three times from France. In time Kaiser Wilhelm would go so far as to put a price on the head of the editor, making sure at the same time that his own weekly copy of *Punch* was delivered in a plain wrapper via the diplomatic pouch.

As the years went by it became an honor to be knocked about in print by Mr. Punch and caricatured by John Tenniel. Politicians tried everything from cajolery to bribery to get into the paper's columns. Grudges were never held. It was best to be on the good side of Mr. Punch.

A large part of the paper was devoted to domestic problems curiously similar to those now in existence, found every day in the *New York Times*, and probably not dissimilar to those that existed in Athens, Rome, or ancient Thebes. Air and water pollution were poisoning the atmosphere, and ecological improvements were called for. Mugging (called "garotting") was rife in city streets after dark. The poor needed adequate social welfare legislation. Education was not what it had been. A drought caused a shortage of drinking water. There was a taxicab strike and an influenza epidemic. The lower classes were getting above themselves, demanding trade unions, going to the opera, reading novels.

With the full support of the proprietors, *Punch* pulled out all the stops. Lemon assigned regular production minimums to his well-fed writers. Jerrold was required to do six and a half columns a week. À Beckett had five and a quarter. Leigh, Horace Mayhew, and later Tom Taylor were assigned two. Thackeray was given the odd number of one and ten-thirteenths. With the exception of the untemperamental and highly professional à Beckett, none of them ever achieved his full quota. Leech was always late getting his wood blocks to the engravers. Lemon was kept busy dashing around London wheedling, lashing, and coaxing his temperamental staff into action.

Punch set the standards for high-quality humorous journalism. When success arrived, imitators followed. Magazines in *Punch*'s image sprang up like mushrooms. There was Tom Hood's *Fun*, *Joe Miller*, *The Tomahawk*, *The Great Gun*, *The Arrow*, and *Lika Joko*. Some, like the *Squib*, were short-lived. Others, like *The Man in the Moon* and *Fun*,

PUNCH TURNED OUT OF FRANCE!

These cartoons were drawn to celebrate Punch's being banned from France for some months (and later forgiven) as a result of a drawing by Thackeray representing the French king as a "pauvre malheurex [sic]." Punch was also banned at different times in Russia, Austria, and Germany. (Above, John Leech, 1843; below, John Leech, 1844)

AFFECTING RECONCILIATION WITH OUR BROTHER OF FRANCE.

lasted longer. Occasionally they siphoned off a small, barely significant portion of *Punch*'s readership, but never for very long. Across the Atlantic, where strict copyright laws had not yet been enacted, low quality items such as *Punchinello*, *American Punch*, and *Southern Punch* appeared briefly and vanished without a trace.

Punch started out as an anti-Catholic, anti-Jewish, fiercely radical paper, slashing in its criticism of privilege and pomposity. With increasing maturity and affluence, it moved gradually to the right. Lemon's policy of a highly restricted staff and Table membership kept out new blood, young men with fresh ideas. New staff members were hired only to replace the originals, who were firmly resolved to work for *Punch* until they died. Under Lemon's editorship only three young men were added to the staff: Henry Silver, who could be depended on to reflect the thinking of Lemon; Shirley Brooks, who kept quiet and did as he was told; and Francis Burnand, who did not join until 1863. Du Maurier was also a comparative youngster, but he was not involved in the political side at all, devoting himself almost entirely to light social commentary.

When *Punch* was founded in 1841, the average age of the staff was twenty-eight. Jerrold was the oldest at thirty-eight, and Leech was the youngest at twenty-four. Silver replaced Jerrold at his death, and du Maurier replaced Leech. As the magazine grew older, the staff grew older. In a decade, it was being written and illustrated by men in their thirties, and ten years later it reflected the opinions of a staff in its forties. Had the Punchites not been prone to early deaths, the magazine might have reached World War I with a staff of ancient boozers in their nineties. It would not have been impossible for them all to die in their sixties within a year or two of one another, leaving the paper with no staff at all.

The result of this rigid personnel policy was that the passionate, courageous radicalism of youth vanished with the ripening of the staff's years. *Punch* became True Blue, representing the majority opinion of the middle and upper classes on social and political matters. And anti-establishment Punchites, who once would have been thrown into prison in France or Germany, began to acquire knighthoods.

In the nineteenth century *Punch* passed through two, separate phases. In the first, the writing was all-important. Artwork was incidental, an attempt to cash in on Herbert Ingram's happy discovery that a paper with pictures sells more copies than one without regardless of whether the pictures have any significance. During the second phase the cartoons became more important than the prose and poetry. People bought *Punch* to chuckle at Keene and du Maurier and to nod approvingly at Tenniel's political comments. The rest of the paper they read afterward. Because of this, the writing was of better quality in the early Victorian years than it was later.

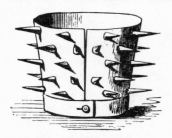

EFFECT OF THE ANTIGAROTTE COLLAR ON A GARROTTEER.

Garroters, the Victorian equivalent of muggers, were everywhere in London after dark. Their tactic was to strangle from behind with a piece of cord and then rob their victims. The Punchites, for some reason, found humor in this, and garroting jokes were popular for a number of years. (Left, Charles Keene, 1856; facing page, T. Harrington Wilson, 1856)

MR. TREMBLE BORROWS A HINT FROM HIS WIFE'S CRINOLINE, AND INVENTS WHAT HE CALLS HIS " PATENT ANTI-GAROTTE OVERCOAT," WHICH PLACES HIM COMPLETELY OUT OF H-ARM'S REACH IN HIS WALKS HOME FROM THE CITY.

Punch was part funny, part serious. The humor was in the comic articles and poems and the social cartoons, each with its cackle. The serious part was in the parliamentary reports and the theater and later the book reviews. A lot of the humor was based on snobbery. The poor, so passionately defended at first, were later shown to be coarse, bestial, unintelligent brutes, resisting any attempt to improve them. The lower and lower-middle working classes were represented as pretentious and absurd.

From its formerly unassailable position as the *enfant terrible* of British journalism, the champion of justice, the crusader against poverty, the defender of the weak and oppressed, *Punch* gradually became the repository of bland, drawing-room jokes and harmless wisecracks. By 1889 it had lost its outrage. It became stuffy and imperialistic, a totally establishment paper, dull and highly repectable, with only an occasional flash of its old magic. It was not until World War I that *Punch* came back into its own again.

The magazine's influence in its early years brought social acceptance to its employees of a kind rarely before enjoyed by journalists. They were welcomed in great houses where they sometimes hobnobbed with royalty.

Titles for journalists and comic artists were still in the future, but they were definitely on the way.

An excellent medium for blending intelligent men and women, regardless of social class, was the popular custom of amateur theatricals. In the early and mid-Victorian period the professional theater was, for the most part, unsatisfactory. The public was bombarded with pantomimes, farces, cheap tragedy, and melodrama, or endless representations of Shakespeare. Amateur productions were usually of better quality than the fare offered in public playhouses. They provided a source of recreation for their genteel casts and audiences. They were also an excellent way of raising funds for charitable purposes. Since pension plans for practitioners of the arts were nonexistent, it was customary for a dead artist's friends to produce a benefit and turn over the proceeds to the widow.

A good example of this custom was the benefit put on by the Punchites and their friends for the widow and nine children of the contributing artist C. H. Bennett. The program included Sir Francis Burnand's adaptation of Maddison Morton's *Box and Cox*, set to music by Sir Arthur Sullivan and cleverly renamed *Cox and Box*. Box was played by du Maurier, Quentin Twiss played Cox, and Arthur Blunt was Bouncer. This was followed by an address in verse by Shirley Brooks, and Tom Taylor's play, *A Wolf in Sheep's Clothing*, with a cast that included Lemon, Tenniel, Taylor, Ponny Mayhew, Silver, Burnand, Brooks, and the Terry sisters—Kate, Florence, and Ellen. The evening ended with two short playlets, Jacques Offenbach's musical *Les Deux Aveugles* and John Oxenford's *A Family Failing*, sung and acted by Punchites. The tickets were a guinea apiece and the house was packed. Tenniel was the star of the evening as Colonel Lord Churchill of the Life Guards and got a standing ovation.

Theatrical parties were as popular with the upper classes as they were in Bohemian or artistic circles. However, the best were considered to be those given by Burnand and his wife, and by the wealthy Regent Street draper Arthur Lewis, who later married Kate Terry. The friends who came to Lewis's Kensington house, Moray Lodge, and acted in plays there in the 1860s were known as the Moray Minstrels. This elite group of amateurs included a social mix of actors, lawyers, publishers, artists, writers, musicians, and stagestruck businessmen. Holman Hunt and Rosetti were members, as were Dickens and Wilkie Collins, Thackeray, Sir John Millais, Sir Edwin Landseer, Anthony Trollope, Henry Poole the Savile Row tailor, and Tattersall the horse auctioneer.

The Minstrels were sometimes joined by members of the aristocracy and courtiers. Leslie Ward, who achieved celebrity as a caricaturist in *Vanity Fair* under the pseudonym of "Spy," recalls in his memoirs another *Cox and Box* in 1867 in which du Maurier shared the stage with Sir Spencer Ponsonby as Cox, and Sir Henry de Bathe as Bouncer. De Bathe was a rich, theater-minded baronet who was to disinherit his son Hugo for marrying the notorious Lily Langtry, sometime mistress of Edward VII. According to Henry Silver he was known to the Punchites as "Sir Henry de Bagnio" because he had had sexual intercourse with a girl on the colors of his regiment while on guard duty at the Tower. This ceremony was apparently a regimental custom carried out the first time a young officer mounted guard. Ponsonby was comptroller in the office of the Lord Chamberlain, a ceremonial post whose duties included carrying the crown from the Tower to the House of Lords for the opening of Parliament.

Leslie Ward, who was sixteen years old at the time of the benefit for Bennett, remembers that the production was "a most artistic one and attracted a very distinguished audience; everybody of any consequence in the world of art, literature, and the stage flocked to see *Punch* behind the footlights."

John Tenniel, who was usually the star performer in these revels, was a tall, shy, kindly man with a splendid drooping moustache which he grew to tease Leech, who disapproved of moustaches on civilians. He was courteous and dignified, with a deep, melodious voice that was rarely heard at the dinners or anywhere else except on the amateur stage. His silence was proverbial. In the descriptions of the Table conversations recorded in Silver's diary, there is hardly ever a mention of Tenniel participating in the arguments, the political squabbles, or the ribald jokes. Occasionally he would make some gentle remark or propose a technical change in a big cut, but he rarely made cartoon suggestions himself. He accepted all Table decisions without objection, admitting to no political opinions of his own (although he tended toward the Conservative), maintaining that whatever *Punch* supported or opposed was good enough for him.

Between 1851 and 1901 Tenniel executed about two thousand full-page or double-page cartoons as well as a great many small cuts, socials, initial letters, and illustrations. Outside of *Punch* he achieved international celebrity for the illustrations for *Alice in Wonderland* and *Through the Looking-Glass* and for the wonderful original designs for the cards used in the children's game *Happy Families* ("Mr. Bones the Butcher" et al.).

Tenniel had the knack of being able to lampoon a political notable without malice or vulgarity, at the time a wholly new development in journalistic art. He had a splendid sense of composition and a bold, inventive style. It was Tenniel who created the British Lion as a symbol of

THE FEDERAL PHŒNIX.

Punch *sided with the South during the American Civil War because it was the more gentlemanly side. The Punchites disliked Abraham Lincoln until he was assassinated. Over the objections of Shirley Brooks,* Punch *printed an apology in verse by Tom Taylor, who was also the author of the play Lincoln was watching when he was killed. (Above, John Tenniel, 1864; facing page: drawing by John Tenniel, 1861; poem by Tom Taylor, 1865)*

ONE GOOD TURN DESERVES ANOTHER.

OLD ABE. "WHY I DU DECLARE IT'S MY DEAR OLD FRIEND SAMBO! COURSE YOU'LL FIGHT FOR
US, SAMBO. LEND US A HAND, OLD HOSS, DU!"

Abraham Lincoln.

FOULLY ASSASSINATED, APRIL 14, 1865.

You lay a wreath on murdered LINCOLN'S bier,
    You, who with mocking pencil wont to trace,
Broad for the self-complacent British sneer,
    His length of shambling limb, his furrowed face,

His gaunt, gnarled hands, his unkempt, bristling hair,
    His garb uncouth, his bearing ill at ease,
His lack of all we prize as debonair,
    Of power or will to shine, of art to please.

You, whose smart pen backed up the pencil's laugh,
    Judging each step, as though the way were plain:
Reckless, so it could point its paragraph,
    Of chief's perplexity, or people's pain.

Beside this corpse, that bears for winding-sheet
    The Stars and Stripes he lived to rear anew,
Between the mourners at his head and feet,
    Say, scurril-jester, is there room for *you?*

Yes, he had lived to shame me from my sneer,
    To lame my pencil, and confute my pen—
To make me own this kind of princes peer,
    This rail-splitter a true-born king of men.

My shallow judgment I had learnt to rue,
    Noting how to occasion's height he rose,
How his quaint wit made home-truth seem more true,
    How, iron-like, his temper grew by blows.

How humble yet how hopeful he could be:
    How in good fortune and in ill the same:

Nor bitter in success, nor boastful he,
    Thirsty for gold, nor feverish for fame.

He went about his work—such work as few
    Ever had laid on head and heart and hand—
As one who knows, where there's a task to do,
    Man's honest will must Heaven's good grace command;

Who trusts the strength will with the burden grow,
    That God makes instruments to work his will,
If but that will we can arrive to know,
    Nor tamper with the weights of good and ill.

So he went forth to battle, on the side
    That he felt clear was Liberty's and Right's,
As in his peasant boyhood he had plied
    His warfare with rude Nature's thwarting mights—

The uncleared forest, the unbroken soil,
    The iron-bark, that turns the lumberer's axe,
The rapid, that o'erbears the boatman's toil,
    The prairie, hiding the mazed wanderer's tracks,

The ambushed Indian, and the prowling bear—
    Such were the needs that helped his youth to train:
Rough culture—but such trees large fruit may bear,
    If but their stocks be of right girth and grain.

So he grew up, a destined work to do,
    And lived to do it: four long-suffering years'
Ill-fate, ill-feeling, ill-report, lived through,
    And then he heard the hisses change to cheers,

The taunts to tribute, the abuse to praise,
    And took both with the same unwavering mood:
Till, as he came on light, from darkling days,
    And seemed to touch the goal from where he stood,

British might, and he popularized the stout, hearty John Bull, although he was not the creator of the character.*

His drawing has been criticized for coldness. It has been said that he drew the features of things without showing their personality; that he was too formal and classical. While there was some validity to these criticisms, it may have been just those qualities that made his cartoons so distinctive and so memorable, and which eventually earned him a knighthood, while his more artistic colleague Charles Keene was ignored except by a devoted cultural elite.

The most striking facets of Tenniel's style were the sharp precision of his drawing and the statuesque quality of his figures. ("If only I could draw boots like Tenniel," John Leech would say enviously.) His illustrations for the 1861 edition of Thomas Moore's *Lalla Rookh* are generally regarded as his best work, superior in conception and technical skill to the *Alice* illustrations. He also did the Leonardo da Vinci mosaic in the south court of the Victoria and Albert Museum.

Tenniel always worked in pencil, making a rough sketch which he then transferred to the wood block with tracing paper. The sketches were often completed later and sold separately. He never used pen-and-ink except on rare occasions, for an almanack or pocket-book picture. As a result, his sketches had a pleasant, soft gray quality that no engraver could reproduce. It was Swain, the engraver, who was responsible for the bold, incisive black lines for which Tenniel was famous.

Tenniel prided himself on never having to use a model, either for the human figure or for backgrounds, relying only on his excellent memory or photographs. (He did not actually see Disraeli or Gladstone until at least ten years after he first began to draw them for *Punch*.) His reliance on memory was responsible for some criticism in his later years, because his representations of items such as bicycles and railway trains did not reflect the latest technological changes. In addition, his public figures seemed never to grow older or fatter. Nonetheless, it was Tenniel's work that was most responsible for raising *Punch* to the high status it eventually achieved.

Tenniel came to *Punch* at Christmas 1850, at the suggestion of Jerrold, who was impressed with his illustrations for *Aesop's Fables*. He was hired to replace Richard Doyle, a Catholic artist who had joined *Punch* as principal cartoonist in 1843 and left abruptly in 1850 in protest against the paper's violent campaign against "papal agression." The Punchites believed, and probably with some justification, that the London

*The popular representation of England as John Bull was the invention of Dr. John Arbuthnot in 1712.

archdiocese had exerted pressure and possibly even the threat of ex-communication on Doyle to make him offer his resignation, hoping that Lemon would find him so irreplaceable that he would modify *Punch*'s anti-Catholic policy. If this was true, the stratagem didn't work. Lemon thought circulation would drop (it didn't), but he confided to Silver that he was sure his firm tone with Doyle had showed the public that *Punch* was "in earnest, and something more than a buffoon."

It was Richard Doyle who designed the familiar *Punch* cover, first used in 1849 and retained until Malcolm Muggeridge replaced it 107 years later. When he left, he took with him one of the paper's more popular series, "The Continental Tours of Brown, Jones and Robinson." He went on to illustrate some of Dickens's books and Thackeray's *The Newcomes*, as well as Ruskin's *The King of the Golden River*.

Doyle's departure left the paper with a number of incomplete projects, but Tenniel pitched in with a will. He completed the work in fine style in plenty of time for the deadline. After a brief trial period of initial letters and small cuts, he gradually began to take over full responsibility for the political cartoons to the delight of Leech, who preferred to devote himself entirely to the socials. Among Tenniel's most famous cartoons are "The British Lion's Revenge on the Bengal Tiger," which fanned an already outraged British public into a white heat of vengeful rage against the Sepoys (and raised *Punch*'s circulation); and for what is probably the most famous *Punch* cartoon of all time, "Dropping the Pilot."

Over the years, "Dropping the Pilot" has been discussed, reprinted, and reproduced in numerous variations—more than any other drawing in or out of *Punch*. The original sketch was purchased by Lord Rosebery who later presented it to Prince Bismarck. The cartoon showed the young German emperor dismissing Bismarck, his old mentor, and preparing to carry on alone. Both Bismarck and the emperor were pleased with it. *Punch* has printed at least eight variations of it, and it has appeared in different forms in such papers as *Private Eye*, which issued a Ronald Searle variation in 1967 showing Mr. Punch dropping Malcolm Muggeridge.

The idea for "Dropping the Pilot" was not Tenniel's, and a great many people have claimed credit for it. Henry Silver and his wonderful diary had long since departed, so there is no eyewitness account, but *Punch* historians, especially Spielmann, credit the idea to Gilbert à Beckett's son, Gilbert Arthur à Beckett. According to "Spy," Linley Sambourne suggested it to Tenniel at a Table dinner. The idea's origina-tor will probably remain a *Punch* mystery forever.

In spite of his reluctance to speak, Tenniel was regarded as a charming and genial Table companion. He was a good listener and did, in fact,

DROPPING THE PILOT.

John Tenniel, 1890

contribute to the conversation occasionally when he thought there was something worth saying. On those especially convivial occasions when contributions to the general gaiety were demanded, he kept in reserve a jolly song which he was never shy about singing in his rich baritone voice. It was called "The Sailor's Adieu to the Ladies of Spain." He sang it admirably and it never failed to delight his audience.

When he retired, a testimonial dinner was arranged for him with Arthur Balfour as chairman. He was toasted by Balfour, and when he rose to reply, the diners settled back to hear what they believed would be the first major public statement by the taciturn Tenniel. The historic moment never came. He got as far as "My Lords and Gentlemen . . . " when words failed him and he sat down again. Burnand, describing the incident later, attributed Tenniel's silence to emotion and said "the effect was marvellous."

Tenniel was a self-educated, Royal Art School dropout. He had attended occasional life classes, at one of which he made the acquaintance of Charles Keene, who was to become a lifelong friend and colleague. Keene was probably the finest artist and draughtsman ever to work for *Punch*, discounting the rare Almanack appearances of Sir John Millais. Sickert regarded Keene as the first of the great moderns, and he was highly admired in Paris. Unfortunately, he was a little too good for the technical reproduction methods in use at the time. Engravers had a difficult time with his subtle shadings and fine lines.

Like artists a century or more earlier, Keene liked to mix his own inks. He experimented with different kinds of special drawing papers and traveled long distances to find just the right background for a picture. Du Maurier wrote of his collaboration with Keene on the social cartoons in *Punch* that Keene "takes the masses, and I take the classes." He pronounced Keene's cabmen, costermongers, and policemen "inimitable," and "as for his busses and cabs, I really cannot find words to express my admiration of them."

> Somehow, one liked the man who drew these strange people even without knowing him; when you knew him you loved him very much—so much that no room was left in you for envy of his unattainable mastery of his art. For of this there can be no doubt—no greater or more finished master in black and white has devoted his life to the illustration of the manners and humours of his time.

Keene was the quintessential eccentric Bohemian in the latter-day flattering sense of the term. He was the typical artist, a confirmed bachelor living in cluttered, paint-spattered studios in unfashionable

FLATTERING!

First Rustic. "'STR'OR'NARY WAY O' GETTIN' YER LIVIN'! AIN'T IT, JOE!"
Second Ditto. "AYE, THAT 'T BE, WILLIAM. *CRIPPLES O' SOME SORT MOST ON 'EM, YOU MAY DEPEND!*"

Charles Keene, 1865

"BROTHER BRUSH."

Ship-Painter. "NICE DRYIN' WEATHER FOR OUR BUSINESS, AIN'T IT, SIR!"
Amateur (disconcerted). "YA–A–S!"——   [*Takes a dislike to the place.*

Charles Keene, 1867

neighborhoods. He was hard-working and, unlike his *Punch* colleagues, a moderate drinker, taking no interest in food and wine, preferring good books and music to the conviviality of the Table. An intensely shy, quiet man, he had no use for clubs, and disliked the weekly dinners. He had very little humor and contributed nothing to the general Table hilarity except for occasional long jokes that were not at all funny and in response to which his companions were forced to laugh nervously and change the subject.

Most of Keene's joke ideas came from other people—in some cases Henry Silver, but usually his old friend, the artist Joseph Crowhall, who collected comic ideas in a notebook and passed them on to Keene. Crowhall was responsible for at least 250 *Punch* cartoons, for which he got neither credit nor payment but only the pleasure of having helped his friend.

Keene, who admitted to Tory sentiments, first came to *Punch* in 1851 at the instigation of his friend Henry Silver. With much reluctance he submitted a drawing in December 1851 from a suggestion by Silver. It was entitled "Sketch of Patent Street-Sweeping Machine Lately Introduced at Paris" and showed several cannons aimed at a spot from which the artist was supposed to have speedily departed. Keene did not think the joke was funny and refused to submit it until Silver agreed to take full credit for both idea and drawing. It was accepted by Lemon and published. Unfortunately, a version of the joke had previously appeared in the *Man in the Moon*, and that paper gleefully took *Punch* to task for joke stealing, portraying Mr. Punch as a ragpicker, calling out "Any jokes? Any old jokes?" In spite of this, Lemon asked for more, and Silver was forced to represent himself as the creator of Keene's next three efforts, two illustrations and the cartoon "The Advantage of an Inundation." Lemon was delighted.

It was obvious that Silver could not go on week after week accepting praise for another man's work. He pointed this out to Keene, who refused again to admit authorship of the cartoons, and it was not until 1854 that Keene finally agreed to put his initials on a drawing.

After nine years as an outside contributor, Keene was asked to join the Table in 1860, even though the Punchites thought him "peculiar." However, he refused to join the staff on a full-time basis. Lemon offered him a salary again and again, but he preferred the freedom of free-lance work and never accepted. He finally left *Punch*, as Thackeray and Doyle had done before him, on a point of editorial policy: He was the only Punchite to disagree with the paper's attitude on the Russo-Turkish War.

Keene loved to draw the lower classes. He did what J. B. Priestley called "superb drawings for what were often rather poor jokes."

Although many critics considered him superior to Leech, Ruskin, who adored Leech, never mentioned Keene at all.

Like many of his temperamental Table colleagues, Keene was painfully sensitive to criticism. He carried on a constant grumbling war with Lemon about cartoon ideas rejected by "our Philistine editor," as he called Lemon, after he had rejected as "brutal" a drawing of a bereaved husband, forced to get into the first funeral carriage with his mother-in-law ("But it will ruin my day!"), and other cartoons of a similar nature.

During his years as a Punchite, Keene submitted between five and six thousand cartoons. He was praised by Lord Leighton for his splendid portrayals of "humble English life." Surprisingly enough, he was a gentleman in the sense of Thackeray, Mayhew, and the rest, being the son of a solicitor and educated for the legal profession. Like Henry Mayhew, he dropped out quickly and worked briefly as a trainee architect and later as an apprentice wood engraver. He had a fine singing voice and played the bagpipe. In 1858 he joined Arthur Lewis's Moray Minstrels, and it was he who introduced du Maurier to that group.

During its late Victorian plateau of complacent prosperity, *Punch*'s major attraction was George Louis Palmella Busson du Maurier. With Leech dead and Tenniel established as the political cartoonist, Keene was assigned as the paper's comic, to specialize in jokes about the lower orders, Irishmen, Scotsmen, and the problems of people attempting to go from one place to another in cabs and omnibuses. Over the objections of Tom Taylor, who thought him an upstart, du Maurier was hired by Lemon to give the readers the "beautiful." Let others be funny, Lemon told him, his job was to be graceful and poetical. In the *Punch* ensemble du Maurier would be the romantic tenor.

Du Maurier concentrated on high life, the world of balls, drawing rooms, and country houses. His characters were aristocrats, millionaires, social climbers, young swells, and beautiful women. According to J. B. Priestley:

> While he could afford to laugh at some aspects of English upper class life in his drawings, he flattered its members by *deliberately elongating* them. Either interest or experience told him that these men and women loved to think of themselves as being taller than the common herd, and that is how he represented them.

This interpretation of du Maurier's motives is an interesting one but probably inaccurate. It seems more likely that du Maurier simply liked to draw tall people. He loved long-legged women with shapely feet, and that

118

THRIFT.

Peebles Body (to Townsman who was supposed to be in London on a visit). "E—EH, MAC! YE'RE SUNE HAME AGAIN!"

Mac. "E—EH, IT'S JUST A RUINOUS PLACE, THAT! MUN, A HAD NA' BEEN THE-ERRE ABUNE TWA HOOURS WHEN—*BANG*—WENT SAXPENCE!!!"

Charles Keene, 1868

CATECHISM UNDER DIFFICULTIES.

Free Kirk Elder (preparatory to presenting a Tract). "MY FRIEND, DO YOU KNOW THE CHIEF END OF MAN?"

Piper (innocently). "NA, I DINNA MIND THE CHUNE! CAN YE NO WHUSTLE IT?"!!

Charles Keene, 1872

is exactly what he produced in drawing after drawing. He loved women in black stockings, and soon black stockings became a London fashion.

Du Maurier himself was a short man, handsome and sweet natured, possessed of an excellent sense of humor and the ability to see comic possibilities everywhere. He was a devoted husband and father. His wife, Emma, was his favorite model, and his five children and their pets romped unchecked about his studio as he worked. Victorians loved his many drawings of the du Maurier children at play or saying quaint, funny, childish things.

He hated pomposity of any kind, pretension, or social cruelty. Above all he detested London hostesses who invited celebrities to dinner but made sure that their probably unsuitable wives were left at home. Du Maurier went to parties with Emma or not at all. When prosperity came, he bought a large house in Hampstead, and its rooms and gardens appear in many of his drawings.

Du Maurier was born in Paris in 1834 into what he believed to be an aristocratic French family of ancient lineage. Later researches by his granddaughter, the novelist Daphne du Maurier, revealed that this was not so. The early du Mauriers were simple tradespeople, a fact that would have distressed him had he lived to learn of it. After failing his examination for the *baccalaureat* he studied chemistry in England, but 1856 found him in Paris again, studying art at the Atelier Gleyre. His hopes of becoming a serious painter evaporated when he lost most of the sight of his left eye.

Du Maurier was drawing from life one afternoon, when the model's head suddenly seemed to shrink to the size of a walnut. Covering first one eye and then the other with his hand, he realized that something was very wrong. He had probably suffered a detached retina, but Victorian doctors were not able to diagnose or cure his ailment. For a while it looked as though his right eye would be affected too. For the rest of his life du Maurier had a morbid fear of blindness.

He was advised to give up his studies and rest. While he was convalescing, he received a copy of the *Punch* Almanack, containing drawings by Leech. He was impressed and decided that since he could no longer paint, he would become a black-and-white artist. As soon as he could make some suitable drawings, he submitted them to Mark Lemon, who turned them down as "hurried and incompetent" but was sufficiently affected to recommend him to *Once a Week*. At last, in 1860, Lemon conceded that he had mastered his medium enough to be ready for *Punch*. He bought a cartoon in which du Maurier had drawn himself and his old Paris art-school friends Thomas Reynolds Lamont and James McNeill Whistler entering the premises of a photographer and being

EXPERIENTIA DOCET.

Elder of Fourteen. "WHERE'S BABY, MADGE?"   *Madge.* "IN THE OTHER ROOM, I THINK, EMILY."
Elder of Fourteen. "GO DIRECTLY, AND SEE WHAT SHE'S DOING, AND TELL HER SHE MUSTN'T!"

DELICATE CONSIDERATION.

Mamma. "WHAT A DIN YOU'RE MAKING, CHICKS! WHAT *ARE* YOU PLAYING AT?"
Trixy. "O, MAMMA, WE'RE PLAYING AT RAILWAY TRAINS. *I'M* THE ENGINE, AND GUY'S A FIRST-CLASS CARRIAGE, AND SYLVIA'S A SECOND-CLASS CARRIAGE, AND MAY'S A THIRD-CLASS CARRIAGE, AND GERALD, HE'S A THIRD-CLASS CARRIAGE, TOO— THAT IS, HE'S REALLY ONLY A *TRUCK*, YOU KNOW, ONLY YOU MUSTN'T TELL HIM SO, AS IT WOULD OFFEND HIM!"

*Du Maurier loved to use his own family as models. The "third-class carriage,"
who was really only a truck, would later grow up to be Sir Gerald du Maurier, the
celebrated actor-manager. (George du Maurier: above, 1872; below, 1873)*

summarily ordered not to smoke because "This is not a common har-tist's studio!''

The three "hartists" and other of du Maurier's friends appeared often in his drawings. He especially loved to draw Whistler, a diversion that later drew him into one of the paranoid artist's many ridiculous and spiteful lawsuits. Du Maurier's earliest *Punch* assignments were initial letters, which paid badly, and an occasional half-page drawing. The in-frequency and low level of his submissions was due to the enmity of Tom Taylor. However, the amiable Henry Silver helped as much as he could by sending him the initial letters for his drama-criticism columns and by speaking up for him at the Table dinners.

At long last, on December 7, 1864, Lemon handed du Maurier the traditional knife and invited him to carve his initials on the Table. His first dinner did little to enhance his popularity with the Punchites. Assuming that his membership gave him instant equality with the superstars, he waded into the conversation as though they had been his cronies all his life. He chattered egotistically about Rossetti and Whistler and was the first to suggest a big cut (which was turned down).

Mark Lemon found him "cocky," but Shirley Brooks defended him, saying that that was exactly what a talented young fellow should be ("I hate your Blifils ''). Even his friend and sponsor Henry Silver, something of a Blifil himself in the majestic presence of his idols, was made un-comfortable by the smug garrulity of his protégé, who embarrassed the Table further by getting up to make a thank-you speech and talking about his blind eye. Brooks rose and pointed out good-naturedly that Tenniel had a bad eye, too [the result of a fencing accident in his youth], and that two good eyes between them were better than a score of bad ones. The subject was not brought up again.

Du Maurier's brashness, the probable result of insecurity or shyness, not unusual in the presence of immortals (Silver had disapproved of Burnand for behaving in the same way at his first dinner and calling the Punchites by their Christian names), soon vanished. Du Maurier was easily assimilated. After the initial dinner, he wrote:

> Old Mark I like immensely, the most genial fellow that ever lived; Shirley Brooks is a deuced amusing fellow, but rather snarling & sarcastic; Sir Tom de Taylor, very jolly too, but so beastly well-informed that he rather im-beasts one at times; the nicest of all is Percival Leigh I think and old Evans whom we call Pater, next to whom I sit . . . Tenniel is a delightful fellow though very quiet—Burnand very amusing, Horace Mayhew often very drunk; *bon enfant mais bete*. Silver rarely opens his lips, at which I wonder for he's got lots to say for himself. Our dear old stiff-necked Keene doesn't

get quite in tune with the others, and I think these dinners haven't as much charm for him as for this child.

He loved the dinners and attended every Wednesday, contributing happily to the bawdy chitchat, the loud arguments, and the jokes. When the big cut discussion began, he would hold private conversations in a stage whisper or subside into his chair in a kind of coma, a handkerchief over his face, pretending to sleep but actually resting his weak eyes and protecting them from the heavy pipe and cigar smoke. He could never bear to be out of the limelight for very long.

Du Maurier was invited to join *Punch* (and the Table) to replace John Leech, whom he knew well from having acted and sung with him and Keene at the Moray Minstrels parties. Leech's sudden death had left Lemon with an unfinished Almanack in 1864. Du Maurier, Keene, and Millais took over and completed it. In the following year du Maurier began to submit prose and poetry as well as artwork. His first written contribution was "L'Onglay à Paris," a comic poem. In 1866 he had two satires in *Punch*: the splendid "A Legend of Camelot," a parody of Pre-Raphaelite art and poetry that is still fresh and funny today; and "A Ballad of Blunders," a burlesque of Swinburne.

In the 1870s and 1880s du Maurier turned the full force of his satire on the aesthetic movement, of which Oscar Wilde was the leader, cruelly lampooning the practitioners of that style with their passion for blue-and-white china and languid attitudes. His wonderful characters, Jellaby Postlethwaite the poet; Maudle the dreadful painter; and their hanger-on and self-styled art expert, Prigsby (not to be confused with his Grigsby, the plain man who follows aestheticism because he wants to be trendy), are devastating portraits of London poseurs with more pretension than talent.

Postlethwaite was said to be a caricature of Wilde, but du Maurier denied this, saying that the poet was really an amalgam of a number of people. Mrs. Cimabue Brown, the well-to-do arty hostess on whom these characters feed (believed by Mrs. Comyns Carr, wife of the director of the Grosvenor Gallery, to be a satire on herself) is a marvelously funny creation. The two climbers—Sir Gorgius Midas, crude, *h*-dropping multimillionaire; and the beautiful and brilliant Mrs. Ponsonby de Tomkyns, a delightful schemer who knew all the tricks—are superb indictments of London snobbery.

Unlike most of the other *Punch* artists, du Maurier preferred to supply his own jokes and write his own cackles, although some were supplied by his friends. (The famous "Curate's Egg" cartoon came from an idea given to him by Canon Alfred Ainger of St. Paul's.) Anstey Guthrie, who

A SMART YOUTH.

Cousin Millicent (with smothered indignation). "Good-bye. Robert! And since it seems you found Nothing fitter than my Favourite bit of Japanese Enamel to drop your Cigar Ashes in, last Night, perhaps you'll accept it as a Gift! It has no further Value for me, after such Desecration!"

Cousin Robert. "Tha-anks, Millicent! And if *that's* the way Articles of Priceless Value are disposed of in your Branch of the Family, I can only Regret I didn't make an 'Ash-Pan of your *Hand!*"

WHAT NEXT INDEED!

Grateful Recipient. "Bless you, my Lady! May we Meet in Heaven!"

Haughty Donor. "Good Gracious!! Drive on, Jarvis!!!"

[*She had evidently read Dr. Johnson, who "didn't want to meet certain people anywhere"*

The "smart youth" was based on Whistler, who was involved in a similar incident and was heard by du Maurier to make the same remark. (George du Maurier: above, 1870; below, 1873) would later become a Table companion of du Maurier's, wrote that in the few lines of letterpress that made up his cartoon captions the artist had brought the art of précis-writing to perfection. They were beautifully concise and to the point.

Unfortunately, his novels were not as well written as his cackles, but they brought him the wealth and comfort he had always longed for—for himself and his family. *Trilby*, published in 1894, was a grand success on both sides of the Atlantic. It was made into a popular play in which his son Gerald played a leading role, and would, after his death, become a film starring John Barrymore as Svengali. It was *Trilby* that inspired the Whistler lawsuit, which resulted in the removal in some editions of the novel of a character based on the irascible artist. *Peter Ibbetson* (1892) and the posthumously published *The Martian* (1897) were romantically overwritten, but they brought him critical acclaim nevertheless.

Du Maurier attended his last *Punch* dinner in July 1896. Henry Lucy, a Table member of the nineties, recalls that he was "curiously grey in the face . . . and, to begin with, was unusually quiet. But he brisked up when cigarette time came [he was a chain-smoker and frequently consumed forty a day], and stayed late in his merriest mood." He had been a Table member for just thirty years. By the 1890s he was almost blind, but he still contributed drawings, which revealed his decline and his inability to capture his former style. Burnand, who was editor at the time, never failed to print them.

Du Maurier died on October 7, 1896, one of the rare Punchites to have known a happy, comfortable, successful life, secure in the love of his wife and children and satisfied with his achievements. He was sixty-two years old. At his own request, he was cremated.

To supplement the work of the Olympians who graced the Table, Punch had a number of nonstaff contributors, or "outsiders," most of whom Lemon had spotted in other publications and proselytized with an invitation to send him examples of their work. Unsolicited contributions were rarely accepted, although a great many of them poured in each week (and still do). Sometimes patronage was extended to the friend or relation of a Punchite, but only if his efforts were suitable for a National Institution. If they were good, but not of *Punch* quality, Lemon would often recommend the author (as he did with du Maurier) to another paper for seasoning. Surprisingly enough, the other editors usually accepted them, happy to have *Punch*'s rejects.

A good many of these outsiders achieved celebrity on their own, either in journalism or in other professions. Thomas Hood, of course, was a star and a brilliant editor in his own right (*Fun* and others). The success of his

"Song of the Shirt" overshadowed his other *Punch* contributions, but he did a great many anonymous one- and two-line puns and conundrums and the two immensely popular poems "A Drop of Gin" and "The Pauper's Christmas Carol."

Among others considered good enough to appear in the pages of *Punch* were Dr. Edward Vaughan Kennedy, the celebrated barrister who defended the grotesque Tichborne Claimant. His major submission seems to have been a translation into Greek of "The King of the Cannibal Islands." Others were the novelist Charles Lever, one of the targets of Thackeray's "Punch's Prize Novels"; Laman Blanchard; Matthew J. Higgins ("Jacob Omnium"); and the Very Reverend Reynolds Hole, dean of Rochester. (Mrs. Hole, in her riding habit, was the model for many of Leech's hunting cartoons.)

Charles Dickens submitted an article deploring polluted suburban water supplies which was declined with thanks by Lemon. He never offered to write for *Punch* again, deterred, perhaps, less by the rejection than by the paper's enforced policy of anonymity for writers. Another outsider was Charles L. Eastlake ("Jack Easel") Keeper of the National Gallery, who wrote a hilarious "Royal Academy Exhibition" parody. There were also Frederick Locker-Lampson; R. F. Sketchley, librarian of the Dyce and Forster Collection at the South Kensington Museum; and W. S. Gilbert, mentioned earlier herein, who had a few short pieces and drawings printed before quarreling with Lemon and taking his "Bab Ballads" to *Fun*.

In the 1860s two new and surprising categories of outsiders were added to the regulars. One was *Punch*'s first woman writer, a Miss M. Bentham-Edwards, to whom Lemon assigned the series "Mrs. Punch's Letters to her Daughter" in 1868. Unfortunately for the advancement of female equality in the arts, she was not as highly regarded by Brooks as she had been by Lemon. He froze her out when Lemon died in 1870. The other *Punch* innovation was the paper's first American, Charles F. Browne, better known in his own country as Artemus Ward. In time he might have been the first Yankee to carve his initials in the Table, but when his first submission appeared in *Punch* he was already in the grip of a terminal illness. He died after only eight successful contributions.

There were as many able and celebrated artist-outsiders as there were writers. Sir John Millais and Sir John Gilbert, R. A., have already been mentioned. Frederick Walter, R. A., was a brief contributor as were Birket Foster, Phiz, and Watts Phillips. George Cruikshank, a fanatical teetotaler, refused Lemon's invitation because he considered the Table dinners to be "orgies."

The Reverend Edward Bradley ("Cuthbert Bede"), author of the con-

GENTLE OVERTURES TOWARDS FRIENDSHIP.

First Stranger. "I DECLARE, SIR, THAT WOMEN ARE GETTING MORE OUTRAGEOUSLY DECOLTAY EVERY DAY. JUST LOOK OVER THERE, AT THAT PRODIGIOUS OLD PORPOISE WITH THE EYEGLASS!"

Second Stranger. "HUM! HA! YES! I CAN'T HELP THINKING SHE'S A MORE FESTIVE-LOOKING OBJECT THAN THAT FUNEREAL OLD FRUMP WITH THE FAN!"

First Stranger. "THE 'FUNEREAL OLD FRUMP''S *MY WIFE*, SIR!"

Second Stranger. "THE 'PRODIGIOUS OLD PORPOISE' IS *MINE*! LET'S GO AND HAVE SOME TEA!"

George du Maurier, 1872

TRUE HUMILITY.

Right Reverend Host. "I'M AFRAID YOU'VE GOT A BAD EGG, MR. JONES!"

The Curate. "OH NO, MY LORD, I ASSURE YOU! PARTS OF IT ARE EXCELLENT!"

George du Maurier, 1895

temporary humorous best-seller, *The Adventures of Mr. Verdant Green*, was an outsider who achieved lasting fame and is venerated to the present day as the developer (although not the inventor) of the Double-Crostic.* He contributed prose and poetry to *Punch* as well as drawings.

One of the paper's ablest and most popular artists was C. H. Bennett. He was, in fact, asked to join the Table and carve his initials, but he got only as far as the letter *H*. Illness kept him from the subsequent dinners and he died before he could carve the final letter. R. T. Pritchett, a Moray Minstrel, was an artist-outsider who also developed and manufactured the durable Enfield rifle, used by British and American soldiers in both world wars. A grateful government awarded him a prize of one thousand pounds for this achievement.

Captain E. Howard, who signed his cartoons with a little trident, was a clever draughtsman who expected to be asked to replace Leech when he died. When du Maurier was chosen instead, he was deeply disappointed and did not draw for *Punch* after 1867. Other popular nonstaffers were J. Priestman Atkinson of the "Dumb Crambo" series and "Rob Roy" Macgregor ("Prince Albert's Hat").

Lemon also added women to the list of contributing artists, beginning with a Miss Coode in 1859, who did nineteen small drawings. The most important of the female artists was Georgina Bowers, a close friend and possibly a mistress of Shirley Brooks. The frequency of her appearances in *Punch* far outweighed her talents. Her drawings consisted almost entirely of inferior approximations of Leech's hunting cartoons, unfunny equestrian jokes drawn in a scratchy, unsure style. Immediately after Brooks died, the new editor, Tom Taylor, gave her to understand that her services would no longer be required.

There were many others, clergymen, solicitors, major-generals, professors—some of whom were accepted briefly and then cut adrift, others of whom lasted longer. Keene tried to promote his nephew, A. Chantrey Corbould, into a job on the staff and was furious when the editor refused to hire him. Corbould, another horsey cartoonist, also attributed this to the fact that the editor (in this case Burnand) did not like sporting subjects. (Burnand was a passionate horseman and hunted almost every week.)

When Lemon died in 1870, Shirley Brooks slid easily into the editorial chair at the invitation of the proprietors, although for years Percival Leigh had been considered the editor's *locum tenens*. Leigh does not seem to have minded very much. In any event, Brooks had been practically

---

*Acrostics constructed by monks in the Middle Ages have been found in monastery libraries.

running *Punch* in Lemon's final years and had done all of the paper's important writing. When he took over, there was no perceptible change in policy. The Lemon tradition was continued almost as though the Falstaffian editor were still in charge.

Brooks was a brilliant, handsome man, du Maurier's "deucedly amusing fellow, but rather snarling and sarcastic." He was unhappily married and offset his domestic disappointments by surrounding himself with attractive, intelligent young women to whom he could play both daddy and Lord Bountiful, and perhaps a little more. In addition to Georgina Bowers, his other favorites included Louise Romer, Lemon's widowed niece, an artist who preferred oil to *Punch*'s black-and-white; and "Sissie" Frith, the painter's daughter.

Brooks was a native Londoner, intended like so many Punchites for the law. He was articled to a solicitor but realized at the age of twenty-nine that the legal profession was not for him. He turned to journalism and fiction. There were few papers in London that he did not write for at one time or another and no subject he could not write about in a witty, readable style. He was an inveterate gossip and loved scandal. A born humorist, he was able to turn any piece of prose into verse instantly.

Because of his sarcastic manner ("Calls a spade a spade," wrote Silver) he had his enemies. Cecil Hay took him as the model for Mr. Cynical Suave in his *The Club and Drawing Room* in 1870 and wrote:

> He is exceedingly amusing, very sharp, especially if you expose your flank to him by some heedless remark—apparently the soul of geniality and the quintessence of wit, just the sort of man that everyone is certain to like immensely the first time of meeting; to like perhaps with moderation the second time; and cordially to detest the third.

Brooks saw himself as a commercial product, not a crusader, an attitude not calculated to endear him to the early Punchites. Nevertheless, Jerrold admired him, although the Little Wasp had been a favorite Brooks target in the *Man in the Moon*. He called Lemon's attention to Brooks's skill as a writer and a satirist. Lemon, for all his parsimony, knew how to lure a promising talent away from a competitor, especially when that competitor was Albert Smith. He offered Brooks a job on *Punch*.

A pragmatic professional, Brooks suffered no pangs of conscience at making a complete conceptual about-face. From being Smith's anti-*Punch* mouthpiece, he easily assumed the role of Lemon's first assistant and general writer. He took over the "Essence of Parliament" column and wrote it for more than twenty years. He filled in on any and all subjects and created several bright, new features. One was the *Punch* "Nursery

Rhyme,'' which would not be called a limerick for some years to come. The little five-line poems celebrated the adventures of people such as the young man from Devizes or the young woman from Gloucester. Brooks boasted that he would continue them until he had made a rhyme on every village in England.

Another Brooks innovation was the series ''The Naggletons.'' It was written in a dramatic dialogue form and consisted of the bickerings of a married couple on various domestic subjects. Like Jerrold's Caudle series, it won wide popularity. Unlike the Caudles, the Naggletons were evenly matched. Mr. Naggleton, as R. G. G. Price put it, was a ''Caudle who bit back.'' They were of a slightly higher social class than the Caudles, which gave them (according to Brooks's philosophy of the amusements and problems of rich and poor) a good deal more to bicker about. In the end Brooks retired them by the simple device of having them receive a legacy contingent on their agreement to change their name, move to the country, and never quarrel again. A typical drama read as follows:

A DOMESTIC DRAMA.

The Scene represents the Parlour, Hall, and doorsteps of a genteel house in the suburbs of the Metropolis. Various boxes, done up in white and corded, also portmanteaus and carpet bags, also a bonnet-box, and a bundle of umbrellas, sticks, and a fishing-rod, are disposed in the Hall.

Mr. Naggleton (fussing about). NOW, MARIA, it is 9 o'clock.

Mrs. N. (looking as objectionable as a woman always does when she has a traveling dress on, no gloves, and a cross aspect). Well, what if it is?

Mr. N. Train starts at 9:40.

Mrs. N. That's ten minutes to ten.

Mr. N. No, it isn't.

Mrs. N. Yes, it is.

Mr. N. I tell you it is twenty minutes to ten, and we have got to get to the Station.

Mrs. N. You need not tell me that. Do you think I suppose that the train starts from this door?

Mr. N. No; but if we are to catch it, we ought to be off.

Mrs. N. What nonsense! As if we should be three-quarters of an hour going there.

Mr. N. Why no, for if we are, we shall miss the train by five minutes.

Mrs. N. No, we shan't, but you are always in such a fidget, and you like to be an hour before time.

Mr. N. Better so than an hour after it. Are you ready?

Mrs. N. I don't know. What's that noise?

Mr. N. The Cab. I sent for it.

Mrs. N. That you might have to pay the man for waiting half an hour. Just like you.

Mr. N. If you are going to keep him half an hour, say so.

Mrs. N. What then?

Mr. N. Then, I'll go into the City, and we will adjourn our departure till to-morrow.

Mrs. N. If I don't go to-day, I won't go at all.

Mr. N. If you don't go to-day, it will be your own fault.

Mrs. N. No, it will not; it will be yours.

Mr. N. How the ——I mean how do you make that out?

Mrs. N. Why, you keep nagging at me, and bewildering me till I don't know whether I'm on my head or my heels. Have you got the bunch of keys?

Mr. N. I've never seen the bunch of keys.

Mrs. N. I gave 'em to you in the bedroom.

Mr. N. You did nothing of the kind. There they are in your basket.

Mrs. N. Then you must have put 'em there.

Mr. N. How could that be when you had the basket on your arm all the time. But you've got them—what else have you got to dawdle for?

Mrs. N. Oh, there! I declare I had rather stay in town all the rest of my life than be hunted and driven like this. Have you written the directions for the luggage?

Mr. N. Lor, woman, yes, and stuck 'em on an hour ago.

Mrs. N. I dare say they'll all come off in the journey.

Mr. N. I dare say they'll do nothing of the kind.

Mrs. N. You know they all did when we went to Boulogne.

Mr. N. I know that one did, which was your own putting on. Mine I pasted firmly on that occasion, and they are on the boxes now.

Mrs. N. Yes, disfiguring them, and making them look like I don't know what.

Mr. N. Can't we finish the Boulogne dispute in the cab, as the time is getting on? But you like to be late—you think it fine.

Mrs. N. How can you talk such rubbish?

Mr. N. I ask you again what the—what are we waiting for?

Mrs. N. We are waiting till I am ready, and are likely to wait till then.

Mr. N. I wish I knew within half an hour or so how soon that would be, because I would like a stroll and a cigar.

Mrs. N. You would vex the soul out of a saint.

Mr. N. I never had the chance of trying. But, my dear, I should like to go to Worthing to-day, unless you have any strong objection. *(Rings.)*

Mrs. N. What are you ringing for?

Mr. N. SARAH, to see the boxes in the cab.

Mrs. N. She is up-stairs with the children.

Mr. N. What business has she there?

Mrs. N. I sent her.

Mr. N. Pray, what for? Where's MORTON, whose business it is to attend to them?

Mrs. N. Perhaps, HENRY, you will permit me to manage my servants in my own way?·

Mr. N. It seems to me that they manage you.

Mrs. N. I can't answer such vulgarity.

Mr. N. I know you can't answer what I say. But, once more, who is to attend to the boxes, if you send the servants out of the way in this ridiculous manner?

Mrs. N. You have no more feeling for your children than a stone. I desired the servants to stay up-stairs with the poor things, that they might not know that we were going away.

Mr. N. Pack of nonsense, they must know it half-an-hour later, and what's the sense of spoiling children in that absurd way?

Mrs. N. It's very little chance our children have of being spoiled, HENRY. I do not suppose that there is another father in this terrace who would be happy in leaving town without taking his children with him.

Mr. N. Now, how in the name of everything that is—

Mrs. N. Your language is getting perfectly horrible, HENRY. They say such things are a sign of incipient softening of the brain. I hope it may not be true, but DR. WINSLOW is certainly an authority.

Mr. N. Bosh! I was only saying how could the children have gone with us, when JAMES expressly said in his invitation that he had only one room to offer?

Mrs. N. And you were so eager to accept that invitation, while if we had accepted AUNT FLAGGERTY'S, we could all have gone; but AUNT FLAGGERTY doesn't fish, and smoke, and drink gin-and-water in the evening.

Mr. N. It may be so.

Mrs. N. HENRY! If you dare to insult a relative who is so dear to me, in your own mind, common decency might induce you to keep such sentiments to yourself.

Mr. N. I never said a word against the old lady. But I certainly had no great inclination for evenings of reading ALISON, and soda-water and bed-room candles at half-past nine.

Mrs. N. Of course you think of nobody but yourself.

Mr. N. Yes, I think of you, and how pleased and amiable you will look when we get to the terminus and find the doors closed, as we certainly shall.

Mrs. N. We shall do nothing of the kind.

Mr. N. I believe you are right, we shall find them open again, and the clerks giving tickets for the next train, which does not go to Worthing.

Mrs. N. It will be all your own fault if we do, standing here annoying me instead of putting the boxes into the cab.

Mr. N. It's not my business. Let the servants do it.

Mrs. N. There, hold your tongue. I will do it. *(Seizes a vast box.)*

Mr. N. MARIA, are you mad?

Mrs. N. It is enough to make me so, being nagged and worried as I am.

Mr. N. Here *(opens street-door)* Cabman!

Cabman. Here you are, Sir!

Mr. N. I know that, but I want *you* here. Put these things in and about the cab.

Cabman. Heavy load, rather, Sir, ain't it, Sir? How many might be going, Sir?

Mr. N. There might be twenty, but there are but two.

Mrs. N. That is right, HENRY, and just like you. Standing to exchange wretched jokes with the lower orders, and every minute valuable, if we are to catch the train.

Mr. N. Go ahead, my good fellow. I'll make it right.

Cabman. All serene, Sir.   [*Attacks the boxes*]

Mrs. N. That's just like you, HENRY. First you joke with an inferior, and then, of course, you undertake to pay him whatever he may try to extort. Yesterday, poor PETER could not have a new cart, because it was throwing away money, but his father can give anything to an insolent cabman.

Mr. N. We shall have a break-down with all that luggage as sure as eggs is eggs. Ah, the first MRS. NAGGLETON travelled with one portmanteau.

Mrs. N. The second MRS. NAGGLETON happens to be a Lady.

[*At this point the conversation of course begins to grow too terrible for publication, but they get off at last.*]

A few excerpts from Henry Silver's diary are indicative of Brooks's off-stage personality. At the dinners he dealt heavily in bawdy jokes, gossip, and strong opinions. Some of them are worth looking at in the light of his choice as editor of a National Institution.

On sex in relation to class: "Percival Leigh says as man develops his higher faculties, he loses his taste for the exercise of his lower. Animals have an instinct which limits their breeding. Man's reason should supply this. [Brooks] says, 'But man doesn't reason in bed.— Poor people have two pleasures, to get children and to get drunk. Rich people have dinners, horses, shooting boxes, sodomy, and small talk—but these luxuries are

"TRAIN UP A CHILD," &c.

"MAMMA, DON'T YOU THINK PUG OUGHT TO BE VACCINATED?"
"WHAT NONSENSE, DEAR! THEY ONLY VACCINATE HUMAN BEINGS!"
"WHY, LADY FAKEAWAY'S HAD ALL HER *SERVANTS* VACCINATED, MAMMA!"

George du Maurier, 1871

George du Maurier, 1873

AN INCOMPLETE EDUCATION.

"WHAT! SHIVERING IN THE MIDDLE OF AUGUST! HOW'S THAT?"
"O, SIR, PLEASE, SIR, WE WAS ONLY TAUGHT 'OW TO BEG IN THE *WINTER* TIME, SIR!"

not allowed to the poor. So you cannot wonder at their having large families though they have nothing to live on and know that half their sons must either steal or starve.' ''

On poverty: ''S. B. emits some aristocratic nonsense about the vice of poverty, to the effect that all poor people are scamps and scoundrels and degraded beasts. D[u Maurier] says it makes his blood boil to hear such bosh (and H. S. agrees with him). S. B. denies that the poor have any feelings but those of an animal.''

On Shakespeare: ''Discussion on whether Shakespeare was a bugger. [Brooks] Sonnets indicate yes. Would a man with natural inclinations write about unnatural ones?''

On Burnand as a playwright: (Burnand, who had been a Table member for several years, was not present on this occasion) ''Shirley despises all actors. Pitches into Burnand's *Cupid and Psyche* as the stupidest and most imbecile burlesque ever written 'And I mean to tell him so.' ''

Brooks, the hater of actors, who had admitted to Silver that he bit his tongue at the theater to keep from weeping at the sad parts (while Silver wept unashamedly at his side) had his own ideas about the function of a weekly paper. He protested when Taylor wrote an apologetic poem after the assassination of Abraham Lincoln, regretting the harsh treatment *Punch* had accorded the martyred president. ''*Punch* has *not* been blind and shallow,'' he insisted, ''and even if it had we ought not to own it!'' Lemon, taking the moderate view as always, contended that Taylor's confession that *Punch* had been ''a bit mistaken'' was manly and just.

Brooks served as editor for only four years, between Lemon's death and his own in 1874. The period was not characterized by any radical changes or noticeable improvements. The paper retained its usual format (which did not change when Taylor became editor in 1874). There was, as always, the big cut by Tenniel, surrounded by comic articles of less than a page in length, a Parliament column, drama criticism, and the spaces filled in with pars and socials that dealt with the funny side of hunting, housekeeping, social climbing, or the idiocies of servants, cabmen, and lower-class drunks. To all intents and purposes, it was as though Lemon had not died at all, but was still directing *Punch* by remote control from some ghostly paradise for magazine editors.

During his reign, Brooks made only one significant addition to the staff. He hired Linley Sambourne, who had contributed small drawings as an outsider. Sambourne began to send work to *Punch* in 1867 at the age of twenty-two and became a staff and Table member in 1871. He was an excellent draughtsman, and his illustrations for Brooks's ''Essence of Parliament'' column were delightful, but showed that he was strongly influenced by Keene, Leech, and Tenniel.

Sambourne, like Tenniel, adhered to the classical style, fanciful but solid. Like Tenniel, he was criticized for the coldness of his drawings. Some critics called them harsh and unfeeling. He had started out as an engineering draughtsman, but soon switched to illustrating, bringing with him to *Punch* the painstaking detail of the blueprint.

He had a collection of some ten thousand photographs of subjects of all kinds, which he used for planning his drawings. Like Keene he was a perfectionist. In one of his drawings of Britannia he used four different models to get her exactly the way he wanted her. His figures were always drawn first in the nude, after which he would carefully dress them, line by line. His memory was encyclopedic, and he had a tremendous fund of recondite information. E. V. Lucas, who wrote Sambourne's *éloge* in *Punch*, described him as follows:

> Others of us could remember that Tenniel, say, had once used a certain fable in a cartoon, but it was Sammy who could remark, 'If you turn to March 1863 you will find it.' Others might fancy that they knew what, say, a German forage cap was like; it was Sammy who, with a few strokes of his pencil, set it down accurately for the guidance of the junior cartoonist.

Droll and mischievous, the fun-loving Sambourne was a delightful dinner companion, taking intense pleasure in making himself the target of the teasing. He loved vintage jokes and enjoyed hearing them over and over again. He was most familiar for his malapropisms which were widely repeated. No one was ever able to determine whether they were inadvertent or whether he had contrived them for the amusement of his companions at the Table.

To Burnand he would say, "Oh, by the way, Frank, before I think of it . . . ," or he would explain, "It was so quiet you could have picked up a pin." Lucas remembers him describing a burden suffered by some public personage as "a white elephant round the man's neck." He informed the Table one evening that "Egypt was the crater of civilization."

Sambourne, who illustrated Charles Kingsley's *The Water Babies,* inherited the big cut from Tenniel in 1900, by which time he had been a Punchite for more than thirty years. His kindly white-haired presence at the Table was said to resemble portraits of Sir Walter Scott, and the other Punchites did not hesitate to tease him about the likeness. Sambourne's house in Stafford Terrace, Kensington, has been maintained by the South Kensington Association as a kind of museum of Victorian decor. His drawing room with its stained-glass windows can still be seen today, crammed with bits and pieces of period china, silver-framed photographs, horse's hoof inkstands, and other nineteenth-century adornments.

136

When Brooks died, the editorial mantle descended on the shoulders of Tom Taylor, who had been a Table member for thirty years. Taylor was born in Sunderland, the son of a self-educated workingman who, by dint of hard labor and more than usual intelligence, had raised himself to the ownership of a successful brewery. Taylor was always accused of being, like his father, a man obsessed with the desire to climb socially. He was fifty-seven when he became editor of *Punch*.

Taylor was the first genuine scholar and intellectual to assume command of *Punch*. As a result, the paper quickly sank in popularity. He was a learned man, but he simply wasn't funny. Spielmann has applied the adjective ''ponderous'' to his editorship with some justification.

> In humour slow, though sharp and keen his mind;
> His hand was heavy, though his heart was kind.

The kindly Spielmann, who had only praise for anyone even remotely associated with his beloved *Punch*, was forced to admit that Taylor was ''too scholarly and well-ordered, too veiled, deliberate . . . and under him *Punch* touched its lowest point.'' He was a moderate drinker but a good companion. As an editor he was hard to work with, impatient and nervous, incapable of quick decisions and entirely without Lemon's natural flair. Nevertheless, he was popular with the other Punchites, who respected his knowledge and his abilities.

In Brooks's time *Punch* had fallen into complacency, relying too heavily on its superstars to maintain its high position in the journalistic world. There were no contingency plans for replacement in case the luminaries should, for one reason or another, become unavailable. During Taylor's six-year tenure, the paper consisted almost entirely of the aging Tenniel, du Maurier's socials, and Taylor's ''Essence of Parliament,'' which he inherited from Brooks and attempted to make more interesting by adding contrived puns and facetious whimsies.

Taylor had been art critic of the *Times* and the *Graphic*, a figure in the art world nearly as powerful as Ruskin. His criticisms singled him out for personal attack in Whistler's *The Gentle Art of Making Enemies* (1890). For two years he held the post of professor of English language and literature at London University. Like many Punchites, he was a barrister. He held an official position on the board of health and was a fellow of Trinity College.

He wrote biographies of well-known painters and about a hundred dramatic pieces. Of all the playwrights who served *Punch* in one capacity or another, Taylor was the best. Several of his dramas were immensely successful in England and the United States (although, as so frequently happened in those days, the managers grew rich on his work but Taylor didn't). He wrote several plays in collaboration with Charles Reade and others.

His prose dramas, such as *The Ticket-of-Leave-Man*, written in 1863 but revived in 1976 in London and New York with notable success, dealt with contemporary Victorian life. They still retain their charm. His historical plays, such as *Ann Boleyn* (1875) and *Joan of Arc* (1871), were written in verse and have a certain style, though they are less amusing than the prose works.

Taylor had the knack of creating wonderful, memorable characters. One was the muddleheaded peer, Lord Dundreary, whose name became an English generic term. Another was the keen-witted hero-sleuth, Hawkshaw the Detective. Unfortunately, Taylor had the dubious honor of being the author of the comedy *Our American Cousin*, at which Abraham Lincoln was chuckling when John Wilkes Booth emptied his pistol into him. Naturally, it was Taylor who wrote *Punch*'s obituary to the martyred president.

In addition to writing the last words ever spoken in the hearing of the Great Emancipator, Taylor achieved another accidental literary laurel. It was he who introduced John Tenniel to his friend Lewis Carroll, with the suggestion that Tenniel illustrate *Alice in Wonderland*. Taylor had wisely turned down a Carroll offering for *Punch*, a poetic parody that began, "I never loved a dear gazelle," and felt, perhaps, that he owed Carroll some sort of recompense.

"Spy," who had a sharp eye for details of character even as a small boy, reminisces in his autobiography about Taylor, who was a friend of his parents.

At dinner his appearance was remarkable, for he usually wore a black velvet evening suit. A curious trait was his absent-minded manner and forgetfulness of conversation. Sometimes when walking in the street with a friend, he would grow interested, and to emphasize his remarks, turned to look more directly into the face of his companion, at the same time placing his arm around his waist. In the case of a lady, this habit sometimes proved rather embarrassing.

Mr. Tom Taylor was a man of unbounded kindness in helping everybody who was in need of money or in trouble; his generosity probably made him the object of attentions from all sorts and conditions of people, a fact very soon discovered by his domestics, for one day Mr. and Mrs. Taylor returned from a walk to be met by a startled parlour-maid who announced the presence of a strange-looking man who was waiting to see them. Her suspicions being aroused by his wild appearance, she had him shown into the pantry, fearing to leave him in the drawing room. On repairing to the pantry with curiosity not unmixed with wonder, they discovered . . . Tennyson . . . quite at home and immensely tickled by his situation.

Taylor rose at six every morning and worked hard for three hours in order to be able to spend his evenings with his wife. This was unusual devotion in a Victorian husband. Unlike his colleagues he was not a very clubbable man, although he took part in *Punch* outings and meetings of the Moray Minstrels, at which the attractive Mrs. Taylor was always a welcome guest.

Even at the Table dinners, it was difficult for him to escape being scholarly. To him they were business meetings and their purpose was a serious one. Silver recalls him pontificating on parliamentary reform:

> T. T. says if you extend suffrage you will lower the tone of Parliament and damage its efficiency. Defends Imperial government on the grounds of economy. If Bright's [reform] bill passed, it would assimilate Imperial government to parochial—there would be an infusion of the demagogic element which in time would oust the gentlemanly and the educated—and the last state of the House would be worse than the first. The House always listens to lower-class members if well-informed.

Taylor and Leech were the first Punchites to volunteer for military service as members of an auxiliary unit. "The Brook-Green Volunteers" had been a source of great fun in Leech's cartoons, *Punch*'s innate snobbery enjoying to the fullest the attempts of middle-class burghers to ape the airs of the regular military. Taylor was teased by his colleagues for his drills and his uniforms. Silver wrote in his diary March 21, 1860:

> Captain Taylor marched in from drill in uniform—grey with silver clasp on crossbelt about as big as a coffin plate, whistle attached by chain long enough for a dog chain (N.B. and this is what they call a quiet uniform). Leech, who has also been at drill, proposes that the Table be called the MESS.

On rare occasions Taylor showed a spark of life, especially when he drank a little too much at the Table. Silver recalls a notable incident when the abstemious T. T. consumed a bit too much hot punch prepared by Pater Evans and Mark Lemon and got very jolly, talking "like a dozen" and proposing a trip to the Derby in "a hearse or in a van with a trombone."

He died in 1880 and with him died a *Punch* era. The paper nurtured and developed by Mark Lemon would never be quite the same again.

You must be clear about Punch's politics. He is a polite whig, with a sentimental respect for the Crown, and a practical respect for property. He steadily flatters Lord Palmerston, from his heart adores Mr. Gladstone, steadily but not virulently caricatures Mr. Disraeli; violently and virulently castigates assault on property in any kind, and holds up for the general idea of perfection, to be aimed at by the children of Heaven and earth, the British Hunting Squire, the British Colonel, and the British sailor.

—John Ruskin

hen Francis Cowley Burnand took over the editorship of *Punch* in 1880, British soldiers were fighting Zulus in Africa and Afghans in Kabul. Boer farmers were being tiresome in the Transvaal and would soon have to be "taught a lesson." The Mahdi was making a nuisance of himself in the Sudan. Worse still, from the English point of view, and much too close to home, the outrageously ungrateful Irish were maiming cattle at home and setting off bombs in London.

Punch sailed along in its politically ambiguous fashion, not so much neutral between parties as ambidextrously hostile, as R. G. G. Price described it. The turn of the century saw a marked upswing in imperialistic sentiment, trumpeted by Rudyard Kipling (and echoed by *Punch*) until Britons had had time to evaluate the lessons learned from the foolish Boer War and the machinations of Cecil Rhodes. English writers began to write self-criticism and to recognize that perhaps Englishmen were not always right about everything. Socialists began to pop up in the most unlikely places.

The so-called Gay Nineties are usually described as opulently wicked and elegantly depraved; characterized by sharp contrast between the dissolute rich and the miserably downtrodden poor. In fact, the rich were no more vulgar or self-indulgent than they are today. The poor, taking into account the inflation factor, were no poorer. As Henry George sensibly pointed out, when one kind of poverty is abolished, another kind is created. Victorian reformers, including Punchites, believed that as soon as everybody had three meals a day, hot running water, and an indoor lavatory, poverty would disappear forever. As we have seen, they were wrong.

Douglas Jerrold's grandson and namesake, commenting on the prewar period, wrote, "the line between the mondaine and the demi-mondaine was much sharper. One seldom met one's aunt and never one's sister at an Edwardian night club, and the middle class had not yet begun to dance." Whether or not this was an indication that things were better in the old days has been a debatable point for many decades.

When Burnand assumed the editorial mantle, *Punch* was still the showcase of British humor and a power in the land. The paper's image as a staple in dentists' waiting rooms was still far in the future. Nevertheless, Tom Taylor's heavy hand had started a decline. Rumors were abroad that the paper had begun to die, that only older readers still subscribed and that the young looked for amusement and instruction elsewhere. Burnand's first priority was to excise the dry rot and freshen the paper's image with new writers and artists.

Burnand toned down the political fervor in favor of domestic family fun. The old Jerrold-style savagery was banished forever. He made some minor changes in format, rendering *Punch* more attractively up-to-date and easier to read. For the first time there was a book-review section. The amount of verse was increased. A new column of collected bits and pieces, called "Charivaria," would become a favorite feature for decades. Bigotry was thrown out. Anti-Catholic jokes were taboo (Burnand was a Catholic). Du Maurier talked him into permitting Jewish jokes, and Keene pressured him into allowing jokes about drunks. Otherwise, Punch became jolly kindness itself.

Through the eighties and nineties *Punch* remained scholarly, avuncular, mild, and middle-aged. Everyone smiled at the jokes but few laughed aloud. A visitor from another planet reading *Punch* would have thought England was an enormous hunting field populated by grotesque and inept equestrians, all of whom lived in large houses filled with disobedient servants. Like his predecessors, Burnand steadfastly refused to recognize that sex had humorous potential, except, of course, behind closed doors at the Table dinners. The ultra-propriety of the Lemon years, when jokes were refused because they contained the name of the Lord; or the Brooks years, when a par was turned down because it dealt with the tendency of crinolines to pop up so that "we now see more of our friends than formerly," still applied.

The readers, regardless of what they did or thought in their leisure time, would not have had *Punch* any other way. It was still a family magazine, and the writers and artists were members of the family,

MILITARY EDUCATION.

General. "MR. DE BRIDOON, WHAT IS THE GENERAL USE OF CAVALRY I MODERN WARFARE?"

Mr. de Bridoon. "WELL, I SUPPOSE TO GIVE TONE TO WHAT WOULD OTHE WISE BE A MERE VULGAR BRAWL!"

Reginald Cleaver, 189

beloved, jovial cousins to every household in England. Reminiscing about wartime *Punch*, A. A. Milne recalled:

> *Punch* readers are delightfully responsive. At a crisis in the war I wrote some pathetic verses called 'The Last Pot' and never lacked for marmalade again. When I had exhausted the benevolence or the larders of English women, the nearer colonies and the more distant dominions took up the torch, so that the Empire became for me a place in which marmalade is always setting.

In the autumn of 1908, T. W. H. Crosland, commenting in the *Academy* on *Punch* readers, wrote that the character of a journal can be judged from its advertisers. ''Ergo, *Punch* readers must suffer from bad legs, indigestion, nits, fleas. . . . They must be bald or nearly bald or craving alcohol.'' This novel concept may not have been entirely wrong.

Burnand brought to the Table some of the brighter young outsiders from Taylor's day. Owen Seaman, who would replace him as editor in 1906, assumed the responsibility for the general donkeywork. Rudolph Lehmann, who had founded the *Granta* at Cambridge, and Anstey Guthrie, who wrote as ''F. Anstey,'' placed their initials on the surface of the venerable board. The wonderful Phil May, whose deft style brought the social cartoon into harmony with the twentieth century, joined the staff. E. J. Milliken and E. T. Reed came into the *Punch* limelight after some years as occasional contributors. Henry Lucy took on the ''Essence of Parliament'' column.

Burnand tried to get W. S. Gilbert to leave *Fun* and write for *Punch*, but Gilbert was still smarting from Lemon's refusal of his poem ''The Rhyme of the Nancy Bell'' as ''too cannibalistic.'' It made no difference to him that Lemon had been dead for fifteen years; *Punch* was still an enemy. Moreover, Burnand had added another insult by referring to one of Gilbert's favorite but least successful plays, *Broken Hearts*, as ''Broken Parts.'' The gibe had been repeated in the *Daily Telegraph* and Gilbert never forgave him. Burnand would never entirely forgive Gilbert for replacing him as Sullivan's librettist, but he was willing to overlook a personal grievance if it would benefit *Punch*. Gilbert was not.

Burnand was able to secure the services of one of Gilbert and Sullivan's finest musical comedy stars, George Grossmith, who, with his brother Weedon, wrote the funny and wildly successful ''Diary of a Nobody'' series which very nearly equalled the popularity of the Caudles and which is still heard occasionally on BBC radio. He also hired that ''graceless young whelp,'' Mark Lemon's longtime bête noir, George Augustus Sala.

The dynastic character of the paper was continued by the presence at the Table of Gilbert à Beckett's sons, Gilbert and Arthur, and by the employment of Brooks's son, Reginald, and Sambourne's daughter, Maude.

Burnand insisted that he had no political sentiments. The Table represented as nice a mix of varying philosophies as Parliament itself. Of the more important policy-making Punchites, Tenniel, Arthur à Beckett, and Anstey Guthrie were conservatives. Milliken, Henry Lucy, Rudie Lehmann, and E. T. Reed were radicals. Sambourne was a unionist. When political matters were discussed, the Table talk was lively.

New sources of humor began to materialize in the latter part of Burnand's editorship. Automobiles appeared in city streets and country lanes, creating problems of traffic control and a favorable side effect—the permanent decline of *Punch*'s horse jokes. The houses of the well-to-do and even the sacrosanct precincts of Windsor Castle blossomed out in electric lights and telephones. There were new fashions in costumes and new fads, including a craze for a card game called bridge, which *Punch* predicted would certainly replace whist.

While he was redesigning *Punch*, Burnand also created a new style in English and American humor. He invented the short chronicle of personal misadventure, the little domestic disaster in which the first-person narrator is the wretched victim of some embarrassment beyond his ability to control: the loss of a collar button or the arrival at a country house for the weekend without one's white dress tie, necessitating the use of a borrowed one three sizes too large—things that could happen to any *Punch* reader who, of course, would be better able to cope than the absurd young man in Burnand's "Happy Thoughts" series. This was a brand new concept. The narrator had never before been the butt in humorous stories. The device was received enthusiastically and has been used successfully ever since by such writers as Robert Benchley, S. J. Perelman, Stephen Leacock, and generations of later Punchites. It was the prototype that led to Bertie Wooster and brought success to such entertainers as Jack Benny and Woody Allen.

The "Happy Thoughts" series was the precursor of this comic genre. Disasters were punctuated at the moment of greatest crisis with the narrator's arrival at a "happy thought," which eased the situation in his favor. The phrase *happy thought* became a catchword of sophisticated London party talk. After a few years the series was followed by "More Happy Thoughts" in which Burnand's bachelor protagonist married his beloved Fridoline, opening up a whole new supply of young-married-man situations. The series was published in book form and is still funny today. E. V. Lucas wrote, "If 'Happy Thoughts' had been taken seriously by its author, it might, without losing any of its fun, be one of the great psychological works of the world. Burnand did not know how good his material was; he played with it and dropped it all too soon.''

Burnand was forty-three when he became editor of *Punch*. His selection was predictable. He had kept the magazine going with his lively pieces during Taylor's dull, heavy tenure. He was the obvious choice, although du Maurier, ever brash, had expected to get the job himself. Burnand had no chance, he wrote, ''for he is a Roman Catholic, and everyone is aware of the emphatic stand Punch has always taken against Romanism.'' Du Maurier was never in the running at all. On the fateful afternoon, the proprietors met with a selection committee made up of Tenniel, Arthur à Beckett, and Percival Leigh. The unanimous choice was Burnand.

He was the son of a rich stockbroker, educated at Eton and Trinity, where he founded the Amateur Dramatic Club. His first choice of a career on leaving Cambridge was the church. He studied under Cardinal Manning, but it soon became apparent that he had no vocation for the priesthood. He left to read law and was called to the Bar in 1862. But the lure of the theater was too much for him, and like so many Punchites before and after him, he left the legal profession to follow the lively arts. He began to write comedies and burlesques, some by himself and some in collaboration with W. S. Gilbert and others. He also contributed to *Fun*, where his work caught the ever-vigilant eye of Mark Lemon.

In 1863 the *London Journal* was serializing a number of luridly written and illustrated novels. Burnand suggested to Lemon that *Punch* publish parodies of the *Journal* thrillers. The result was ''Mokeanna'' which appeared on February 21, 1863. It was a great success. The *Journal* novels were illustrated by John Gilbert, Millais, Keene, and du Maurier; and Lemon conceived the idea of having the artists burlesque their own work rather than have the parodies done by others. The illustrators had a marvelous time making fun of themselves.

At first sight, readers were fooled for a moment into believing that *Punch* had actually decided to publish sensational fiction. The proprietors were appalled, thinking that pages of the *Journal* had accidentally gotten bound into *Punch* at the printers. Lemon was delighted, and Burnand became a permanent fixture. He would remain one for forty-three years.

Burnand's stage comedies poured out in great numbers, deluging the racier side of the London theater. In 1866 he scored a hit with a parody of Douglas Jerrold's *Black-eyed Susan*. Over the years Burnand wrote more than a hundred burlesques, many of which were successful, if lacking in artistic value. Frank Harris, who was editor of the *Saturday Review* at the time, dropped in to see his *Blue Beard*. He wrote:

The play was worse than absurd, incredibly trivial—Mr. Burnand's hero keeps a note book for getting down the addresses of interesting young women; otherwise he is not much of a monster. His mysterious Blue Chamber contains nothing more terrible than hair dye. He is a beardless lad of one-and-twenty; has, however, a blue lock to show; but it's a fraud. His wife and father-in-law are to lose their heads for discovering his secret; the catastrophe is averted by the timely arrival of troops of young ladies in fantastic martial costumes that reveal the most shapely figures.

Miss Nelly Farren is the Baron Abomélique de Barbe Bleue, and Miss Kate Vaughan is Lili, the Baron's bride. Here is the first verse of her song in the second act:

> French language is a bother,
>   To learn it I don't care,
> Don't like to hear my mother
>   Called by the French a *mère*.
> I like a husband to myself
>   But the dear one is my *chère*,
> Though I've only got one father,
>   Yet they swear he is a *père* . . .

Then Kate danced . . . with inimitable grace; and the way she picks up her dress and shows dainty ankles and a hint of lovely limbs is a poem in itself, and all about her beautiful smiling girls in costumes that reveal every charm, sway or turn or dance as if inspired by her delightful gaiety. In another scene she imitates Sarah Bernhardt . . . someone else mimics Irving and all this in a rain of the most terrible puns and verbal acrobatics ever heard on any stage—an unforgettable evening which made me put Burnand down as one of the men I must get to know as soon as possible, for he was evidently a force to count with, a verbal contortionist, at least, of most extraordinary agility.

In point of fact, Burnand's burlesques were awful, but they were exactly what the theater-going Londoner wanted to see. His dreadful puns had a hard time competing with Kate Vaughan's legs and the smiling ladies of the chorus, but nobody cared. He knew how to blend both to the public taste.

Harris did get to know "handsome little Frank," as he called Burnand, and found him "as kindly pleasant as he was good-looking and witty, and that's saying a good deal." The two did not become good friends but met from time to time in London clubs and exchanged off-color jokes.

Burnand was short, good-looking, and charming, resembling in his

A "B. AND S." AT THE SAVOY.

A GREAT deal is expected from the collaboration of Sir ARTHUR SULLIVAN and Mr. F. C. BURNAND, more especially when the work is

Sir Arthur. "Then *Box*——"   *Sir Author.* "And *Cox*——"
Both. "Are satisfied!"   [*Curtain.*

"Up in the morning early."

stared at 'the Savoy, and is brought out under the direction of Mr. D'OYLY CARTE. The brilliant audience that gathered on Wednesday night for the first performance of *The Chieftain* evidently came full of expectation, and as evidently went away filled with satisfaction. Twenty-seven years ago, when they were boys together, B. and S. (that sounds friendly and refreshing) brought out an early version of the opera which they called *The Contrabandista.* After the rehearsal of the new piece had gone forward for some weeks, ARTHUR SULLIVAN stumbled over this rather difficult word and sprained his ankle. Whereupon F. C. B., with characteristic promptitude and originality, changed the name to *The Chieftain.* That is the call-boy's narrative of events. However it be, since the opera has been entirely re-written, enlarged and beautified, it was natural to bestow upon it a new title. On the first night *The Chieftain* stormed the passes to public favour, and appears likely to occupy them for some time. Nothing brighter in colour, fuller of life, more musical, more mirthful, has been seen at the Savoy since its palmiest days. Sir ARTHUR and Sir Author are perfectly mated, F. C. B. brimming over with genuine humour, and A. S. pre-eminently displaying his rare gift of expressing humour in musical notes. The cast is a very strong one, which is fortunate, seeing the appetite of the audience is insatiable, and only exceptional strength could meet the demand for encores. Where all excel it is difficult to particularise merit. But Miss FLORENCE ST. JOHN and Mr. COURTICE POUNDS in the French duet, Mr. PASSMORE from first to last (especially in his Bolero dance, one of the funniest things for a long time seen on the operatic stage), Miss EMMIE OWEN in her graceful movements, and the sextet with its merry music and its laughing dance, are things to see and hear.

ENGLISH AS SHE IS CRAMMED.

¡THE Oxford Board of Studies will conduct an examination in 1896 for the new Final School of English Language and Literature. The following preliminary paper is to be set :—

ENGLISH LANGUAGE AND LITERATURE.

Time allowed—18 months.

[Questions are to be answered either in Gothic or Icelandic, according to the taste and fancy of the candidate. The dates of the *vivâ voce* "Chatter about SHELLEY," and "Scandal about Queen ELIZABETH," will be announced shortly. Evening dress optional. Smoking and Bohemian Concert to follow. See Handbills.]

1. Write out the English Alphabet as inaccurately as possible ; and distinguish between great A and the track of a duck.
2. Translate the following unheard-of passage from BEOWULF:—

Tuinchael . . . . lytl . . .
Haui onedr hwatuar
Uppabuvye wereld sohi
Lika . . . ynneye . . .

Supply the *lacunæ* in the text. Candidates may send in as many solutions as they please, provided each is accompanied with a shilling Postal Order. The total amount subscribed will be pooled among the winners, less ten per cent. for our commission.
3. Discuss the following :—
(a) When is a door not a negress ?
(β) What is the difference between hearing recitation and being bored ?
(γ) Why is HALL CAINE like a tenpenny nail ?
Any replies to the above will be most thankfully received, and paid for at our usual rates.
4. "There was a very foolish, fond old man,
Fourscore and upward, dwelling at Liskeard,
Who said, I am not in my perfect mind ;
It is just as I feared, in very sooth,
For, to deal plainly, four larks and a hen,
Two hooting owls, and one small wren to boot,
Did each one lodge last night within my beard."

King Lear, Act IV., Sc. 6.

Hence show, by internal evidence, that EDWARD LEAR wrote BAKESPEARE.
5. State the various questions to the following answer:—
" Because there's a 'b' in both.'
6. Give the meaning, if any, to the subjoined flowers of speech :—*cheese your patter, perform the negative, a runcible cat, cow-chilo, do a drag, a pale paradox, going tommy-dodd, dead-lurk a crib, the hush of the corn, ferjunt rarm, the momeraths outgrabe,* and *filling up the cup.*
7. Trace the origin of the following legends :—(a) The old lady who travelled twice round the Inner Circle Railway against her wish ; (b) The conversation between TOOLE and St. Peter about HENRY IRVING ; (c) The leading journalist whose nose cost him £8,000 to colour ; and mention any other chestnuts you may know of.
8. Compose a leader in the *Times* style on Ballet-girls and their Little Ways ; in *D. T.* phraseology on Quaternions ; *à la Pink'Un* on the Delights of Sunday School ; and in the best *Guardian* manner in Defence of Prize-fighting.
9. Write down all you don't know about any mortal subject you are most ignorant of, provided it has nothing to do with the English language and literature.

"IN spite of all temptation," MARCUS WARD & Co. remain true Englishmen, and have had their dainty Christmas cards, and other delightful novelties, "not printed in Germany." The support of the loyal British shopper should be their re-*Ward*. But C. W. FAULKNER & Co. evidently think that a foreign name is more attractive, and have christened their new table-game "Malletino." It hardly requires a deep knowledge of Italian to discover that it is played with mallets, and is amusing. Their cards and calendars are quite "up to date"—at least the latter will be next year.

EXCEPTION.—Pleasant Christmas Bills : Bills of Fare.

caricatures by "Spy" and "Ape" (Carlo Pellegrini) a jovial, bright-eyed elf. He was married to a pretty actress who was that strange object of Victorian disapproval, his deceased wife's sister. The match was illegal in Britain for many years for religious reasons.

Burnand's association with Sir Arthur Sullivan began with a chance meeting and the suggestion that the two set Maddison Morton's *Box and Cox* to music. His collaboration with Gilbert on plays makes him probably the only literary figure of the period to work with both of the titans of the London musical stage, but the partnerships brought him neither money nor fame. Gilbert and Sullivan seemed to be unlucky for him, and except for the retitled *Cox and Box*, his collaborations were failures. Both Gilbert and Sullivan (before their quarrel) were frequent visitors at the theater parties given by Burnand and his wife at their house in Belgrave Road.

As an editor Burnand was energetic and a strict disciplinarian, unlike his easygoing predecessors. E. V. Lucas describes him in action:

> As a jovial head of the Table, Burnand could not have been better, and as a chairman of a committee met for the selection of the two cartoons into which at a given hour the regular weekly meal merges, he was admirable. No simple talk, for professional humorists can be garrulous and deviate from the point; but Burnand, while letting everyone have his say, pounced suddenly on the salient idea and quickly fixed the picture.

Henry Silver, who was a little jealous of him, summed him up as "not a bad fellow, albeit a noisy one. . . . Burnand has a loud laugh that in his case does not speak the vacant mind. Neat, natty little fellow he is." In his later years Burnand grew very grand, pointing out to newcomers that the Punchites were professional men and gentlemen, not simply journalists or jokesters. "Frank is such a five-thousand-a-yearer in his habits," du Maurier wrote to a friend.

With increasing success, he grew bored with *Punch*, leaving most of the work to his assistants, with the result that the magazine began a new decline. This inevitably led to problems with the proprietors who wanted to get rid of him and secretly offered the editorship to Henry Lucy. Lucy, who owed his job to Burnand, refused to go behind his editor's back. In any event, Burnand, getting wind of what was happening, managed to mollify the irate proprietors. *Punch* continued to slip, however, going off in its own direction, completely out of touch with the real world. Its power as a molder of political opinion decreased sharply. At last Burnand

148

was forced into retirement at the age of sixty-nine, lured by a fat pension. For a while he toured the lecture circuit, giving his listeners his own biased point of view of his problems with the proprietors. He made his last appearance at the Table the year after his retirement at the dinner honoring Mark Twain.

The accession of Owen Seaman to the editorship in 1906 was not much of a surprise, although it may have been a disappointment to some. An ambitious striver, Seaman had deposed Arthur à Beckett as assistant editor and would cheerfully have murdered his own grandmother for the job. Had Henry Lucy not been so adamant about so fine a point of honor, *Punch* might have moved in an entirely different direction with perhaps more success and certainly with a more liberal political bias.

Lucy had been Burnand's first appointment when he took control of *Punch*. He had come to the editor's notice, like so many excellent Punchites before him, because of work on other publications. His articles in the *Observer*, called ''From the Cross Benches,'' reflected ten years of parliamentary reporting of the best kind. R. G. G. Price calls his employment at *Punch* ''one of Burnand's happier strokes of resuscitation.'' E. V. Lucas described him as having ''no fire and much caution,'' but conceded that as a political journalist he was unequalled with his ''neat descriptive gift and power of summary and his deadly instinct for the use of the spotlight.'' He was keen and outspoken and possessed of an excellent memory, which was not always necessary since he was not above putting his own epigrams in the mouths of politicians who were not bright enough to have thought of them themselves.

His articles gave him sufficient power to criticize without fear of libel prosecution and to broadcast the latest political gossip. He was neither as partisan as Tom Taylor nor as cleverly hostile as Shirley Brooks, but forceful and controversial in his analyses. His parliamentary reports were often more amusing than the writings of the professional humorists in the later years of Burnand's tenure.

Price evaluates Lucy as one of the most valuable Punchites of the period.

> His political articles in the *Gentleman's Magazine* had turned Woodrow Wilson to politics. He was an important figure in the Liberal ''working'' of the press. Prime Ministers sent him notes from Cabinet meetings and resigning Ministers were anxious that he should have their version of the facts. Neither Theodore Roosevelt nor the King of the Belgians read any other Parliamentary Report. Shackleton named a mountain in Antarctica after him. He knew everybody and his dinner parties were important as they were politically neutral and allowed opponents to meet socially.

Lucy had a famous tablecloth that distinguished guests at his dinner parties were invited to sign, a custom borrowed, of course, from the Mahogany Tree itself, and perhaps a trifle more snobbish since the signers were chosen arbitrarily. One of the dinners was given in honor of Gladstone in order to bring him together with the staff of *Punch*, which had supported him for nearly half a century. This led to a comment in a rival publication, written by a pseudonymous author who called himself "Moonshine." He wrote, "It is said that *Punch* has been entertaining Mr. Gladstone. We don't believe a word of it, as we can't conceive that *Punch* ever entertained anybody!" Burnand immediately put out feelers to see if he could find out who Moonshine was, with the purpose of inviting him to contribute. His editor, however, refused to unmask him.

Lucy revised the "Essence" column and added a new subtitle, "The Diary of Toby, M.P." He was given the privilege of suggesting his own illustrator and chose Harry Furniss, whom he took to the House and familiarized with the ins and outs of parliamentary procedure. He also reviewed books in Burnand's new literary criticism feature, under the name the "Baron de Book-Worms." His first *Punch* contribution appeared in January 1881, and he was called to the Table in 1884. In his latter years he wrote six volumes of autobiography, now hard to find, but of considerable historical value for students of the Victorian era.

Arthur à Beckett may have harbored some hopes of becoming editor after Burnand, but he resigned in a huff in 1903 when he was removed from the assistant editorship, traditionally the stepping stone to eventual command. His fury at being replaced in the number two job by Seaman permeates his autobiographical books, *The à Becketts of Punch* and *Confessions of a Humorist*.

A former civil servant, à Beckett had edited two unsuccessful papers before coming to *Punch* at the invitation of Tom Taylor. By the time he left he had submitted more than a thousand prose pieces, reviving his father's "Briefless" series and celebrating the ups and downs of the legal profession, which he had joined in 1881.

He was an indefatigable worker. As a result, the bored Burnand gradually left all the work to him. It was quite natural that he should assume that the editorship would fall to him since he presided at the Table in Burnand's absence. He was probably more than anyone else responsible for the magazine's decline when Burnand lost interest in it. Price has called him a silly old man, and if his autobiographies are any indication, he certainly was just that. He was a stuffy, pompous old buffer. Price's comments on "bufferdom" in *Punch* are worthy of repetition here.

ESSENCE OF PARLIAMENT.
Extracted from the Diary of TOBY, M.P.

House of Commons, Wednesday.—New Session opens to-morrow; 1 one seems to have closed only yesterday. Time coming when e shall refuse to make two bites at cherry, and, meeting on 1st January, shall adjourn on Christmas Eve, as we did last year. und OLD MORALITY here taking last glance round before battle gins. Looks plump and pleasant. Has laid in new stock of copy- ok headings, a few culled from foreign languages.

" A little more flowery some of them," he said, 'affectionately rning over leaves of stout note-book, "but I fancy they'll fit in."

" Heard you were not coming back," I said. "Reported that you re going a step higher to consort with the Barons of England."

"Well, if you listen attentively you may hear a good deal of me at is not actually consonant with truth. Never was any founda- n for this particular fable. Shall never desert the Commons until ey wear me out."

Glad to hear this. OLD MORALITY not as brilliant as DIZZY, nor as quent as GLADSTONE. But everybody likes him, and wishes him ck in the new Session.

Business done.—Going to begin.

MEETING OF THE GODS.

Parliament as Olympus. Zeus is the Marquess of Salisbury, who was the Conservative prime minister. Facing him as Hercules is his predecessor, the Liberal leader William Ewart Gladstone, who would succeed Salisbury again in 1892. Other notables of the political scene are represented as the various gods and goddesses. (Harry Furniss, 1889)

No paper has been so threatened by silly old men as *Punch*. Bufferdom has to accept changes in science and warfare and technology. It digs in its toes when its entertainment is concerned and in entertainment it includes all the arts. . . . Buffers expect all humour, all drawing, all writing, to be much the same as when their taste was formed in childhood. Buffers write in to the paper complaining of the absence of contributors long since dead or discarded and attacking contributors who try to do anything new. . . . While they remained a minority of readers they could be replied to politely or ignored and the policy of the paper could develop organically. The trouble began when they got right into the office. Percival Leigh became a buffer young, but his contributions were dropped. Taylor had a bit of the buffer in him but he was a man of sufficiently varied public life to prevent his sinking altogether into the elderly clubman. The buffers really got into the works with à Beckett, and even he had been quite light and entertaining in his youth.

Another Table member who might have hoped to rise in the *Punch* hierarchy was E. J. Milliken, a businessman turned journalist who was Tom Taylor's most valuable acquisition. In the later Taylor years and the early and middle Burnand period, it was Milliken who suggested most of the ideas for political cartoons and wrote the verse or prose commentary that accompanied them—the *Punch* equivalent of an editorial. He also served as chief obituary writer when notables in the literary or political world died.

Milliken started as a contributor in 1875 and was called to the Table in 1877. His first contribution was "A Voice from Venus" on January 2, 1875, for which Taylor paid him the high compliment of demanding a guarantee of originality. He was best known for the " 'Arry Papers," the chronicle of a lower-class bounder who dropped his *H*'s. 'Arry was a hate figure, the fictional replacement for the banned real-life hate figures thrown out in Burnand's campaign against bigotry. In hating 'Arry, the readers were permitted to despise everything he stood for. Spielmann described him as brazen, vulgar, unashamed, mean-souled, swaggering, selfish, cynical, objectionable, insolent, and a self-declared cad.

'Arry was the later counterpart of Thackeray's snobs and Leech's swells, except that he recognized the fact that he was a bounder and the others were unaware of it. In creating him, Milliken said he had combined street boys, costers, cheap clerks, counter-jumpers, excursionists, music hall performers and audiences, and mechanics. 'Arry was an attack, he said, on "the *spirit of Caddishness*, rampant in our days in many grades of life, coarse, corrupting, revolting in all."

'Arry was a popular figure with the readers because he could be despised without threatening anyone. He bore no relationship whatsoever to the real working class, which was currently involved in trade unionism. The word " 'Arryism" became a generic term for caddishness, and 'Arry found his way into the Oxford English Dictionary. Milliken, delighted with his creation's success, began to write about 'Arryism in the middle and upper classes, rather foolishly retaining the Cockney accent. Other 'Arry figures followed, most notably John T. Bedford's "Robert the City Waiter" who appeared in *Punch* a great many times until the joke wore thin. Both 'Arry and Robert were considered to be social satire, but were, in fact, the old *Punch* snobbery peeping through. One critic went so far as to put back the dropped *H*'s and to translate Robert's language into proper English and then demanded to know where the humor had gone.

Superior to both Milliken and Bedford as a taker-off of people who spoke substandard English was Thomas Anstey Guthrie, a kindly little man who wrote under the pseudonym of F. Anstey. He was already well-known as a novelist when he came to *Punch* in 1885 with his first contribution, a short piece called "*Faux et Preterea Nihil.*" He was made a Table member in 1887.

Guthrie's reputation was based almost entirely on one book when he arrived at *Punch*, a farce called *Vice Versa*, written when he was twenty-six. It dealt with a father and schoolboy son who exchange bodies through the intermediary of a magician, retaining their own personalities. The father was forced to undergo the rigors of schoolboy life while the son made a botch of things at home. *Vice Versa*, now in the public domain, still retains its charm. It was borrowed in toto a few years ago by the Walt Disney Studios and made into a dreadfully arch film called *Freaky Friday*, with the protagonists transformed into a modern day mother and teen-aged daughter instead of the original males.

Guthrie's other books, *The Tinted Venus*, *The Black Poodle*, *A Fallen Idol*, and others, brought him celebrity as a humorist and an invitation from Burnand to contribute. His first great success was with "Mr. Punch's Model Music Hall Songs," a collection of parodies many of which were superior to the fare currently offered at London's variety houses.

In "Mr. Punch's Young Reciter" Guthrie produced a number of bombastic or tear-jerking recitations that almost put an end to the custom of after-dinner drawing-room recitation. His poem in which a burglar is reduced to tears by an innocent child is especially hilarious, and the idea was later borrowed for an essay by Robert Benchley ("Editha's Burglar"). He also delighted *Punch* readers with 'Arryism in dramatic form in his *Voces Populi* series, a wonderful social commentary that some called new-fangled although Brooks had used the device in the Naggletons series.

Guthrie got around the Burnand antibigotry edict with his "Jottings and Tittlings" series, the first-person adventures of an Indian gentleman in London to study law. Baboo Hurry Bungsho Jabberjee, B.A., graduate of Calcutta University, who had "passed his courses with fugitive colours" by dint of "nude courage" delighted his English readers with his bizarre syntax. He was a kind of Bengali version of *Private Eye*'s bewildered Australian, Barry McKenzie, of nearly a century later; a colonial in England trying to be English and rendering himself ridiculous in the attempt. Baboo Jabberjee passed his Bar examination at last, but got himself in and out of all sorts of messes including a bungled shoot in Scotland, a breach-of-promise suit with his landlady's buxom daughter, and a blighted love affair. His comments on London customs were delightfully funny.

Guthrie's Table and Cambridge colleague Rudolph Chambers Lehmann joined *Punch* in 1889, becoming a Table member only four months later, a record for newcomers. Lehmann was the grandson of one of the original contributors, W. H. Wills. He was educated at Highgate School and Trinity, where he was president of the Cambridge Union. A passionate oarsman, Lehmann was captain of the first Trinity boat club and served as amateur coach for victorious crews at Oxford, Cambridge, Leander, Dublin, and the *Berliner Ruder Klub*. He also traveled to America to coach the Harvard crew and was awarded a master's degree there.

Sports were his whole life and he was mildly disappointed when his children did not inherit his passion for them. His son John, in his autobiography, recalls that the Lehmann house at Bourne End was cluttered with mementoes of Lehmann's sporting past: dumbbells, fencing equipment, oars, old boxing gloves leaking their stuffing, and similar useless but treasured items.

Lehmann had founded the Cambridge humor magazine, *Granta*, which gave *Punch* Anstey Guthrie, Owen Seaman, A. A. Milne, and Barry Pain. After he left Cambridge he studied law (and was awarded a newspaper prize for the handsomest barrister). Apparently he possessed sufficient private funds to support his large family without having to practice his profession. He certainly lived in a style that could not have been achieved on a *Punch* salary.

In 1905 Lehmann won a landslide election in the Market Harborough division of Leicester and served as liberal-radical member for that constituency for four years. His politics brought him into frequent and acrimonious conflict with Owen Seaman, who did not feel, after he

GOOD ADVERTISEMENT.

"I USED YOUR SOAP TWO YEARS AGO; SINCE THEN I HAVE USED
NO OTHER."

Harry Furniss, 1884

RESTORATION OF BRITISH CYCLIST.
20TH CENTURY.   BRITISH MUSEUM

A WARNING TO ENTHUSIASTS.

E. T. Reed, 1889

became editor, that *Punch* should retain its former political impartiality. He was especially shocked when Lehmann spoke out publicly in favor of the Boers and against the Boer War. In 1901 Lloyd George convinced Lehmann to accept the editorship of the *Daily News*, but he only held the post for a year. It interfered too much with his leisurely life-style.

His contributions to *Punch* were light and pleasant, gentle little verses about sports and country living. His prose articles consisted of relaxed jokes about domestic affairs and husband-wife discussions (never quarrels), or gentlemanly pieces about shooting or rowing. According to his son John:

> It was typical of my father's attitude toward his family that he used us all quite shamelessly, and to the delight of his large circle of readers, as material for the verses and sometimes even for the prose pieces which appeared every week in *Punch*. For some weeks he encouraged Beatrix to tell him stories on their walks together, which he would then rearrange a little and, imitating her own highly individual spelling, serve up to *Punch* under the title "Stories for Uncles."

The Lehmann children all achieved celebrity in the arts, Beatrix as an actress, John as a publisher, and Rosamond as the author of the best-selling novel *Dusty Answer*.

In the last years of the Burnand editorship, a number of stories by notable writers appeared in a feature called "Extra Pages." Somerset Maugham was a contributor, and Frank R. Stockton was another. Henry James's *Mrs. Medwin* appeared as a four-part serial, probably because no one else would accept it. It was not one of his best efforts. The feature was very un-*Punch*-like and was discontinued.

Burnand attracted a number of able if somewhat eccentric artists to *Punch*. Probably the strangest was Harry Furniss, chosen by Lucy to illustrate his parliamentary critiques after Tenniel had proven unable to catch likenesses rapidly. Furniss was able to do a portrait in a few minutes from behind a pillar on a scrap of paper concealed in his pocket. He was much influenced by the style of Richard Doyle and was admired for his book illustrations, which included Lewis Carroll's *Sylvie and Bruno* and a 1911 edition of the complete works of Dickens.

Furniss was a noisy, overbearing Irishman, paranoid to the extent of violence, suspecting insult in every discussion and wearing a permanent chip on his shoulder. Although he was a congenial Table companion, the other Punchites looked forward to his frequent absences, when his lectures on portraiture and "The Humours of Parliament" (with impersonations of leading politicians) took him out of London.

Tom Taylor invited Furniss to submit work in the 1870s but turned down his first drawings as unsuitable. His first accepted *Punch* drawing showed two men in a boat rowing on a flooded meadow, reading a sign that stuck up out of the water saying "Highly Eligible Site to Be Let or Sold for Building." Taylor ordered it redrawn by du Maurier. The furious Furniss refused to work for *Punch* again during Taylor's editorship and conceived a bitter, lifelong jealousy of du Maurier. He joined the *Illustrated London News*, where his drawings were so successful that Burnand invited him to become a regular contributor (although, like Keene, he never became a member of the staff). He was twenty-six years old at the time.

For the next decade he was everywhere in *Punch*, contributing numerous drawings and even dramatic criticism (he was paid by the square inch). His parliamentary sketches were caustic and in many cases insulting, but politicians wooed him with the hope of being displayed by Furniss in *Punch*. Nevertheless, he made many enemies. A particularly biting sketch of a member of Parliament named Swift McNeill brought matters to a head: MacNeill and other members of his party cornered Furniss in the gallery and threatened him with physical violence. The canny Furniss realized that the incident was an attempt to provoke him into striking a member so that the others could then have him barred from the House. For once he kept his temper—and his accreditation too. His enemies finally got him in the end when he left *Punch* and started his own magazine, the weekly *Lika Joko*. His *Punch* parliamentary entry permission expired when he left the magazine, and the authorities refused to issue another for his new journal, thus assuring its failure.

Invited to the Table in 1884, four years after he became a regular contributor, he remained for ten years and then resigned one day by simply leaving, saying he would return in an hour. He never came back. His departure was said to be the result of a controversy with the proprietors over the rights to his drawings. One of his most famous cartoons showed a scruffy, tattered, unwashed tramp scribbling a letter to a soap company, saying "I used your soap two years ago; since then I've used no other." It had a tremendous vogue, and the proprietors sold it to the Pears Soap Company. It became as famous an advertisement as it had been a cartoon. Furniss was furious at others profiting from his work, and the quarrel precipitated his permanent departure from *Punch*. He later wrote novels and art instruction manuals as well as editing *Lika Joko*, and worked for Thomas Edison in the budding film industry as writer, producer, and actor, the first Punchite to appear on the screen.

A new development of the 1880s, advantageous to comic artists, was the use of photography for magazine illustration reproduction. *Punch*'s cartoons and illustrations up to this time were drawn directly on the woodblock (or transferred to it on tracing paper as Tenniel preferred to do) and sent to the engraver for execution. This meant that the drawing itself could not later be sold, since it had to be destroyed to make the illustration. It also meant that artists had to make their drawings the exact size needed for their reproduction on the printed page because the woodblock could not be enlarged or reduced.

The perfection of the process for photographing drawings onto woodblocks enabled artists to make their drawings any size they wished. Tenniel refused to use this method, but it was a blessing to the others, especially du Maurier, whose eyesight grew dimmer as he grew older and who was happy to be able to make very large drawings that could be reduced for *Punch*'s pages. The photographic process was soon followed by the process block, a metal plate on which the drawing was photographed and then etched with acid. For the first time the readers saw what the artists had actually drawn rather than the engraver's approximation of it. *Punch*'s first process block illustration appeared in 1892.

Not long after the appearance of the process block, the halftone appeared, adding shades of gray to the black-and-white lines for which *Punch* was famous. Glass screens etched with vertical and horizontal lines were placed between the camera and the drawing to diffuse the lighter parts into small dots and deepen the darker parts. *Punch*'s first halftone appeared in 1896.

A number of excellent artists passed through *Punch*'s pages in Burnand's time. Whistler contributed a drawing of a butterfly. Sir Frederic Leighton illustrated one article, "The Schoolmaster Abroad," in 1886. There was Gunning King ("Sometimes I sits and thinks, and sometimes I just sits") and the amazingly durable G. L. Stampa, who did cockneys and street urchins for the fifty-six-year period between 1894 and 1950 and qualified as *Punch*'s "Grand Old Man." F. H. Townsend, who had illustrated the 1890 edition of the novels of Thomas Love Peacock, was the magazine's first art editor. He was a fine draughtsman and a shy, kind man who was appointed by the proprietors supposedly without the knowledge of the editor, presumably to make the short-tempered Burnand hand in his resignation. It didn't work. Townsend joined the staff in 1905 and stayed on until after World War I.

E. T. Reed was one of *Punch*'s more memorable staff artists. He made his first appearance in 1889 with "The Parnell Commissioners Enjoying Themselves up the River" and went on to produce a number of wonderfully funny and modern series that looked more like present-day drawings than Edwardian efforts. From heavy-handed jokes like the

"Fancy Portrait of My Laundress," a powerful-looking woman about to belabor his linen with a spiked club, he moved into "Prehistoric Peeps" in the 1893 Christmas number. They were astonishingly accurate and well-researched drawings of prehistoric people and dinosaurs comically coping with modern day situations. The device has been a comic strip favorite for generations and is still being done in magazines and strip cartoons such as "B. C." and "Alley Oop." A favorite Reed device was guessing at how future anthropologists would reconstruct items left behind by present-day citizens. His "reconstructions" of bicycles, hansom cabs, and the like were hilarious. When Furniss left, it was Reed who took over the illustrations of Parliament and did an excellent job with them, although he was never as popular as Furniss had been.

Generally accepted as the finest draughtsman since Keene, and thought by some to be better than Keene, was Phil May. Priestley called him the single figure who, more than anyone else, represented the picturesque and lively nineties. Aubrey Beardsley, Oscar Wilde, Henry Irving, even the Great Dan Leno had, in Priestley's estimation, to take a back seat to May, the raffish, hard-drinking Bohemian who was the most popular comic artist of the period. After decades of opening *Punch* directly to the du Maurier cartoon, English families now adopted May as their favorite. His cockney urchins, costers and pearly queens, portrayed with some compassion because he himself had known poverty, had a wonderfully warm, wry humor.

May's strong point was economy of line. His predecessors had crowded their space with tiny cross-hatchings, fine details, designs, and decorations. May could say what he wanted to say in a few strokes. His lean style was the result of a great many preliminary drawings, from each of which he carefully pruned away all unnecessary lines until it was exactly as he wanted it to be. His drawings were the forerunners of the modern cartoon.

Before May, it had always been necessary for comic artists to show their characters with expressionless faces: A joke situation usually lasted several minutes and required action or speech from a number of individuals, making it impossible to show the speaker by drawing his mouth open or the principal character by making him darker or more detailed. Captions were often five or six lines long. May showed that cartoon characters could get an idea across with facial expression as well as with lengthy, involved cackles.

In his prime, May made a great deal of money. Like most poor boys who become rich, he had no sense of the value of it. He was always surrounded by spongers and hangers-on, and his income vanished as quickly as he made it. When he worked for the *Sketch*, he was said to have

159

Q. E. D.

"What's up wi' Sal?"   "Ain't yer e3d? She's Married agin!"

Phil May, 1894

Passenger (rising politely). "Excuse me, Mum, but do you believe in Woman's Rights?"
New Woman. "Most certainly I do."
Passenger (resuming seat). "Oh well, then Stand up for 'em!"

Phil May, 1896

an arrangement with management under which he could come to the cashier's office, do a quick drawing, and cash it like a check. He always insisted on payment in advance for his work.

Whistler said of him, "Modern black and white art [can] be summed up in two words—Phil May." "Spy" portrayed him in *Vanity Fair* in a bowler and velvet-collared coat, grinning, a cigar cocked at an angle in his mouth and a brimming tumbler in his hand. He was not a sportsman, but he loved to affect the pose and costume of one. He had hoped at one time to be a jockey, but lifelong bad health had prevented him from anything more strenuous than the night life that eventually killed him.

A pale, hollow-chested Yorkshireman from Leeds, he had very little formal schooling and no art training at all. He started at the age of twelve as timekeeper in a foundry. He was an actor, a beggar (for a short while in London), and an odd-job man. At sixteen he found a steady job with a theatrical costume house and contributed drawings to the *St. Stephen's Review* until his doctor advised him to emigrate to Australia for his health. He worked for the *Sydney Bulletin* for three years and returned to London. In his time he was a wallpaper designer, solicitor's clerk, estate agent's clerk, and piano duster in a music shop. After traveling to Rome and Paris at the expense of a generous patron, he devoted himself entirely to drawing. In 1893 he was invited to join *Punch*. He carved his intials on the Table two years later.

Although he was a Table member, he was never really a part of the group. The classic boozing of the forties and fifties was part of the past, and May found the dinners too correct and upper middle class for his enjoyment. He would often drop in for only a few minutes, leaving a cab waiting downstairs, and then leave for somewhere livelier, stealing a menu to show his wife, so that she would think he had spent the evening at *Punch*. In spite of the benevolent influence of the other Punchites and the magazine itself, he never achieved anything like respectability.

He worked hard and played harder, overtaxing his delicate constitution and weak lungs. When he died he was only thirty-nine years old. In the comparatively brief time that he worked for *Punch* he livened up its dignified pages and helped to create a brighter image and to attract new readers.

May was a natural artist. He had a keen sense of character, and although he drew the same types over and over again, every one of his cockneys or drunken old gentlemen was a separate individual. Du Maurier's colonels and lovely ladies all resembled one another, and perhaps their sameness was what had endeared them to the Victorian readers. At the turn of the century people wanted something new, and May gave it to them. His characters came alive, although the backgrounds in which he placed them were sketchy at best, hinted at rather then firmly established. But the settings were not the important part of the joke. Keene, in his travels around England to find just the right meadow, or du Maurier, with his luxurious drawing rooms, had not realized this. May was the first to discover that the point of a joke was more important than a gracefully constructed cackle. Whether today's readers find him funny or not, he had an important influence on many graphic artists who came after him. "Draw firm and be jolly," was his advice to young comic artists, and no one has ever phrased it better.

Another Burnand acquisition was Bernard Partridge, son of the president of the Royal College of Surgeons and nephew of Queen Victoria's personal portrait painter. After a short period at London University, Partridge had worked in an architect's office and then moved on to a junior position in a firm of stained glass designers. He studied drapery and church ornament and moved on to book illustration. Guthrie and du Maurier admired his drawings and recommended him to Burnand as a social cartoonist. His early *Punch* cartoons are funny and well executed, showing the influence of du Maurier, whom Partridge considered his professional master. His work is not as good as du Maurier's (which may be one reason du Maurier was so happy to recommend him), just as his later political cartoons were not as good as Tenniel's. Nevertheless, he was a good, sound draughtsman who did as he was told and got his work in on time.

In time he succeeded to the "cartoon junior," the second political cartoon, leaving socials behind him. In 1910, when Sambourne died, he accepted the post of principal cartoonist only after considerable soul-searching and much against his will. He thought of himself as a hack draughtsman, carrying out other people's ideas in other people's styles because that was what the readers expected. In spite of this attitude, he produced cartoons for nearly fifty years, spanning the period from 1891, when he first joined *Punch*, to World War II, during which he performed the same kind of mayhem on Hitler and Mussolini that he had worked on the kaiser a generation earlier.

He patterned his political cartoons on Tenniel's, but they were grandiose, Teutonic, and curiously lifeless. Most critics feel that his talents would have been better used anywhere except in a comic magazine. Price says that Partridge felt that the political cartoonist of *Punch* should be a grand old man as Tenniel had been, and he became one quite early in life. He has been described by one critic as "a veritable coelocanth among cartoonists—his ornate sesquipedalian style an ossified relic of a bygone age." In actual fact, he simply failed to keep up with the latest fashions in black-and-white art, an understandable and forgivable failing in an elderly artist who has been doing the same job for fifty years. The same thing happened to Tenniel.

Partridge's sturdy Tommies and gallant officers and his horrible Germans and plucky little Belgians earned him his eventual knighthood, which was not undeserved. He loved living in high style, but he was not able to keep up with the inflation rate (nor were the *Punch* salary schedules any help). His original drawings did not command high prices, and at the end of his life he was hard put to make ends meet. He had rooms in the *Punch* building at 10 Bouverie Street for a while, and when he died he left the office his furniture. A few pieces of it still remain there, notably a table and a worn and badly sprung green leather armchair with stuffing leaking out of it, a sad legacy from one of *Punch*'s best-known artists who had to spend his life competing with and overshadowed by the magazine's two most revered immortals.

It is hard to evaluate Partridge's contribution to the magazine's history. What would Tenniel's reputation have been if he had been forced to display his weekly cartoon in the company of work by two artists superior to him in every way? What would Partridge's career have been like if he had left *Punch*, as he wanted to do, and worked as a serious free-lance artist? No one will ever know. In both world wars, and in the period between them, Partridge's heavy and rather pompous style was exactly what was needed for *Punch*'s contemporary image. The editors and proprietors played on his loyalty and his financial position to keep him with them in spite of his repeated attempts to retire as he grew older. He was still working for *Punch* in his eighties. He died in 1945 at the age of eighty-four.

n January 1906, the Conservative party suffered its most crushing defeat since 1833. In addition to a Liberal landslide, the year also marked the accession to *Punch*'s editorship of the Conservative Owen Seaman, a man who equated Radical or Liberal sentiments with high treason.

The election also brought into prominence a brand new feature, not seen before in British politics, a strong and significant third party. Labour held twenty-nine seats in the House and could rely on the support of sympathetic ''Lib-Labs.'' They showed their muscle by securing passage of the Trade Disputes Act, which defined the rights of labor unions to picket and insured them the full protection of the law. Even the traditionally labor-baiting lords left the bill alone.

Oddly enough, the rise of Labour as a powerful new force was accompanied by some of the worst labor troubles in history. In a single month, dock, transport, railway, and mine workers went on strike. Not far behind the working men were the suffragettes, who engaged in harassment of all kinds, chaining themselves to the iron railings of Buckingham Palace and smashing Bond Street shop windows with bricks and paving stones. The country was shocked when suffragettes, imprisoned for violence, went on a hunger strike and were brutally and humiliatingly force-fed by the police.

The major domestic issue of the day was Lloyd George's complicated budget, which contained such innovations as a graduated income tax, death duties, and a land tax. The lords were up in arms. Lloyd George was actually proposing a pension for people over seventy whether they deserved it or not. The Liberals were forced to call for a general election on the budget issue, adding as well a request for the nation's support on limitation of the power of the House of Lords. They won on both counts. The budget passed and the veto power of the House of Lords was permanently checked. The lords fought hard, tacking amendment after amendment onto the legislation, but they were forced to surrender when the King threatened to create three hundred new peers and pack their House with Liberals.

In 1912 the smug complacency of the Britsh medical community was shattered by the introduction of a Health Insurance Bill, which, doctors insisted, would reduce them to beggary and destroy the quality of medical care in England. There was rioting and bloodshed in Ireland and talk of civil war.

With all this going on at home, the English man-in-the-street was not paying too much attention to matters abroad. The armaments race was discussed in the press, but it did not affect the average citizen as much as health insurance or income tax. At the suggestion of Theodore Roosevelt, the nations of Europe met at the Hague to try to iron out their differences, but the peace conference was not a success. The kaiser gave a saber-rattling interview to a correspondent of the London *Daily Telegraph* which strained Anglo-German relations and to which the London press reacted strongly. *Punch*, in a cartoon by Linley Sambourne, represented the German emperor as a clumsy conjuror, trying to pull the dove of peace out of a folded copy of the *Telegraph* and producing a basilisk instead.

Punch tended to regard Labour with some suspicion but not too much concern, a menace with which a firm hand must be taken; after which the lower classes, having released as much steam as they were capable of releasing, would return to their beer. The magazine deplored the suffragettes' guerilla tactics but insisted that they be treated with the courtesy and justice to which all women were entitled. Nevertheless, it was hard for the magazine to take women seriously, in fact, as anything but a source of cartoon humor. *Punch* had always considered women, as Price points out, as a kind of domesticated Irish. By 1918, however, the magazine had made a complete about-face and supported votes for women.

In the period between Seaman's accession to the editorship and the beginning of World War I, *Punch* seemed more an uncommitted reporter of political events than a partisan. The cartoons got milder until the kaiser, a ready-made universal enemy, could be set up as the target. Whether this was a sign that *Punch* had really foregone political comment or whether it was merely the new editor refraining from offending anyone

PROBABLY THE NEXT ABSURDITY

IN LADIES' WINTER COSTUMES.

THE COMING RACE.

Doctor Evangeline. "BY THE BYE, MR. SAWYER, ARE YOU ENGAGED TO-MORROW AFTERNOON? I HAVE RATHER A TICKLISH OPERATION TO PERFORM—AN AMPUTATION, YOU KNOW."

Mr. Sawyer. "I SHALL BE VERY HAPPY TO DO IT FOR YOU."

Dr. Evangeline. "O, NO, NOT *THAT!* BUT WILL YOU KINDLY COME AND ADMINISTER THE CHLOROFORM FOR ME?'"

THE PENITENT.

Mr. PUNCH, ALWAYS READY TO ADMIT HIS EXCEPTIONAL "BLOOMERS," DOES PENANCE FOR HIS ERROR OF THIRTY-FIVE YEARS AGO, AND BEGS TO OFFER HIS RESPECTFUL CONGRATULATIONS TO LADY ASTOR, M.P.

The idea of equality for women tickled the Punchites, who made fun of the suffragettes as often as possible. In these cartoons the magazine suggests the absurdity of such future improbabilities as women lawyers and doctors. By 1919 the Punchites had changed their tune. In Partridge's cartoon Mr. Punch apologizes to Lady Astor for ridiculing her attempts to break the taboo against women in Parliament. In 1919 she was elected to her deceased husband's seat in the Commons —the first woman ever to sit in Parliament. (Top left, Linley Sambourne, 1868; bottom left, George du Maurier, 1872; top right, Bernard Partridge, 1919; bottom right, George du Maurier, 1871)

FLIPPANCY.

Captain Jinks. "WHO IS THE BENEVOLENT-LOOKING GENTLEMAN JUST COMING IN ?"
Mrs. Malapert. "MRS. WITHERINGTON MILDEU, THE FAMOUS ADVOCATE FOR WOMEN'S RIGHTS."
Captain Jinks. "HA, HA ! VERY GOOD ! BUT I MEAN THE LITTLE MAN, WITH THE VELVET COLLAR."
Mrs. Malapert. "O, I BEG YOUR PARDON—THAT'S HER HUSBAND. HE'S A MOST LADY-LIKE PERSON, AND CONSIDERED RATHER PRETTY."

is debatable, but the fact remains that Seaman, after eight years as editor, received a knighthood in 1914.

When Seaman took over, *Punch* was in another of its periodic declines. For some years Burnand had been almost invisible, working at home on his memoirs and dropping in unexpectedly at Bouverie Street on rare occasions. He would sit behind his desk for a while, dreamily shuffle a paper or two, and then vanish quietly. Until 1903 he left the running of the magazine almost entirely in the hands of Arthur à Beckett, who boasted proudly that only one percent of the work of hopeful new contributors got past him to the editor.

A new broom was badly needed to sweep away what remained of the Victorian cobwebs. Seaman swung into action like a new colonel whipping a substandard regiment into shape. The rambling articles and contrived puns of the nineties were banished forever, to no one's regret. A revived sense of discipline pervaded *Punch*'s offices.

Realizing that the major cause of the magazine's decay was Burnand's disinterest, Seaman insisted on seeing everything himself. Rejection slips and form letters were thrown out. Anyone who submitted a promising piece of work to *Punch*, whether it was accepted or not, received a handwritten personal letter from the editor commenting on its quality and making suggestions for its improvement. A. P. Herbert, when he was in his teens and a student at Winchester, made so bold as to submit a poem to the magazine. He was delighted to receive a letter from the editor himself which, although it rejected the poem for publication, analyzed it in detail. "Verse three conflicts with verse one!" the pedantic Seaman pointed out. "I don't like the rhyme!" (Herbert had attempted to rhyme *worn* with *dawn*.) Obviously most Englishmen would pronounce *dawn* and *worn* in the same way, but Scots would not. Suppose the poem were read by a Scot? In order to be perfect, the poem had to be perfect for everybody, not just for one part of the reading public.

Herbert, in spite of his tender years and bruised ego, was forced to admit that Seaman was right. "His discipline has clung to me all my life," he said later, "to my detriment." Herbert was not the only writer who held to that opinion. The anonymous journalist who wrote Seaman's obituary in the *Morning Post* (perhaps one more reincarnation of the vengeful Jenkins) said: "Once he had shaped a humorist to his liking the latter could claim to have achieved a high standard of excellence; and it was only later that he discovered that he had, in becoming the ideal *Punch* contributor, rendered himself precious little use for any other literary purpose."

The tremendous amount of extra work caused by his personal interference in all facets of the magazine's operations was increased for his staff by the fact that he was painfully slow. He insisted on going over copy word by word until he drove his assistant editor, A. A. Milne, half mad with impatience.

> All Owen's past life (or something) came before his eyes as he corrected a page of *Punch*, but through it all he read doggedly, very slow, very sure, until I wanted to scream: 'For Heaven's sake, what's it all about? Time isn't a thing you do this to. . . .'
>
> By one o'clock we were through. It had been interesting to cut ten lines out of somebody else's article, and annoying to have to cut two out of my own. I had verified a quotation, explained the point in one of the paragraphs—
>
> 'Not more than twenty people will see it. Can't you make it clearer?'
> 'Easily, but it will spoil it for the twenty.'
> 'We can't edit a paper for twenty readers.'
> 'Wouldn't it be heavenly if we could? Is that better?'
> 'Hm . . . it isn't too clear now.'
> 'One must keep it funny somehow.'
> 'Oh well, all right. You may find a better one tomorrow.'

As far as Seaman was concerned, cartoons as well as prose and poetry had to meet the standards of logic. Each cartoon was subjected to a close scrutiny. Could the situation in the drawing have really happened? Would people react in the way they seemed to react? E. V. Lucas, in his reminiscences, found him "less swift in his decisions" than Burnand (a kinder verdict than Milne's) but far superior as a literary editor.

One hangover from the Victorians that Seaman was reluctant to discard was *Punch*'s traditional refusal to deal in any material that was in any way sexual or could be considered offensive or in bad taste. Price accuses him of false delicacy, but Seaman, as his knighthood and later his baronetcy proved, knew which side his bread was buttered on. Price quotes the following anecdote as an example of Seaman with respect to the off-color.

> Once when George Morrow was Art Editor, he brought Seaman a drawing that depended on an octopus's flooding the surrounding sea with ink. Seaman liked the caption but looked worried and said, "George, eh, where does the octopus discharge the ink from?" "Well, Owen, I'm afraid it is from the, eh, anus." "What a pity. Then of course we can't use it." "Eh, Owen, I understand that in an octopus the anus is between the eyes." "Oh, in that case, we'll take it."

Although he believed that during his editorship *Punch* was a non-political magazine, free of pressure from the top in either direction, he equated Liberal or Radical sentiments with high treason, or worse, with

THE POST CARD.

Landlady (reads): "'MARLBRO'-HOUSE. DEAR JOE—LOOK IN TO TEA AND SHRIMPS ON YOUR WAY HOME TO-NIGHT. WE'RE ALL ALONE, AND THE PRINCESS AND THE YOUNG ONES 'LL BE DELIGHTED. YOURS EVER, ALBERT EDWARD!'— WELL, IF EVER I DID!—I'D NO IDEA!—— AN' I WAS JUST GOIN' TO GIVE THE POOR, DEAR, YOUNG FELLOW A BIT O' MY MIND ABOUT HIS RENT!"

[N.B. The stratagem was successful.

AWFUL APPARITION!

Mrs. T. (to T., who has been reading the popular novel). "PRAY, MR. TOMKINS, ARE YOU NEVER COMING UP-STAIRS? HOW MUCH LONGER ARE YOU GOING TO SIT UP WITH THAT 'WOMAN IN WHITE?'"

Punch *never failed to take a satirical view of new developments in science, the arts, or daily life. These cartoons celebrate the appearance of the postcard, cod-liver oil, the first mystery thriller best seller (Wilkie Collins's* The Woman in White*), and the furor caused by Charles Darwin's* On the Origin of the Species. *(Top left, Charles, Keene, 1870; bottom left, John Leech, 1861; top right, John Leech, 1861; bottom right, Fritz Eltze, 1865)*

THE LION OF THE SEASON.
ALARMED FLUNKEY. " MR. G-G-G-O-O-O-RILLA ! "

REMARKABLE EFFECT—
THE MAID HAVING BY MISTAKE POLISHED ONE OF THE DINING-ROOM CHAIRS WITH COD-LIVER OIL !

lower-class affectation. A man who was not a Conservative was by definition, according to him, not a gentleman. True, there were Liberals at the Table, but he could find excuses for most of them. Lucas had attended neither a great public school nor a university. Lehmann, a Liberal M.P., had German blood, even if it was extremely remote. But Milne, whom he had handpicked, was unforgivable. Milne had not only been to Westminster, but to Seaman's own university, where, like Seaman, he had written for the *Granta*. His radicalism made him a double traitor, once to his country and once to his class. The war solved the Milne problem for Seaman. When he returned from military service, Milne was given to understand that he would not be welcome if he returned to *Punch*. Fortified by success as a playwright and novelist, Milne departed forever.

Seaman disapproved of the playful, boozy character of the Table. It was he who discontinued the dinners in the twenties, replacing them with working lunches. To him the Table was just another schoolroom situation, a kind of staff meeting at which he could instruct the members in what he expected of them.

He also disapproved of the custom that allowed Table members to submit their copy directly to the printers, so that he saw it first as galley proofs, but there was nothing he could do about it. His solution to the problem was to restrict his Table appointments to men chosen not only for their literary abilities but for their loyalty to himself and his political principles. Milne had been a mistake, and Seaman was not a man to make the same mistake twice. He took the unusual step of replacing a young man with an older one, appointing W. A. Locker, a former newspaper editor, as his assistant, *vice* Milne. Locker, whom Price describes as "a kindly old boy, who enjoyed producing a stream of little puns over his tea," left no mark whatsoever on *Punch*'s history. His negative personality seems to have been just what Seaman had in mind for his assistant editor. Locker became a Tory member of Parliament in 1916.

Seaman was an odd mixture of contradictions: brilliant, insecure, cynical, capricious, sometimes kind, often ill-mannered, a single-minded upward striver. He was the grandson of a mill hand and a farmer's daughter. His father, a self-educated clerk, had raised his status by securing an apprenticeship in the shop of a rich linen-draper uncle. He saved enough money to open a florist's shop of his own on Sloane Street, gradually diversifying until he became "Seaman & Co., Importers of Artificial Flowers, Court Milliners, Dress and Mantle Makers, Corsets, Blouses and Ladies Outfitters."

The establishment was prosperous enough to support a private school for young Owen, who was packed off to Mill Hill, where he carried on the family tradition of upward mobility by winning a scholarship to Shrewsbury. Unfortunately, Seaman & Co. impeded any boyish social pretensions he may have had. He confessed in later years that he experienced ''some snobbery'' at school because his parents were in trade.

The snobbery, so lightly dismissed by the mature and successful Seaman, must have been intense. The schoolboy sense of humor is hardly subtle at best. At Shrewsbury a shop was bad enough, but corsets? It is easy to imagine the tone that was taken in the jokes. They must have galled the bright, ambitious young Seaman beyond endurance. It is possible that the mothers of some of his schoolmates were customers of Seaman & Co. Owen and his companions may even have observed the elder Seaman, bowing and scraping in the traditional posture of the British shopkeeper, swallowing insults from clients of all classes, smiling in the face of arrogance and humiliation. The effect on young Owen was permanent. He would outdo them all somehow, if not in lineage then certainly in wealth or, better still, in power.

The classic defense was hard work. Contemporaries remember him at school as sanctimonious, self-important, and something of a prig. He was not popular with the other boys, but seems to have sought and won the esteem of the masters. The ticket to acceptance at school, as elsewhere in England, was a title. He sweated and strove until he became school captain. After that the corset jokes stopped, at least within his hearing.

At school and in later life Seaman bears an uncanny resemblance to the character Widmerpool in Anthony Powell's novel series *A Dance to the Music of Time*. Powell, who worked at *Punch* under Muggeridge, maintains that the smug, pompous Widmerpool was not based on any one person, but was a combination of many. Nevertheless, Seaman's shrewdness, his pedantry, his drive for acceptance in spite of what he considered his father's distasteful trade, his success in winning the esteem of ''people who count'' and titles and money are strongly reminiscent of Powell's creation.

Unlike Widmerpool, Seaman was successful with women, although he never married. He had mistresses, but they seem to have made little impression on his life. He was not a man to fall in love or even to maintain a lasting emotional relationship. Pearl Craigie, the novelist, loved him, and in her later years wrote of him with the petulance of an intelligent woman who has failed to arouse in the object of her affections any sort of responsive spark except possibly a sexual one.

After Shrewsbury, Seaman won a scholarship to Clare College, Cambridge; not the fashionable Trinity of his predecessors on *Punch*, but still acceptable. He took a first in classical tripos, and participated in gentlemanly sports, becoming captain of the Clare boats in his senior year. He went from Cambridge to a job as a master at the Rossall School and later to Magdalen College School, where he nearly became headmaster. Instead he accepted a lecturership at Durham College in Newcastle-on-Tyne, moving up in two years to the position of professor of literature and classics. The mill worker's grandson had come a long way.

The ambitious Seaman was not ready at twenty-nine to vegetate in the academic world, with the hope of one day becoming a kind of Newcastle Mr. Chips. In his days as a schoolmaster he had begun to send contributions to various papers. In 1887 he issued two books, *Oedipus the Wreck* and *With Double Pipe*, which won him a reputation as an able writer of light, humorous verse.

In 1894 he was pleased to have his poem "The Rhyme of the Kipperling" accepted by *Punch*. It was a clever parody of Kipling's "Rhyme of the Three Sealers" and was published on January 13 of that year. Seaman, who had attracted the notice of the Punchites by his poems in the *Granta*, was introduced to Burnand by Rudie Lehmann at a dinner at which he also met Anstey Guthrie, Linley Sambourne, and E. T. Reed. He knew how to make himself agreeable, and he seems to have made a good impression on Burnand, who invited him to send prose and poetry to the magazine. His work was, apparently, in the one percent that got past Arthur à Beckett.

The year 1897 was a fortunate year for Seaman. He was called to the Bar, freeing himself from shop and classroom forever, and he was invited to the Table to replace the departed Milliken. As it was to so many Punchites, the Table was more seductive than the courtroom. Seaman never practiced as a barrister. Instead he accepted Burnand's invitation to dine at the Table every Wednesday and to supply items for publication for a stipend of ten guineas a week.

It was obvious to the astute Seaman that *Punch* offered avenues to power and importance that pleading cases would not, or at least not without a great deal more time and effort. He deposed the outraged à Beckett five years later, and, as we have seen, got his boss's job in 1906 after the gentlemanly Lucy had turned it down. When he took over as assistant editor, he ran the magazine with a firm hand, carefully avoiding any action that might offend or anger Burnand. He kept the magazine going during the moribund period of Burnand's disinterest and was responsible for bringing in E. V. Lucas and for Milne's first accepted poems in 1904.

No description of Seaman would be complete without the oft-quoted and devastating evaluation of him that appears in Milne's autobiography.

> He was a strange, unlucky man. All the good fairies came to his christening, but the Uninvited Fairy had the last word, so that the talents

found themselves in the wrong napkin and the virtues flourished where graces should have been. Humour was drowned in scholarship. Tact went down before Truth, and the Fighting Qualities gave him not only the will to win but the determination to explain why he hadn't won. . . . He had, truly, a heart of gold, and if it had been ''concealed beneath a rugged exterior'' as so often it is in novels, it would have been more patent to the world than the veneer, which was so nearly gold, allowed it to be.

C. L. Graves, Seaman's friend and fellow Punchite, called Milne's attack a ''mean, ungenerous, and untruthful record.'' Milne would eventually marry Seaman's goddaughter, Dorothy de Sélincourt, but the marriage had no noticeable ameliorating effect on his dislike for his former chief.

As editor of *Punch*, Seaman continued to publish books. His *Horace at Cambridge* in 1894 contained many of his *Punch* verses and is highlighted by his obsession with the humorous possibilities of the appointment of the lackluster Alfred Austin as Poet Laureate over the heads of Swinburne and Sir Edward Arnold. In fact Owen dedicated the opening poem of *In Cap and Bells* to Austin ''in polite imitation of his Jubilee Ode.''

> A nutting went the nimble chimpanzee—
> And what, you ask me, am I driving at?
> Wait on; in less than twenty minutes we
> Shall come to that.

In 1902 his *Borrowed Plumes* parodied the work of George Moore, George Meredith, and Henry James among others. It was well received by the critics. James replied in kind by taking Seaman to pieces in *The Wings of the Dove*, in which the pompous Densher is obviously modeled on *Punch*'s assistant editor. Pearl Craigie, who understandably had an axe to grind (although Seaman is said to have loved her as much as he was capable of loving any woman) wrote:

> Henry James has sent me *The Wings of the Dove*. Clearly the man is meant to be Seaman. It is hard on him. With James I took the bull by the horns. I said, in acknowledging the book, ''I know Densher. But he is far more child-like than you have made him.'' He may take it that I mean ''Densher'' is an eternal type of the weak, smug Englishman. All the same the book runs a bit close to fact.

The work that first established Seaman as a verse parodist did not appear in *Punch*, but in the *World,* to which he contributed poetry under the pseudonym of "Nauticus." It was "A Ballad of a Bun," a satirical takeoff of John Davidson's "Ballad of a Nun," which had been published in John Lane's *Yellow Book*. Commenting on Seaman's parody, Agnes Repplier wrote:

> Mr. Davidson committed the unpardonable sin of taking a medieval figure, simple, typical, easily understood, winning human sympathy and receiving divine forgiveness, and turning her into an introspective hussy, sinning for sin's sake, and demanding praise for her achievement. Seaman in turn stripped this temerarious young woman of every attribute save bewildered modernity. He described her unkindly as desirous of becoming a "sex impressionist" but not knowing how to set about it.

> > Across the sounding City's din
> > She wandered, looking indiscreet,
> > And ultimately landed in
> > The neighborhood of Regent Street.

Like Burnand, Seaman was sure that the magazine could not exist without him, and he was fully prepared to remain as editor until he died, to the dismay of the proprietors. At last, in 1932, he retired after undergoing surgery. He was awarded a baronetcy in December 1932 and died of pneumonia four years later.

Of all the talents attracted to *Punch* by invitation of Seaman, probably the most celebrated was Alan Alexander Milne, author of the immortal *Winnie the Pooh* and other less celebrated but perhaps more worthy works. His articles were light-hearted little chronicles of domestic fun—not as funny as those of P. G. Wodehouse but of the same genre. They were redolent of country houses, croquet lawns, foolish young men in flannels, and pretty girls, and were very popular with the *Punch* readers. According to Lucas,

> not since its foundation in 1841 has *Punch*, in my opinion, printed articles of such unwavering high spirits, fun, and felicity of phrase as those signed "AAM." A new kind of nonsense was his, based upon and blended with the facts of life, never permitting an intruding qualm, and all carried out with apparently effortless ease and the utmost gaiety. The art that conceals art. Anyone sitting down to the portmanteau volume *Those Were the Days*, in which his weekly articles are collected, must agree with me.

Milne began sending poems and stories to *Punch* when he was sixteen, as so many boys before him had done and as schoolboys still do today. They were not accepted. At Cambridge, where he edited the *Granta*, he published in that paper a humorous series called "The Rabbits." He received a letter from Rudie Lehmann asking the name of the author of the series "of which I and many others in London have a very high opinion," in the hope that "work of a similar nature might be put in his way." The delighted Milne, who was twenty at the time, answered at once. "The Rabbits" went back and forth between Milne and Seaman, covered with editorial suggestions and comments, and was finally accepted and given to Burnand, who was busy writing his autobiography. The series was not heard of again. At last Lehmann rescued it and sent it to *John Bull*, which accepted "The Rabbits" at once; but the paper went bankrupt before it could be published.

Two years later some of Milne's verses got past Seaman and were actually published in *Punch*. Milne received the princely sum of sixteen shillings, sixpence, and advice from Philip Agnew that the "honor of writing for *Punch* was sufficient reward." In 1906 he was summoned by Seaman.

> The new editor made as little of the occasion as he could. In his new position he wanted somebody to relieve him of the worst of the donkey work; somebody who came in for, say, a couple of afternoons a week and sorted out the contributions. Naturally I should be on trial at first: naturally I couldn't expect to be put on the *Punch* Table immediately: obviously this and obviously that. But what it came to, however he glided over it, was—How would I like to be Assistant Editor of *Punch*?

The salary was £250 a year, and a similar amount would be paid for weekly contributions. To Milne, who was trying to make his way as a journalist in London without private funds, the offer was a godsend. He loved *Punch* and became one of its most popular writers. He stayed until 1914, when he left, as he thought, temporarily, to enlist in the army in World War I.

After the war Milne felt that he was obligated to return to the magazine, although he could by that time well afford to support himself as a novelist, playwright, and writer of children's books. *Punch* had paid half his assistant editor's salary while he was in the army during the first three years of the war. He felt that he owed the proprietors at least three years before he could honestly go his own way. When he returned to England, he went directly to Bouverie Street to get the required job letter that would hasten his demobilization.

> I burst in on Seaman. He looked up, surprised.
> "Hallo," he said.
> "I've come back," I announced dramatically. . . .

WHEN WE WERE VERY YOUNG.

IV.—PUPPY AND I.

I met a Man as I went walking;
    We got talking.
      Man and I.
" Where are you going to, Man ? " I said.
    (I said to the Man as he went by.)
" Down to the village to get some bread.
    Will you come with me ? " " No, not I."

I met a Horse as I went walking;
    We got talking.
      Horse and I.
" Where are you going to, Horse, to-day ? "
    (I said to the Horse as he went by.)
" Down to the village to get some hay.
    Will you come with me ? " " No, not I."

I met a Woman as I went walking;
    We got talking,
      Woman and I.
" Where are you going to, Woman, so
    early ? "
    (I said to the Woman as she went by.)
" Down to the village to get some barley.
    Will you come with me ? " " No, not I."

I met four Rabbits as I went walking;
    We got talking,
      Rabbits and I.
" Where are you going in your brown fur
    coats ? "
    (I said to the Rabbits as they went by.)
" Down to the village to get some oats.
    Will you come with us ? " " No, not I."

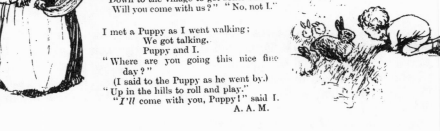

I met a Puppy as I went walking;
    We got talking.
      Puppy and I.
" Where are you going this nice fine
    day ? "
    (I said to the Puppy as he went by.)
" Up in the hills to roll and play."
    " *I'll* come with you, Puppy ! " said I.
              A. A. M.

*Drawing by Ernest Shepard, poem by
A. A. Milne, 1924*

So when I said "I've come back," and Owen, instead of falling on my neck, said coldly, "Oh!" and when it appeared the Proprietors had neither expected nor wanted me back, being not only very well satisfied with my elderly substitute, but also a little annoyed that I had written plays, not *Punch* articles, in my spare time; when, in short, it became clear that I was free to do whatever I liked, which is what I have always wanted to do, I said bitterly and ungratefully to myself, "Kicked out!" But I did know that within a few hours I should be delighted.

Talking of the future, Seaman made it plain to him that there was no possibility of his ever becoming editor ("making it sound like a compliment"). Seaman did publish some of Milne's things after that. *The King's Breakfast* was one, and *When We Were Very Young* first appeared in *Punch* in 1924. It was Seaman who suggested Ernest Shepard as illustrator, as felicitous a combination as Lewis Carroll and Sir John Tenniel. The Shepard illustrations for *Winnie the Pooh* have been a source of enjoyment to children for generations.

The subject of a job at *Punch* must have come up again, after Milne became a celebrity, since we find him writing to E. V. Knox in October 1923: "I could not bear to write regularly for *Punch* again. I'm sorry, but it would make me miserable." The choice of Knox rather than Seaman as ambassador in this case is significant. Milne felt so strongly about the whole matter that he never once was able to mention Locker by name in his autobiography, calling him only "my successor" or "my substitute." Why he extended his bitterness to Locker, who was innocent of any wrongdoing, is a mystery.

Early in World War II, P. G. Wodehouse, another *Punch* contributor recruited by Seaman, had the misfortune to make several innocent broadcasts in Berlin which were seized upon and used for propaganda by the Nazis. Wodehouse was attacked by press and public in England. He was not forgiven or restored to his former popularity at home for many years. Among the most severe of his attackers was Milne, who should have known better.

The insult rankled. A decade later he revenged himself on Milne in a peculiarly Wodehousian way. He wrote a story in which a principal character was an effete versifier who persisted in informing his little boy that bluebells are fairy telephones and wrote dreadful children's poetry.

> Timothy Bobbin has ten little toes,
> He takes them with him wherever he goes,
> And if Timothy gets a cold in his head
> His ten little toes stay with him in bed.

Milne's opinion of the story, which must have been brought to his attention by numerous amused acquaintances, has not been recorded. But the cruelest indictment of Milne's famous works came from Dorothy Parker, writing literary criticism in the *New Yorker* as "Constant Reader." Her review of *The House at Pooh Corner* was "Tonstant Weader fwowed up."

Wodehouse's *Punch* contributions were, sadly enough, very few. His success as a novelist and writer of lyrics for musical comedies brought him prosperity and relocation to America in the twenties. In the late 1950s, after his wartime error had been rectified and his name had been cleared, he served as a kind of occasional transatlantic correspondent. He was invited, at long last, to carve his initials in the Table, an honor delayed almost as long as his knighthood. He replied that he would be delighted to do so. Unfortunately, he was already in his nineties and his traveling days were over. He never did join the roll of *Punch* immortals. He died at his home in Long Island before he could return to his native land.

Probably the man closest to Seaman was C. L. Graves, a "dear old boy," quaint, lovable, and dreadfully boring. Graves, who replaced Locker as assistant editor in 1928, was the brother-in-law of Earl Grey, a connection of undoubted value to Seaman, and an imperialist after the editor's own heart. Seaman, who said that the ultimate test of a nation's greatness was its power to colonize and that England had never had competition in that field "since we outdid Spain at her own work," must have pleased the minister; and the adulation of Graves may have contributed to Seaman's baronetcy.

Graves was also the uncle of Robert Graves, an occasional *Punch* contributor in the fifties, who as a young man admired Seaman's verses. C. L. Graves's writings have not survived the erosions of time; his verses today have about them a flavor of the seasonal greeting card. Perhaps recognizing his own limitations, Graves wrote a number of pieces in partnership with one of *Punch*'s abler all-around writers, Edward Verrall Lucas, a friend and contemporary of his who had worked with him at one time on the *Globe* and also on Harry Furniss's ill-fated *Lika Joko*. Graves, explaining their collaboration in verse, wrote (after six introductory stanzas):

> You know the sequel; how he took
> To Lamb* and Punch, a dreadful diet,
> And published every month a book
> Until his system craved for quiet.

*Lucas had written a biography of Charles Lamb.

> Then realizing that his mind
> > Was overcharged with mere frivolity,
> A second time he came to find
> > In Graves his complemental quality.
>
> And that, as you will understand
> > Is our collaboration's basis;
> I furnished him with lots of sand
> > And he provided the oasis;
> I acted chiefly as accom-
> > Panist when we performed our duet;
> He was the ornamental plum,
> > And I the necessary suet.

Lucas came to *Punch* in Burnand's time with the strong support of Seaman. He joined the Table in 1903, occupying Phil May's old chair between Sir William Agnew and Sir Bernard Partridge. He wrote light, humorous essays on peculiar or amusing current events or adventures that he or his family had experienced. Price has compared his work with Thackeray's "Our Fat Contributor" articles. Alan Dent called him a "mixture of Montaigne and Rabelais," which he certainly wasn't. Lucas himself said that he wrote "bedroom books" in the Victorian rather than the modern sense, meaning that a young and innocent girl could have his work on her bedside table without suffering any moral harm. He knew that he was accused of being a writer of the lavender-and-old-lace school and didn't care. He considered himself an entertainer rather than an artist.

Of humble Quaker background, Lucas attended eleven different schools before he finally gave up education and decided to make his way in the world of literature. The frequent changes were not his fault, but were due almost entirely to differences between his father and various headmasters about payment of tuition bills. He was an oddly tortured man, incapable of dining alone or going to bed early. A quiet evening at home with a book was unthinkable for him. He haunted clubs, restaurants, and music halls. "I have an idea," James Agate wrote in *Ego 3*, "that the serenity of the writer was a mask hiding the torments of a man knowing as much about hell as any of Maupassant's characters or even Maupassant himself." There was never a Punchite whose personal life was so different from the happy, secure life depicted in his essays.

When Seaman was on holiday on the Riviera or shooting at country houses, it was Lucas who sat at the head of the Table as acting editor,

TO ARMS!

Recruiting-Sergeant Punch. "NOW, MY LADS, YOUR COUNTRY WANTS YOU. W
FOR THE FRONT?"

L. Raven Hill, 1914

outranking Milne, Locker, and later Graves. Milne remembers him as having

> as many concerns outside *Punch* as Owen had few, and consequently was as quick as Owen was slow. After the paper was put to bed on Friday night Owen had nowhere to go but home, and a lonely home at that. E. V. had a hundred mysterious activities waiting for him. Only once as we walked down the Strand together did he vary his usual ''Well, I'm going this way. Good night.'' in preface to one of those disappearances to which I was now used, and which had all the air, even if they took him no further than the Garrick Club, of a prelude to adventure.

Lucas was able to work anywhere and under any conditions. His daughter, Audrey, remembers him scribbling away in a music hall during one of the less interesting turns. He was a dreadful hypochondriac and suffered from a perpetual head cold. He was fond of informing his family in portentous tones that ''on only one day in the entire year is it safe to sit on the grass.'' (He never ventured to say what day that was.) He made life miserable for his fellow Punchites and luncheon or dinner companions, tracking down nonexistent drafts and improperly closed doors and windows.

In his later years he wrote lyrics for the wartime revue *Business as Usual*, under the pseudonym ''F. W. Mark.'' In the twenties, when his style had become a charming but faded Victorian anachronism, Seaman set him to writing reviews, although he was usually wrong about literature and the arts. He loved films, and Seaman let him do early film reviews in order (as he wrote to the proprietors) to be ''spared his other contributions at least once a week.'' He understood very little about the cinema, preferring James Cagney and Spencer Tracy to other actors and American films to the more artistic European variety. To him films were, like music halls or his own essays, entertainment, not art. Cinema, theater, the occasional opera, and, failing those, billiards or cricket matches, were merely ways of filling the empty hours in his life which would otherwise have been unbearable.

He published an edition of the works and letters of Charles and Mary Lamb in 1903 and a life of Charles Lamb in 1905. His two anthologies, *The Open Road* (1899) and *The Friendly Town* (1905), are charming period pieces as are his novels, *Over Bemerton's* (1908) and *Listener's Lure* (1911). His autobiography *Reading, Writing and Remembering* was published in 1932 by Methuen, the publishing house at which he had served as an editor for a good many years while on the *Punch* staff and to which he had steered those of his *Punch* colleagues whom he thought had commercial possibilities.

In 1908 an ecclesiastic demagogue, Father Bernard Vaughan, delivered what he thought were fiery sermons from the pulpit attacking the "Smart Set"—youthful forerunners of the Flaming Youth of the twenties, the Beautiful People of the sixties and the Jet Set of the seventies. The sermons caused quite a stir in the period before the war, as weighty pronouncements against the fortunate people of the world always do. The Smart Set was a ready-made target, but Father Vaughan was not the Savanarola to scorch them.

Punch, always ready to side with the upper classes, was quick to satirize him. Graves and Lucas wrote this devastating parody of one of his maladroit sermons.

More Wise Words on Wedlock
Father Vaughan Tupper's Great Sermon

We have been fortunate in obtaining the manuscript of the searching and vivid sermon on "Marriage: Its Trials, Failures, and Triumphs," delivered by that inspired yet caustic observer of modern life, Father Vaughan Tupper, at the headquarters of the Mayfair Roman Catholics on Sunday. We print his scathing remarks and profoundly shrewd counsels just as they issued from his lips, but the readers of cold type necessarily lose the fire and spirit of this great and original preacher—his fervour, his sarcasm, his irony.

"Marriage is a lottery. I say it with all caution after hours of thought on the matter. Marriage is a lottery. You *may* get a good wife, you *may* not; and (here I address myself to the ladies), you *may* get a good husband, you *may* not. Yes, my friends, marriage is a lottery. A lottery.

"When a man goes forth to get a wife he should be guided by good sense. He should not choose a showy, flighty, smoking-room girl, but one whom he can admire and respect. If she is beautiful so much the better; but probably he will think her beautiful, and that will do as well.

"I will not say that the man is the superior, or the woman the superior. In every case time will show.

"Men and women are so different that there are almost certain to be moments when they disagree. The fewer and briefer are these periods of disagreement the happier is the marriage. I say it deliberately—the fewer and the briefer are these periods of disagreement the happier is the marriage.

"Nothing can so assist the husband and wife as good advice. Let me give you some. I am full of it. Also I am by my office a bachelor, and therefore the best judge.

"To the husband I would say: Do not interrupt your wife and say sarcastic things to her. Let her talk on. Give her sympathy. Give her ornaments and clothes, if you can afford them. Love her. Be kind to her.

"To the wife I would say: Don't nag. Don't scold. Don't cry. That husbands dislike tears is a truth that has been borne in upon me. Never mind what other people say, but take it from me that husbands dislike tears. Don't keep a bad cook. Husbands like good dinners. Were I, in fact, to speak in a more vulgar phrase, I might say, at the risk of shocking you by my originality and homeliness, feed the brute. Dress well. Do not be slovenly. See that the house is well kept.

"To put the whole matter briefly, I should say to husbands: Husbands, do not do anything to annoy or disappoint or alienate your wives; and to the wives, Wives, do not lose your husbands' love.

"Only thus can there be happy marriages."

If *Punch* was Douglas Jerrold at first, John Leech in the sixties, and du Maurier in the eighties, the magazine was Alan Patrick Herbert during most of Seaman's tenure. Herbert was a man of limitless energy. He hurled himself headlong into everything he did; from leading a troop of landlocked sailors in the Dardanelles in World War I to fighting for better written English in government reports.

Educated at Winchester and New College, Oxford, Herbert was published in the *Observer*, the *Pall Mall Gazette*, and *Vanity Fair* while he was still an undergraduate. His first *Punch* contribution, a poem called "Stones of Venus," appeared in 1910. He received a guinea in payment.

He was a vigorous, untidy, nervous man with a prominent, down-curved nose. In his youth he resembled the late Basil Rathbone. As he grew older, as happened to so many senior Punchites, he began to look like Mr. Punch. Tall and stoop-shouldered, he had a peculiar habit of jerking his head, the result of a childhood accident, which earned him the school nickname of "Peck." He had a nervous blink and a slight stammer. Nevertheless, he was a forceful and vigorous public speaker.

Herbert was a passionate adherent of causes. He seems never to have known a moment of noninvolvement; he was always attacking or supporting some momentous issue. He wrote more than a thousand letters to the *Times* which the editors were happy to print—probably not so much because of the timeliness of their contents, as of the fact that the paper was getting the work of a popular and high-priced author for nothing.

Elected to Parliament in 1935 as an Independent for Oxford University, he set himself up as the gadfly of the House, in opposition to whichever party happened to have a majority. He was fond of representing himself as a "crusted Tory," although his political sympathies shuttled back and forth according to the issue that happened to interest him at the moment.

He came out strongly for road safety and violently opposed daylight saving time. He stumped unsuccessfully for self-government for Newfoundland, and successfully for the reform of obsolete divorce and marriage laws.

He struggled for legal aid for the indigent and sane licensing laws. He opposed censorship of publications, obscene or otherwise; entertainment taxes; and most especially the 1940 wartime 12 percent tax on books. He attacked the new problem of airplane noise twenty years before it became a major political issue. He began a lifelong battle with the tax authorities by demanding that all artists be exempted from income taxes.

When Herbert began to prosper as a writer, he found to his horror that the government was unfairly insisting that money received as an advance for a book that might take several years to write be taxed as the income received in a single year. He fought them in and out of the House of Commons. Receiving an ultimatum from the tax commissioners one day, stating that he was behind in payment of his surtax, he drafted a check, written entirely in verse, on a sheet of his own letterhead writing paper and drawn on his bankers.

> Dear Bankers, PAY the undermentioned hounds
> The shameful sum of FIVE-AND-EIGHTY POUNDS.
> By 'hounds,' of course, by custom, one refers
> To SPECIAL INCOME TAX COMMISSIONERS:
> And these progenitors of woe and worry
> You'll find at LYNWOOD ROAD, THAMES DITTON, SURREY.

The poem went on for another twenty lines of complaint about the injustice with which he was treated by the cruel tax people, who not only raided his little income but demanded a surtax too. The poem ended with the lines ''And let the good old custom be enforced / Don't cash this cheque, unless it is endorsed.''

A few weeks later he was amazed to receive in an official envelope from the Office for the Special Commissioners for Income Tax:

S.T.H. 31097/40

> Dear Sir,
> It is with pleasure that I thank
> You for your letter, and the order to your bank
> To pay the sum of five and eighty pounds
> To those here whom you designate as hounds.
> Their appetite is satisfied. In fact
> You paid too much and I am forced to act

186

Not to repay you, as perchance you dream,
Though such a course is easy, it would seem.
Your liability for later years
Is giving your accountants many tears:
And till such time as they and we can come
To amicable settlement on the sum
That represents your tax bill to the State
I'll leave the overpayment to its fate.
I do not think this step will make you frown:
The sum involved is only half-a-crown.

Yours faithfully,
A. L. Grove

Herbert was not about to allow himself to be bested at his own game by the bureaucrat Grove. Refusing to surrender, he insisted on having the last word.

Your ref. S.T.H. 31097/40
I thank you, Sir, but am afraid
Of such a rival in my trade:
One never should encourage those—
In future I shall pay in prose.

Writing bizarre checks was a favorite eccentricity of Herbert's. He would dash one off on the label of a champagne bottle or a menu, a theater program, or any sort of scrap that happened to be within reach. The checks were, of course, legal, if unusual, and were always honored by his long-suffering bankers.

In spite of his many outside activities, Herbert still found time to be a prolific *Punch* contributor, to write books, to write advertising copy, to maintain his barge-houseboat, *Water Gipsy,* as a part of the Thames community of river dwellers, to engage in a rich social life replete with clubs, dinners, speaking engagements, and historic pubs, to serve in two world wars, and to write West End revues for the impresario Sir Charles B. Cochran. The large amount of energy expended in giving his best to all of these projects resulted in periodic bouts of nervous exhaustion, but he always bounced back in top form ready to tilt with another windmill. He was still at it when he died in 1971 at the age of eighty-one.

Although he did not hit his stride as a Punchite or join the Table until after World War I, Herbert's contributions appeared fairly regularly until 1914 when he joined the Royal Naval Volunteer Reserve, achieving the rank of sublieutenant. In 1915 he was posted to combat service, becom-

Medical Officer (London practitioner in private life). "WOULD YOU COME TO ME WITH SUCH A TRIVIAL COMPLAINT IN CIVIL LIFE?"
Private. "NO, SIR. I SHOULD SEND FOR YOU."

F. H. Townsend, 1918

Fred Pegram, 1916

Tommy (dictating letter to be sent to his wife). "THE NURSES HERE ARE A VERY PLAIN LOT——"
Nurse. "OH, COME! I SAY! THAT'S NOT VERY POLITE TO US."
Tommy. "NEVER MIND, NURSE, PUT IT DOWN. IT'LL PLEASE HER!"

ing one of "Mr. Punch's young men" reporting from the battlefronts, like E. V. Knox, A. A. Milne, Kenneth Bird, and others. He devoted the same wholehearted interest to the navy that he would later bring to Parliament.

He landed at Gallipoli with a detachment of sailors attached for some reason to the army command there and after a period of fighting appeared on "Mr. Punch's Roll of Honour" as "Wounded at the Dardanelles." In fact, he had been invalided home with a bad case of virulent enteritis. He really was wounded in 1917—in the buttock—by a projectile that also shattered his hip flask. He always maintained afterward that he had been saved from gangrene by the antiseptic quality of the brandy in the flask. Seaman, sticking to the standards he had formerly applied in the case of the octopus, did not choose to describe either of Herbert's disabilities in *Punch*.

Like the other Punchites at the front, Herbert sent periodic dispatches to Bouverie Street during his active duty. This gave him an oddly ambivalent status in his organization; since he was both a very junior officer and the working representative of one of the most influential press media in England. He did not hesitate to use his power on occasions when he felt it could be helpful. In the Dardanelles, his commanding officer, a regular army brigadier, was outraged that one of the young naval officers had a beard and demanded that it be shaved off (the navy allowed beards, the army didn't). The following week, to his utter dismay, the brigadier found himself the ludicrous subject of a comic poem in *Punch*, describing in rhyme the Great Beard Controversy. The subject was dropped at once, but the brigadier was for some time an object of ridicule among his brother senior officers in the mess.

It was characteristic of Herbert that although he was only a volunteer reserve, he considered himself navy to the marrow of his bones, rating (publicly) his army divisional commander as "somewhat less important than the managing director of Harrod's." He would never have lampooned an admiral in *Punch*, no matter what the provocation, nor would he have laid the senior service open to ridicule. He served again in World War II, when he was in his fifties, as a petty officer in command of his own *Water Gipsy*, which he had turned over to the navy for river patrol.

Unlike the unfortunate Milne, Herbert was enthusiastically welcomed back to *Punch* after the war. In 1924 Seaman invited him to join the staff on a full-time basis and contribute an article a week for a stipend of fifty pounds weekly. "A valuable youth," John Galsworthy wrote to the editor when he heard of Herbert's appointment, "who hits things that ought to be hit nice and hard."

He made a tremendous success at once with his series "Misleading

Cases,'' reports from a fictitious law review on obscure and funny points of jurisprudence, written in a parody of legal language that was so subtle that distinguished lawyers on both sides of the Atlantic sometimes quoted the cases as the real thing. Like so many other Punchites, Herbert was a member of the Bar and had taken a first in jurisprudence at Oxford, so he knew what he was doing. Some of the ''Misleading Cases'' have been rewritten for television and are still shown on BBC–TV. At the same time, he wrote the revues *Riverside Nights* and *The White Witch*, which opened at the Haymarket in 1926.

Probably his most often quoted poem is one in which he deflates officious, self-important minor functionaries: members of useless committees, municipal councilmen, and similar petty would-be leaders of men. The poem has not only transcended the years without losing any of its sting, it has actually improved with age, and is even more pertinent now than it was when Herbert wrote it in 1928.

> Let's stop everybody from doing something!
> Everybody does too much.
> People seem to think they have a right to eat and drink,
> Talk and walk and respirate and rink,
> Bicycle and bathe and such.
> So let's have a lot of little regulations,
> Let's make laws and jobs for our relations,
> There's too much kissing at the railway stations,
> Let's find out what everyone is doing,
> And then stop everyone from doing it. . . .

Possibly even more famous is his classic set of erotic verses, quoted in locker rooms and barracks everywhere, often by people who never heard of A. P. Herbert or, for that matter, of *Punch*. His ''Lines on a Book Borrowed from the Ship's Doctor'' was a favorite:

> The portions of a woman that appeal to man's depravity
> Are constructed with considerable care,
> And what appears to you to be a simple cavity
> Is really quite an elaborate affair. . . .

The poem had an international underground success and caused him to be credited with the authorship of a good deal of lewd poetry written by other people. His ''Ode to a Seagull,'' also disseminated widely without having appeared in the austere pages of *Punch*, had a similar success. Written for fun during a sea voyage, it delighted both passengers and crew.

Oh seagull, we're grieving
To see you relieving
Yourself on the merchant marine.
You have very good sight
And should see, in this light
The *Otranto* is not a latrine.
God gave you the oceans
For your little motions,
And Spain's a convenient po;
But if it feels finer
To aim at a liner—
Well, why not a nice P & O?

For a while Herbert, who adored the movies, was assigned with Lucas to write film reviews. His critiques were superior to Lucas's, although, like Lucas, he had not the slightest idea of the artistic values of the cinema or, for that matter, of cinema acting. His comparison of Marion Davies and Greta Garbo, appearing in a double feature silent release, is a good example of Herbert as critic.

> I went to the palatial Tivoli to see a well-advertised film called *Love*, based on the book *Anna Karenina* and "starring" a famous charmer called GRETA GARBO, "Filmland's Most Attractive Woman." There was a curtain-raiser called *The Politic Flapper*, featuring MARION DAVIES. The curtain raiser lasted about an hour-and-a-half and *Love* about an hour only. But I thoroughly enjoyed the *hors d'oeuvre* and was rather bored by the *pièce de résistance*. Indeed, I left the building before the climax of the tragedy was reached, so that, not having read, I confess, TOLSTOY'S book, I still do not know what happened to the beautiful wife, or the elderly husband, or the dull young man (who seemed scarcely worth the trouble and expense anyhow) or who died or what. [N.B. The dull young man was played by John Gilbert.]
>
> And the awful thing is that I do not really care. But I cared enormously what happened to MARION DAVIES as the politic flapper. Your GRETA is certainly a seductive creature in a wax-model kind of way, and she may be Filmland's First Fascinator, but MARION DAVIES in my humble judgment is Filmland's Funniest Female. And much more than that. GRETA can act, but MARION knocks the spots off her as an artist. She is the only film-woman I ever saw that I would mention on the same day as CHARLIE CHAPLIN.

It was typical of the *Punch* reviews of the period. The readers wanted to know what to see for an evening of rattling good entertainment with, if possible, a few laughs or a thrill or two. Art was for the stage. Movies were for fun.

His novel *The Secret Battle* (1919) was said by many, including Lloyd George and Winston Churchill, to be one of the finest antiwar books ever written. In *The Water Gipsies*, in which the *Times Literary Supplement* discovered a ''Dickensian fecundity,'' he expressed his love of life on the river. His operettas, except for *Bless the Bride* which ran for more than two years, were praised by the critics, but were not financial successes.

In the late forties his energies began to diminish at last, or perhaps he had taken on more than he could handle. His *Punch* contributions decreased in quality. When Kenneth Bird (''Fougasse'') became editor, and later under Muggeridge, steps were taken to induce him to retire, but without success.

When Bernard Hollowood became editor in the sixties, rejection of Herbert's articles increased sharply. Between 1961 and 1963 *Punch* refused thirty-five of his pieces. Hollowood wrote to him with some asperity, ''We can't go on saying that nothing new is any good when we are trying to lure new young readers.''

After the United Newspapers takeover, there was a brief reconciliation. Davis, who knew the publicity value of living legends, tried to reestablish the aging Herbert as a *Punch* drawing card, but it was too late. He was approaching eighty, and his value to a modern magazine trying to upgrade its image was zero. But *Punch* did not forget him. In 1970, his sixtieth year as a Punchite, the staff was observed leading a cow into the Holborn branch of Barclay's Bank. Painted on its flank was Pay A. P. Herbert £5. Underneath was the signature of William Davis. The bank honored the check. Reading about it in the newspapers the next day, very few people under the age of forty knew what the joke was about.

Herbert's last *Punch* contribution followed not long after the cow incident. He died in November 1971. Many of his crusades had resulted in constructive changes in British jurisprudence. Backed by the undoubted power of *Punch*, his ''Misleading Cases'' had used humor to force the alteration of silly, obsolete laws. He was not able to stop daylight saving time, but people could now, if they so desired, get married after three o'clock in the afternoon. They could divorce without committing adultery or without engaging in illegal collusion to pretend they had.

At this point it is pertinent to leave the individual Punchites to comment on the magazine's performance as a morale raiser and propaganda instrument during World War I. Up to the time that Kaiser Wilhelm II ''dropped the pilot'' in 1890, *Punch* had always found Germans to be funny. During the Schleswig-Holstein controversy in 1864,

192

Mr. Punch had presented the king of Prussia, Wilhelm I, with the "Order of St. Gibbet." In 1873, after the Franco-Prussian War, Tenniel produced his prophetic cartoon showing the end of the German occupation with a defeated but proud France coolly bidding the Prussians au revoir.

From 1892 the Kaiser became the magazine's prime target of satire, outstripping even the luckless Lord Brougham in the number and variety of guises in which he was drawn by Tenniel, Partridge, Raven Hill, and others. He was an "Imperial Jack-in-the-Box," a "Modern Alexander" (for which the magazine was summarily, but temporarily, banned from the Imperial Palace), "*Struwwelpeter*" ("Fidgety Will"), an actor-manager casting himself for *Un Voyage en Chine*, and a "Cook's Crusader," siding with the Turks on Crete. He became the "Moor of Potsdam" on the Moroccan question and the "Sower of Tares," after a painting by Millais. When the war began, he was shown weekly as a cowardly butcher of women and children and a megalomaniacal bungler. *Punch*'s cartoons of Wilhelm II had an interesting side effect. British officers' moustaches, still full and curled in the Victorian manner, grew smaller and neater in order to avoid comparison with the German emperor's upswept waxed points.

The war opened a new source of humor for *Punch*. It was easy to make fun of temporary reserve officers, fresh out of banks and stockbrokers' offices, swaggering about with monocles screwed into their eyes and falling off their horses. Great fun could be had with outraged sergeant majors trying to make soldiers out of maladroit clodhoppers. Almost as soon as the first British blood was spilled in France the tenor of the jokes began to change. It was impossible to make fun of people who were dying. The cartoon officers became unbelievably gallant and courageous. Lower-class 'Arry in uniform grew taller and handsomer, performing prodigies of valor, still dropping his *H*'s but in a brave and gallant fashion. The brutality of *Punch*'s former snobbery was toned down and replaced with a kind of admiring banter, half condescension and half hero worship.

"In the shock of discovery" (that the world was really at war) interpreted by C. L. Graves, "Mr. Punch thought seriously of putting up his shutters." There is some doubt, of course, as to whether Seaman ever seriously thought of suspending the magazine's operations although he may have felt embarrassment that a humorous paper had no place in a country whose sons were being systematically mowed down at the front. Nevertheless, *Punch* never stopped congratulating itself for carrying on instead of closing up shop. It also never stopped making excuses.

In December 1914, Mr. Punch is shown making a trip to the front wearing the uniform of an "Honorary Cornet-Major of the Bouverie

HERO-WORSHIP.

Slightly soiled Urchin. "PLEASE, MR. GENERAL, IF YER WOULDN'T MIND BENDIN' DAHN A BIT, ME AN' EMMA 'D LIKE TO GIVE YER A K—

G. L. Stampa, 191

Fred Pegram, 1916

Visitor (at private hospital). "CAN I SEE LIEUTENANT BARKER, PLEASE?"
Matron. "WE DO NOT ALLOW ORDINARY VISITING. MAY I ASK IF YOU'RE A RELATIVE?"
Visitor (boldly). "OH, YES! I'M HIS SISTER."
Matron. "DEAR ME! I'M VERY GLAD TO MEET YOU. I'M HIS MOTHER."

Street Roughriders.'' He pops into a trench to chat with a ''very young subaltern'' (*Punch* was still speaking on terms of equality to officers only) and discusses the subject of *Punch*'s wartime value.

> ''I'll tell you a true story,'' he [the subaltern] said quietly. ''There was a man in this trench who had his leg shot off. They couldn't get him away till night, and here he had to wait for the whole of the day. . . . He stuck it out. . . . And what do you think he stuck it out on?''
> ''Morphia?'' suggested Mr. Punch.
> ''Partly on morphia, and partly on something else.''
> ''Yes?'' said Mr. Punch breathlessly.
> ''Yes—*you*. He read . . . and he laughed . . . and by-and-by the night came.
> A silence came over them both. Then Mr. Punch got up quietly.
> ''Good-bye,'' he said, holding out his hand, ''And thank you . . .''

Whether in actual fact a soldier really did subsist on morphia and *Punch* until the medics were able to patch up his severed limb is questionable. Seaman did not choose to include the man's name and regiment, in deference to wartime censorship perhaps, although he would have violated no seal of secrecy since the soldier would, by publication time, have been removed to a hospital in England. *Punch*'s detractors had a God-given opportunity to comment on the magazine's soporific qualities, as a subsitute for chloroform in deadening a patient's abilities to feel pain or anything else. They were kind enough to let the chance pass them by. Jokes at the expense of the seriously wounded had died with Gilbert and Thomas Hood.

The incident, apocryphal or not, may have been a personal apology by Seaman himself for not being in uniform. In his vigorous fifties when the war began, he led *Punch* in fierce recruiting drives, savagely attacking ''shirkers and slackers and scaremongers, callous pleasure-seekers, faint-hearted pacifists, rebels and traitors,'' among whom he included everyone, regardless of reason, who was not in uniform. *Punch*'s cartoons celebrated the courage of men who were too old, too young, too tall or short, too ill, or lacking in teeth, sight, hearing, or any other necessary qualities, yet lied bravely to the recruiting officer in order to join the armed forces.

Seaman joined a group of middle-aged lawyer volunteers recruited from the Inns of Court and went to weekly drill sesssions. The group was turned down when it applied for inclusion in the regular army. This was certainly foreseeable, especially to so astute an observer as Seaman, but it gave him a perfect alibi: He had tried to get into the fight, but he hadn't been accepted. It seems obvious that Seaman, who knew personally everyone in a position of authority from the prime minister to the chief of staff, could certainly have gotten himself into uniform if he had wished to do so.

He did visit the front briefly on one occasion, as a personal guest of the commanding general. Having thus established himself as a "war correspondent," Seaman went back to his desk and continued to point out as often as possible, that it was "not only a privilege but a duty to minister to mirth at times when one hastened to laugh for fear of being obliged to weep."

It can be said in Seaman's favor that the authorities who did not insist on his taking on some government duty were probably well advised. *Punch* was an important morale builder. Mothers, fathers, and sweethearts sent copies to loved ones in the front lines. *Punch* meant home as much as Ivor Novello's *Keep the Home Fires Burning* did, and jokes about country villages, golf, and young wives carrying on in spite of rationing did force a great many laughs that masked homesick tears. It is likely that Seaman at the front or even in a staff job in the War Office would have been considerably less useful to the nation than Seaman in command of the "Bouverie Street Roughriders."

With the editor's status as a wartime asset firmly established, the paper attacked the Germans and other enemies with fists flying. Proudly pointing out that Punchites were in the thick of it from the western front to India, the magazine praised the bravery of territorial troops and poked gentle fun at staff officers and other brass hats at home. There were bitter complaints about censorship keeping people from getting timely news from the battlefields and blimpish bleats about the universities which were given to "a handful of Rhodes Scholars, reluctant crocks, and coloured students." Boat Race Day was definitely not what it used to be. Before long the black men and the Rhodes scholars would be gone, too, and it would be worse.

Women, of course, were what was left on the home front, and Mr. Punch chuckled as they took over the jobs of postal and bank clerks, truck drivers, farm laborers, and factory workers. Imagine women in such jobs! It was a delicious source of cartoon fun.

A stiff upper lip was kept at Bouverie Street with respect to food rationing, margarine ("*C'est magnifique, mais ce n'est pas le beurre!*"), and a severe shortage of sausage skins. Mr. Punch kept his usual sharp eye on Parliament, noting that "the Cabinet has decided not to be cinematographed"; that unnecessary whistling for taxis was to be suppressed; and that Mr. Swift McNeill, the same who had threatened Harry Furniss with bodily harm, had extracted from the prime minister a promise to remove British titles from enemy dukes.

Through it all, the paper kept up a steady barrage of anti-German, antikaiser jokes which stimulated an article in the *Kölnische Zeitung* to the effect that *Punch*'s "cartoons are lacking in modest refinement" and that their treatment of the kaiser "savours of blasphemy." This attitude did not prevent the German propaganda authorities from concocting a counterfeit *Punch* for distribution in the United States. Using the well-known Doyle cover, the top margin, usually given over to an advertiser, said in large black letters AS ENGLAND SEES U.S. The bottom margin added: "Some Famous and Forgotten Cartoons that the Present Generation of Americans Should See." The first and only issue contained a collection of real *Punch* political cartoons by Leech, Tenniel, and Doyle dating back to the 1850s, in which the United States came off badly. The cartoons dealt with slavery, the *Trent* and *Alabama* controversies, the Civil War, lynching, the Mexican War, and even a cartoon showing English contempt for the Irish. Put out by "the American Truth Society of 1133 Broadway, New York," the German *Punch* cannot have excited anything more than ridicule in America.

On the home front, *Punch* deplored the fact that "lonely soldiers" were being "victimized by fair correspondents" promising affection but making off with pay packets. "A new and dangerous ally of the enemy" was working to undermine British fortitude at home, where citizens and soldiers alike were contending with Drink. The ever-pompous Milne wrote an angry letter to G. K. Chesterton, taking him sternly to task for advocating that pubs be allowed to stay open after 9:00 P.M. He implored Chesterton to lay off, at least for the duration of the war. The closing hour, he explained, was not meant to keep people moral, but merely to keep them sober, and was highly necessary for "silly young soldiers" away from home for the first time.

Almost as frequently and bitterly lampooned as the kaiser was Woodrow Wilson, who, according to *Punch*, was dragging his feet about bringing America into the war. He appeared in cartoons as Hamlet, Noah, Rodin's "The Thinker," and "a Byzantine logothite" among others. He became a heroic policeman after the Americans finally came in on the Allied side. Until the United States actually declared war, *Punch* rarely missed a week without raising the ghastly remains of the *Lusitania*.

Up to the very end *Punch* was a paragon of flag-waving patriotism. Every issue contained a heavily inspirational poem by "O.S."; a condescending tribute to the courageous Tommy characterized by Bert Thomas in his "'Arf a mo', Kaiser!" cartoon*; tributes to the navy, the infantry, or the Royal Flying Corps ("These airy fellows talk of war as if it

---

*This cartoon was widely reprinted on posters and postcards. It showed a cocky British private directing the German emperor to hold up the war so that he could light his pipe. " 'Arf a mo', Kaiser'' became an unofficial camp slogan like "Kilroy was here" in World War II.

197

were a day's shooting''); and to ''the cheerfulness of the limbless men in blue.'' The hate-the-enemy campaign never faltered.

The tone of the magazine was almost sulky when the Germans surrendered and suddenly it was all over. *Punch* experienced nearly as severe a nervous reaction to the peace as the weary Tommies, home from the muddy trenches. Bernard Partridge celebrated the end of hostilities with his standard heroic stained-glass figure in medieval armor atop a charging war-horse, accompanied by a winged, laurel-crowned goddess, and titled VICTORY! The same figure, holding a trident instead of a sword and knee-deep in water, was called ''In Honour of the British Navy.'' Mr. Punch, secure in the knowledge that he had won the war, prepared to cope with the peace.

As to Punch—I've seen him . . . in all sorts of out-of-the-way places where he represents England in all its varieties to men who, because they are far removed, see and remember it more keenly . . . it is perfectly true that he has become urbane, which he was not, even as late as the Sixties, or thirty years back, when he used to whack me on the head on general principles. But he can hit quite hard enough when he likes.

—*Rudyard Kipling*

n spite of his weaknesses, Seaman was not a totally unattractive character. He was admired and respected by many, and he knew how to make himself likeable. He had a charming, unpredictable sense of humor and would frequently collapse in helpless and highly contagious laughter over some silly or unscholarly joke. He may have been autocratic, a kind of editorial monolith, but he was also brilliant and hardworking.

He was kindhearted, but with the benevolence of a man who has never known real financial hardship. He exercised a benign, avuncular supervision over the lives of the younger Punchites, frequently causing consternation by inviting himself to dinner at their houses, oblivious of the fact that his young hosts and their wives might have to undergo painful sacrifices to supply food and drink suitable for the editor of a National Institution.

Eric Keown, who wrote the theater page in the twenties, recalls a sojourn in the hospital where he was amazed to receive a visit from Seaman, bearing armfuls of books and bottles of champagne. Sometimes Seaman would cadge a lift home in Keown's tiny Austin, his bulk jammed into the miniscule front seat from which he had to be extracted, shouting with laughter, by his hall porter.

If Seaman is to be faulted at all, it is for his inability to adapt rapidly to change. This seems to be an endemic malady of *Punch* editors. It can be said in his defense that there were more dramatic changes during the three decades of his editorship than had occurred at any time in British history. Mark Lemon, whose tenure was about the same length as Seaman's, could be reasonably certain that each Victorian year would be very much like the previous one, give or take the odd remote war or change of prime minister. In Lemon's day *Punch* could thunder against poverty or raise its eyebrows over bloomers, whiskers, or loud street musicians. In Seaman's time the forces that controlled British life shifted with such dizzying speed that a middle-aged Tory editor, winding down mentally and physically with the years, simply could not cope with it all.

During Seaman's editorship the horse, which figured in so much of *Punch*'s humor, gave way to the motorcar. The science-fiction fantasy of heavier-than-air flight moved into the age of the Wright brothers and on through zeppelin raids to become a major part of international commerce. Seaman's passionate odes in praise of Cecil Rhodes and Kaiser Wilhelm II as a keeper of world peace had to be withdrawn in embarrassment. (He would later publish equally passionate verses attacking Mussolini, who responded by putting him on the Fascist blacklist. The delighted Seaman promptly wrote a second poem, to tell the world about it.)

Punch kept its usual jaundiced eye on British women's fashions, always ultraconservative and always ten years behind. Seaman's editorship saw the disappearance of the du Maurier woman, exposing her pretty ankle or exciting the disapproval of Queen Alexandra, who found it indecent that the actress who played the part of Trilby should appear on the stage barefoot. Ladies in corsets, leg-of-mutton sleeves, chignons, and Dolly Varden hats vanished to be replaced by slender, cigarette-smoking flappers in mini-dresses and "pneumonia blouses."

Seaman's answer to coping with postwar changes was simply not to cope, but to keep *Punch* as near to what it had been at the turn of the century as logic would allow. Once again, the inevitable decline began, stimulated as always by editorial menopause.

With the war safely in the past, *Punch* lumbered unsteadily into the twenties. Lloyd George and Bonar Law gave way to Stanley Baldwin and Ramsay MacDonald, and the nation had its first Labour government, but the long-expected workingman's utopia did not automatically follow. Instead there were strikes, unemployment, and the depression. With thousands on the dole, *Punch* was still chuckling good-naturedly about foolish servant girls and golf course misadventures.

Fortunately the decline in the magazine's quality was not accompanied by financial crisis in spite of the general slump. In the years immediately before the war, the growing young advertising industry had discovered that *Punch*'s pages were a potential gold mine. The proprietors had always limited advertising to six pages, but under pressure they relented, and soon income from the sale of space outstripped revenues from sales and subscriptions. As advertising increased, so did the size of the editorial

Frank Reynolds, 1931

"WHERE ARE YOU OFF TO?"
"TO THE DOCTOR. I DON'T LIKE THE LOOK OF MY WIFE."
"I'LL COME WITH YOU. I HATE THE SIGHT OF MINE."

Serious Politician. "UTOPIA WILL NEVER BE ACHIEVED BY A SINGLE PARTY."
Gay Young Thing. "OH, NO—THERE WOULD HAVE TO BE A PARTY EVERY NIGHT."

H. M. Brock, 1934

part of the magazine, which grew from sixteen pages to twenty-eight by 1924.

For the first time in its history *Punch* hired an advertising manager, Roy Somerville, who held that job from 1910 to 1922. As a noncreative employee, he never achieved Table membership. He was succeeded by Marion Jean Lyon, one of the first great, shrewd, tough career women, as authoritarian in her department as Seaman was in his. A staunch and incorruptible Puritan, she saw to it that advertisements for ladies' undergarments were presented with absolute decorum and banned alcoholic beverages from the magazine's pages.

Advertisements were grouped into two sections, the first and last in each issue, so that readers who did not want to be bothered could skip over them entirely. Complaints or suggestions from the clients who bought the space for their products were not taken kindly. With *Punch*, you were on a take-it-or-leave-it basis. The advertisers took it and considered themselves lucky. Being a woman, Miss Lyon was, of course, ineligible for the Table, but she approached it from another angle. She married a Table member, the cartoonist Raven Hill.

Marriage to the dragon of the advertising department does not seem to have affected Raven Hill adversely. He was well able to hold his own, being just as irascible as his wife. He was said to have been the hardest Punchite to get along with since Harry Furniss. He was a short, rotund, fierce-tempered Welshman whose dour, biting political cartoons hit hard without the gentle humor of Tenniel's or the heavy grandeur of Partridge's. When Partridge moved into the principal cartoonist position at Sambourne's death in 1910, Raven Hill succeeded him as second cartoonist and stayed in that job for twenty-five years. He was succeeded in turn by Ernest Shepard in 1935. He never did achieve the number one spot, monopolized for a century by Tenniel, Sambourne, and Partridge. But he contributed a good many socials, and his work was sought after by other papers and magazines. Rudyard Kipling, a personal family friend, chose him to illustrate *Stalky & Co.* (1899).

As Punch grew in size in the twenties, the number of people who contributed to its pages increased. Where Lemon had been able to turn out an outstanding paper with four or five colleagues, by the end of World War I *Punch* was accepting regular contributions from more than forty writers and artists, and a great many occasional submitters of verse, articles, and illustrations. A number of them were important to the magazine's development and deserve a place in its history. A few were added to the Table.

Walter Emanuel, a lawyer and probably *Punch*'s first regular Jewish staff member, took over what Harold Nicolson called "that distressing page entitled *Charivaria.*'' This catchall section consisted of ponderous commentary on excerpts from other papers or odd bits of news which contained unusual associations of ideas. Nicolson was right. It was distressing, and to Americans, often incomprehensible.

> A dog belonging to a resident of Bromley is alleged to have bitten three postmen. Its owner has been advised to change the animal's diet.

> Much sympathy is felt for the man who was last week crossing the Strand and, not noticing that the road wasn't up, tripped and fell.

The ''Charivaria'' page was inherited by C. H. Bretherton when Emanuel died in 1915, but remained distressing until the forties, when J. B. Boothroyd improved it. Seaman believed that it amused the older readers, who loved to send in their own items for possible publication.

Most of the big guns of *Punch* in the twenties are now forgotten, with the exception of A. P. Herbert, whose poems are still fun to read. There was no one to replace Milne or Wodehouse, much less Thackeray or Jerrold. In 1926 Bretherton took over the ''Essence of Parliament'' page from Locker, writing under the pseudonym ''Algol.'' It was not hard to be more amusing than Locker, even with Seaman watching closely for signs of irreverence to Tory principles. The illustrations were done by the South African artist A. W. Lloyd, a clever caricaturist who wove bits of fantasy into his drawings of public figures. Bretherton was also a prolific versifier, less polished than Seaman and not overly talented. In spite of this, he had a large following among the readers.

Drama criticisms were written by J. Thorp, who signed his page with the initial *T*. Thorp succeeded Milne when he left and was supposed to be first-string reviewer, but he was often superseded by Seaman or by E. V. Knox when there was a play that either of them particularly wanted to see. He was a spoiled Jesuit who involved himself in esoteric societies and offbeat charitable endeavors (at one of which he first met Seaman). Like Burnand, he gave up the chance of priesthood for want of a proper vocation. Instead he went into advertising and industrial design. His drama reviews lacked Milne's finesse or the erudition which later made Eric Keown's reputation. Seaman advised him to ''say what you think but sometimes remind yourself that the actors earn their living at this business, and give them the benefit of the doubt,'' a sage piece of counsel that critics of any sort should always have pinned up over their typewriters. It may have been the reason that actors and producers did not take *Punch*'s drama page too seriously until Keown arrived.

Eric Keown was a *Granta* boy whose duties at *Punch* ranged over a wide spectrum. He was literary critic, parliamentary reporter, and general-purpose writer, as well as play reviewer. He wrote for *Punch* for thirty-five years, until his death in 1963. Keown's humorous pieces were similar to those of Wodehouse and Milne, but not as funny. His humor depended on exaggeration of some small incident, turning a minor mishap into what appeared to the narrator to be a great drama. A few pickets knocked out of his fence becomes a Sherlock Holmes mystery until the culprit is found to be a strayed gypsy pony. A monkey snatches off a lady's wig and a whole French village deliberates on how to get it back, in the style of a de Maupassant story. A bath chair goes out of control with the narrator in it. Two gentlemen try out a scene in a forthcoming novel written by one of them, which calls for a marriage proposal to be delivered on two escalators going in opposite directions, to the amazement of commuters in the Piccadilly tube station.

Keown's stories hit pay dirt when one of them was made into the wonderful Robert Donat film *The Ghost Goes West.* After that, presumably, he no longer had to struggle along on a *Punch* salary. It can only be assumed that he still attended the Wednesday Table lunches.

Anthony Marshall and A. A. ("Anthony Armstrong") Willis were general-purpose writers of the typical *Punch* article. Marshall's popular "Simple Stories" series began in 1926. The stories were light, little, once-upon-a-time fairy tales applying the technique of children's books to adult problems. The technique was an innovation at the time but has been widely imitated since. Armstrong wrote bits and pieces of humor which, in my estimation, rarely ever succeeded. His subjects were the cliché contretemps of country life, golf, amateur theatricals, night clubs, and the like. He stayed with *Punch* until the end of World War II.

Major John Kendall, who wrote as "Dum-Dum," wrote stuffy little poems and articles that do not hold up well in the seventies. As late as 1936, the era of Jean Harlow and Carole Lombard, Dum-Dum was still deploring such storms-in-a-teacup as women wearing lipstick. He did not really belong in the twenties. He belonged in 1894. In due course, his writings disappeared and are now forgotten.

W. C. Sellar and R. J. Yeatman delighted the readers with the well-written and popular *1066 and All That*, and Lieutenant Colonel John McCrae brought tears to many an eye with his immortal poem "In Flanders Fields," which first appeared in *Punch*. F. O. Langley, who, like Gilbert à Beckett, was a police magistrate, earned a wide following with his series "The Watch Dogs," about territorial troops abroad. There were a number of women contributors, too, notably Jessie Pope, Eleanor Farjeon, and Rose Fyleman.

The artists of the twenties were superior in talent to the writers and poets of *Punch*. Some critics bemoaned the loss of the old detailed draughtsmanship, personified by Keene and du Maurier. A. P. Herbert was unable to come to terms with the modern slapdash technique of drawing a comic situation with a few black lines and a scribble or two of background.

> What is the matter with the comic draughtsmen?
> They do not seem to like the human race.
> They may be funny; they may be good craftsmen
> But can't they draw an ordinary face?

In reply, the cartoonist H. M. Bateman pointed out that public standards and taste had declined, obviously the result of the rise of socialism; that in the twenties artists studied until they learned a few basic tricks and then used them over and over.

Bateman was probably what Herbert was complaining about, although he does not seem to have realized it. The faces in his cartoons were distorted with outrage or fear. They could never have been described as ordinary. One of his better cartoons shows an art instructor seeing for the first time that his pupil has become a better artist than he is himself. His face is a masterpiece of bitter rage and hatred.

Bateman was famous for irate colonels and for his "The Man Who . . ." series. He often used the strip method of cartooning, leading up to a punch line with a large number of small drawings each contributing to the joke. In a 1921 issue he covered four full pages with fifty-eight drawings showing a day in the life of a musician whose job was to play a single note on a clarinet during a symphony concert. Similar lengthy jokes showed the problems of a plumber fixing a leak, and a man driven insane by the advice of a crowd of friends on what sort of car he ought to buy. The strip technique was not original with Bateman. It had been used earlier in *Punch* by J. Priestman Atkinson in the "Dumb Crambo" series. It would be used later, to better effect, by Kenneth Bird, who drew as "Fougasse."

One of the most popular and amusing cartoonists of the twenties was Lewis Baumer, who specialized in flappers and precocious children. *Punch* reminiscers tend to underrate Baumer, but I found him to be one of the few postwar cartoonists who is as funny today as he was then. His drawing was swift and sure and showed exactly the effect he wanted it to. Leech's plump little darlings were adorable, and du Maurier's women were lovely, but Baumer's girls were the sexiest ever to grace the magazine's pages. They were slender, self-assured little debutantes in clinging little wisps of dresses; with straight, short, bell-shaped hair and

THE GUEST WHO WAS TOLD TO MAKE HIMSELF QUITE AT HOME, AND DID SO.

H. M. Bateman, 1922

THE MAID WHO WAS BUT HUMAN.

H. M. Bateman, 1922

wide innocent eyes, wonderfully desirable and eminently kissable. They personified the New Woman of the twenties—beautiful but projecting a kind of delectable idiocy, liberated for the first time in history but without the foggiest idea of what to do with her freedom other than smoke in public and go to night clubs. Baumer was the perfect cartoonist for a Jazz Age humor magazine. By the standards of the era, his drawings were modern and young; and if he was no Keene, May, or du Maurier, as Douglas Jerrold so wisely pointed out a century earlier, "who wants Rubens on *Punch?*" Baumer was the first Punchite to produce his own films, a series of short motion pictures entitled *Potted Films*, which he issued in 1916.

Frank Reynolds joined the Table in 1919, after having been a contributor since Seaman's arrival in 1906. After Townsend's death in 1920, he became art editor and remained in that job for ten years. One of his most talked-about cartoons appeared during the war and showed a German family at the breakfast table, "enjoying its morning hate." It was enormously popular and was cut out and pinned up by hundreds of English families.

Reynolds's cartoons dealt mostly with the pitfalls of suburban life and with inept golfers and cricketers. When he became art editor, he clashed with Seaman, who felt that his duties should consist mainly of throwing out poor work and submitting the rest to him for selection. Reynolds disagreed. He also tangled with Seaman on his rigid principle of logic in cartoon situations. He was able, on both counts, to bend the usually inflexible Seaman. It was thanks to Reynolds that some of the modern "crazy" humor finally leaked into *Punch*.

Toward the end of his tenure as art editor, Reynolds was stricken with a long illness and was forced to relinquish his duties to George Morrow, who substituted for him for a while and then replaced him as editor in 1930, retaining the job for seven years. Morrow had been a Table member since 1922. He was a shy, talented, hardworking man, as quiet and withdrawn as Tenniel had been. A. P. Herbert maintained that in his years at the Table no one, except the man sitting next to him, had ever heard Morrow utter a single word.

Morrow helped Seaman with the editorial chores after the departures of Milne, Graves, and Lucas and served as a kind of lieutenant to him in the latter years of his editorship. Like Frank Reynolds, he contributed his first cartoon in 1906. As the years passed, he developed a soft, wavy line with a distinctly modern flair, unlike the old wood-engraving style for which *Punch*'s cartoons were famous. His cartoons were cheerful and good-humored, avoiding controversial subjects and cruelty to suburbanites and

THE SWING OF THE PENDULUM.

IT IS PERHAPS JUST AS WELL—

THAT THE TWENTIETH-CENTURY
GIRL,—

AFTER HAVING BOBBED
HER HAIR—

THEN SHINGLED IT—

THEN ADOPTED THE ETON CROP—

NEVER QUITE REACHED THE
DARTMOOR SHAVE—

AND IS NOW STARTING TO GROW IT
(AND HER DRESS) AGAIN.

Lewis Baumer, 1928

golfers. His jokes were based on antique whimsy, light fantasy, and the application of modern standards to situations brought forward from former centuries.

His "Entertainments at Which We Have Not Assisted" showed such scenes as English villagers solemnly involved in the ceremony of "hopping the clod," to determine the prize-winning clodhopper of the year, or a party of chartered accountants competing in a contest of "balancing the books" like circus jugglers.

Another stalwart of the period was Ernest Shepard, who achieved a wide reputation as a superb illustrator of children's books with his delightful drawings for *Winnie the Pooh*, *Now We Are Six*, and Kenneth Grahame's *The Wind in the Willows*. He became a regular contributor of charming, funny socials in 1921, and replaced Raven Hill as second political cartoonist in 1935. Shepard was one of the few Punchites trained at the Royal Academy schools, where he studied in 1896. In another *Punch* intermarriage, Shepard's daughter became E. V. Knox's second wife in 1936.

One of the first *Punch* artists to eschew the hard black ink or pencil line, George Belcher drew in chalk or soft charcoal. Overenthusiastic critics have compared him with Phil May, although there is little similarity between them, except that Belcher often drew costers and charwomen. His funniest cartoons concerned portly, middle-aged, lower-middle-class businessmen. He had, unfortunately, not much sense of humor and depended largely on jokes supplied by other people. He appears to have been luckier with them than Phil May, who once paid five pounds for a collection of drawable jokes, only to discover that they were all cribbed from old copies of *Punch*.

Price quotes a well-known Belcher anecdote in which the artist was given a joke situation that depended entirely on the fact that its principal character was a fishmonger. When the cartoon was finished, it was discovered that Belcher had made him a greengrocer, rendering the joke meaningless. Asked why he had done this, Belcher explained that there was a wonderful greengrocer in his neighborhood whom he had been itching to draw for a long time. He was amazed when he was told the cartoon was not usable.

In support of the stars were the usual featured players: Charles Grave who joined *Punch* in 1912 and specialized in jokes about sailors, ships, and seaports; Bert Thomas, famous for his wartime " 'Arf a mo', Kaiser!" cartoon; and Arthur Watts, who was the first *Punch* artist to abandon the frontal proscenium angle and draw his situations from above, as though he were suspended from a scaffold looking down at the action. D. L. Ghilchick regularly contributed domestic situation socials. The durable Stampa was still there. G. D. Armour carried on a tenuous connection with the days of John Leech with the last of the horse cartoons until Thelwell arrived with his fat ponies a generation later.

Jack Yeats, the younger brother of W. B. Yeats, submitted cartoons as "W. Bird." He was a strong proponent of lunatic humor. Madness lurked in every corner of his drawings. Price called him a genius and a fine serious painter, the comic artist who best gave *Punch* its unique character. I regret to say I am unable to agree. I found Yeats's work clumsy, badly drawn, and not particularly funny. Nor was he popular with anthologists. Bird's work would not be acceptable to most comic magazines today, unlike much of Baumer, Stampa, Ghilchick, and even du Maurier.

J. H. Dowd carried on the du Maurier tradition of jokes based on the funny sayings of children. H. M. Brock and his brother R. H. Brock were funny in the classic, gentlemanly *Punch* tradition of jokes based on officers and clubmen. Claude Sheperson, who was to become an associate of the Royal Academy, and Wallis Mills were merely adequate, perhaps published because of some connection with Seaman. W. L. Ridgewell and G. S. Sherwood were notable principally for breaking away from the traditional *Punch*-type cartoon and developing individual styles of their own, but they were not assigned very much space. W. K. Haselden illustrated the theater page with caricatures of well-known actors that sometimes resembled their models and sometimes did not.

Of course the best and the brightest of the postwar Punchites were E. V. Knox among the writers and Kenneth Bird ("Fougasse") of the artists. Both were to contribute greatly to the history and development of *Punch* as future editors. For this reason I have not lumped them in with others who worked under Seaman. They deserve to be considered separately.

With Seaman gone at long last, there was a splendid opportunity for radical change. The odor of decay had to be aired out of the Bouverie Street corridors. A vigorous young editor was needed to alter the magazine's stodgy character and attract young subscribers. *Punch* could now recruit someone who was attuned to the times and in touch with reality.

Instead of hiring such a man, the proprietors clung to tradition, promoting from the inside as usual, leaning heavily on seniority and what they felt to be suitability. The selection of a new editor had always amounted to a minor shuffling of the seating arrangement of the Table. In this case, the obvious choice was Edmund George Valpy Knox who wrote as "Evoe," a crossword puzzle word meaning "a Bacchanalian cry" and pronounced in the Greek fashion "eee-veee" rather than "eee-voh." The name itself boded ill for the future—an obscure, inside joke to be enjoyed only by classicists or dons.

211

When he moved to the head of the Table, Knox was already fifty-two years old. He had been a contributor and a Seaman favorite for thirty years. It was apparent that *Punch* had calcified into a kind of imitation of an obscure branch of the Civil Service in which the senior person earns promotion (provided he is a gentleman and a graduate of the right schools) regardless of management ability.

Knox was an amiable, sweet-natured man, liked by everyone. The strict schoolroom discipline of Seaman's editorship evaporated, replaced by a kind of lazy informality. If Seaman's *Punch* was run like a sixth form classroom, Knox's *Punch* was like the common room of one of the better colleges, with Knox himself as the beloved professor surrounded by admiring students.

He was the son and grandson of bishops. His ancestry was heavily loaded with rectors, vicars, deans, and chaplains. Two of his brothers were distinguished churchmen. One of them, Monsignor Ronald Knox, was a celebrity in church circles, but not at home, where he was in disgrace for becoming a Catholic. *Punch*'s future editor was educated at Rugby and Corpus Christi College, Oxford. Unlike Seaman, he had never experienced a moment of social insecurity. He was unsnubbable from birth and was accustomed to hearing his senior relatives addressed with great deference as "My Lord." There was no need for Knox to undergo the insecurity, the perpetual defensivenesss, the craving for acceptance and position that characterized Seaman's existence. He wasn't Henry James's Densher or Widmerpool or anyone else except himself. He didn't have to be.

As happens so frequently with the children of clerics, Evoe rebelled against all the sanctity at home and went through a dandy-playboy period at Oxford. He distinguished himself by sneaking a music hall actress, Miss Mabel Love, into his college rooms after hours, earning the admiration of his contemporaries. It was obvious that he would never make a vicar, much less a bishop. His father decided that the best place for him was the Indian Civil Service, a safe distance from home. He was ordered to direct his studies toward that end.

In 1905, while he was still at Oxford, Evoe submitted some verses to *Punch*, receiving ten shillings, sixpence, for them. He determined to try his luck at writing and informed his family that he would not be happy as a civil servant in India or elsewhere. In 1906, after a brief stint as a schoolmaster, he headed for Fleet Street to try his hand at journalism. At some time during that period he appears to have called on Seaman in Bouverie Street. A man who knew how to talk to bishops could hardly have failed to impress Seaman. Although there was nothing open at *Punch*, Seaman helped him get a job as assistant to Sir Douglas Straight of the *Pall Mall Magazine*.

Two years later war was declared. Evoe was thirty-four, a bit elderly for active duty, but he joined the Lincolnshire Regiment and was commissioned a second lieutenant, to the delight of Seaman, who wrote to him, ''I am very glad for your sake (not for my own, except as a matter of *Punch* family pride) that you have got a commission.'' Seaman added happily, in strictest confidence, that he himself was under surveillance by German intelligence.

Although he was only an outside contributor, Knox was now (according to Seaman) one of ''Mr. Punch's young men'' at the battlefront. He soon became eligible for ''Mr. Punch's Roll of Honour'' when a sniper wounded him severely in the shoulder at Passchendaele. In 1919 he was shipped back to England and discharged from the army. To support his family, he took a job at the Ministry of Labour, but spent a good deal of his free time in Bouverie Street doing odd jobs in the hope of landing a permanent job. A year later he was invited to join the Table and soon after that became a member of the regular *Punch* staff.

Two of his Table colleagues have tried to describe Evoe in his *Punch* days. E. V. Lucas remembers him and A. P. Herbert as ''two of the brightest jewels in Mr. Punch's present day (1932) crown.''

> Evoe, whose mordant brilliance both in prose and verse, is one of the most remarkable features of *Punch* today, and whose physiognomical formation is so like that of the busts of Voltaire, has serious depths which it is wise not to stir. Owen Seaman having latterly directed his muse chiefly towards events of the week upon which she turns a steady and sometimes withering gaze, it has been left to Evoe to keep burning the pure flame of parody, and he has been signally successful.

R. G. G. Price compared him with the early Percival Leigh. Commenting on Knox as a contributor, Price wrote:

> At times he was rather too elaborately surprised that there were little people living in new suburbs whom any comparison based on Lemprière would astound. . . . There was too much iteration of the oddness of having to use the Tube, of having to work for one's living, of having few and inefficient servants. However, under the rather factitious boredom and the pose of the young man-about-town hampered by financial stringencies, was an enthusiasm and gaiety, of which at times he seemed rather ashamed. Some very ordinary article about the minor trials of life would suddenly have its surface broken by a kind of mad poetry and it was at these increasingly frequent moments that the differences between Evoe and the other *Punch* writers suddenly appeared.

MY ENJOYMENT OF A PLAY -

ALWAYS CEASES—

WHEN FIREARMS APPEAR ON
THE STAGE.

I NEVER KNOW IF THEY'RE
GOING TO GO OFF—

OR, IF SO, WHEN THEY'RE
GOING TO GO OFF—

OR, IF SO, HOW OFTEN THEY'R
GOING TO GO OFF—

OR, IF SO, WHAT SORT OF
NOISE THEY'LL MAKE WHEN
THEY DO GO OFF—

OR, IF SO, IF I SHALL JUMP
WHEN THEY DO GO OFF—

OR IF, WHEN I'M ALL BRACE
UP AND READY FOR THEM T
GO OFF—

THEY WON'T GO OFF -

OR IF, WHEN I LEAST EXPECT
THEM TO GO OFF—

THEY - - AND OF COURSE
THAT'S JUST WHEN THEY
DO GO OFF!!!

Fougasse, 1928

Bernard Hollowood calls him a quiet genius with a flair for spotting talented newcomers. Reginald Pound, the biographer of A. P. Herbert, referred to him as a "man of rueful countenance and subtle humour" who patiently endured classification as a comic versifier although he was an accomplished poet, "almost a banned term in the [*Punch*)] office." Herbert makes very little mention of Knox in his autobiography. There was apparently bad blood between them going back to 1924, when Herbert first joined *Punch* and Knox objected strenuously to the fifty pounds a week Seaman had offered him as being much too high. Herbert never forgave him.

When Evoe first submitted verses to *Punch*, they were imitations of Calverly and Barry Pain, which he explained away with the principle that imitation is good for beginning writers because it increases the vocabulary. Later his work could very easily have been taken for Seaman's, although it was less robust and lacked Seaman's frequent effusions of righteous indignation.

Seaman was delighted with Evoe's work, accepting its similarity to his own poetry (which Bernard Shaw once said "could have been written by a contractor") as a sign of great talent. He was able to overlook Evoe's Liberal tendencies as youthful exuberance. (Evoe later became a Churchillian Tory.) Seaman assigned him drama criticism, general articles, and (to his dismay) the coverage of the Wembley Empire Exhibition of 1924, with Raven Hill as his illustrator. In addition to his wide-ranging *Punch* duties, he published twelve books of verses, essays, and parodies before he became editor in 1932. His parodies, collected in the volume *Parodies Regained* in 1921, were very funny and popular with the readers. They include a remarkable account of a golf match, narrated in the style of John Masefield, and takeoffs of Tennyson, Walter de la Mare, and many others. Edgar Rice Burroughs, delighted with Knox's Tarzan parody, wrote to him, "You have saved me from oblivion!"

On July 15, 1931, Seaman, who had announced his decision to retire, published a poem called "To Mr. Punch on His Ninetieth Birthday," praising the famous puppet for "changing not his style" and for adhering to standards laid down nearly a century earlier. In November 1932, he took his seat at the head of the Table for the last time. He gave his blessing to "the friend and colleague who succeeds me." There was no laughter. Jokes were not attempted or even thought of.

The proprietors (with Seaman's approval) offered Evoe a ten-year contract at three thousand pounds a year with bonuses for special numbers and almanacks and, for the first time in *Punch* history, an assured retirement pension. After thirty years of association with all facets of the magazine's operations, he had no trouble in assuming its leadership. There were many things on which he and Seaman were not in complete agreement, but Evoe made almost no immediate changes out of respect to his predecessor. He felt that radical alterations would be insulting to Seaman's memory and allowed the magazine to move on in its usual way.

In Evoe's time, *Punch* improved in some ways but declined in others. Unlike Seaman, he was a delegator. He hated detail, preferring to choose an efficient and trustworthy staff to handle it for him, with as little supervision as possible. The *Punch* office came to resemble a relaxed gentlemen's club, its members dozing, reading, or daydreaming at their desks. Sometimes a visitor would find no one there at all. It came to life only as press night approached and the staff realized that there was a strong possibility that the proofs would not be ready in time.

Sex jokes were still banned. As far as Knox was concerned, their time had not yet come for *Punch*, although in America *Esquire* had acquired a huge readership with the naughtinesses of Peter Arno, E. Simms Campbell, and a group of uninhibited writers. *Punch* had to remain a family magazine for a while longer.

Of the senior writers, almost nobody remained from the Seaman days except Herbert, who appears to have had the knack of getting along with all editors, except possibly Hollowood; and Eric Keown, who had developed from a *Granta* recruit into a valuable staff member. Evoe added H. F. Ellis and Richard Mallett to do general writing and criticism. Mallett was appointed to succeed the departed E. V. Lucas as movie critic. Keown took over the "Essence of Parliament," and J. Thorp was replaced on the theater beat by Douglas Woodruff and later by Keown. The most startling innovation was the inclusion of a crossword puzzle, written by Evoe himself. It was a failure, some said because it was too difficult and others, because it was allotted so little space that the squares and clues were too small for *Punch*'s elderly readers to see properly.

Evoe perked up the ponderous "Charivaria" and shortened the captions under the cartoons, sometimes eliminating them entirely. Reaching out for new blood he found the cartoonist "Paul Crum" (Roger Pettiward) and convinced Heath Robinson, A. E. Coppard, and Lord Dunsany to contribute. One of his finest acquisitions was Graham Laidler, who drew remarkable cartoons under the pseudonym "Pont." E. M. Delafield, later famous as a novelist, joined the staff, and contributions came in from Alfred Noyes, author of *The Highwayman*.

Attracting young readers was an acute problem in the thirties because of the appearance of a new dimension in humorous journalism. The *New Yorker* had caught on, on both sides of the Atlantic. In London especially it was fashionable to decry the stuffiness of poor old *Punch* and to point out that one was only amused by the *New Yorker*, which was, after all, eighty years younger and, better still, imported. There was snob value in the thirties in *not* reading *Punch*.

But *Punch* had fought and won battles before and would continue to do so. Evoe turned his attention to larger problems. He took over as editor at the peak of the depression. He won for himself the reputation of the softest touch on Fleet Street. There was always a handout if not a bit of work for free-lance artists and writers who were down on their luck. His own writing, now that he had nobody left to imitate, developed into good, high-level magazine prose, editorial comment of the best kind, and sturdy little poems about news that had cropped up during the current week. *Punch* and Evoe were far ahead of the government in condemning fascism and dictators.

Outside contributors were encouraged to submit work, but Knox insulated himself from them. For some reason he refused to meet them personally, perhaps fearing a request for the loan of a fiver he knew he would be unable to refuse. Many good outsiders, interpreting his aloofness and refusal to praise their work as disapproval, went elsewhere. This always surprised him. He felt that people capable of really good work did not need to be told they were good.

Evoe retained the short comic "typical *Punch*" articles of personal misadventure but followed the *New Yorker* in the new prose style of lunatic humor (à la Perelman) which Seaman had considered too American for *Punch*. He discontinued the practice of recruiting good men while they were still students and training them in the ways of *Punch*, which Seaman had introduced before the war. He was incapable of planning for the future at all, perhaps the result of his ecclesiastical upbringing. He had unshakable faith that God would provide *Punch* with the necessary geniuses generation after generation.

Except for the stars mentioned *supra* and a few others such as Hugh Kingsmill, who wrote the book page, and Ernest Bramah, who contributed a few of his Kai Lung stories in the forties, the staff recruited by Evoe was commonplace. A careless copy reader could easily have interchanged the initials or pseudonyms under the poems and stories and no one would ever have been the wiser. The typical *Punch* article was written by typical *Punch* writers, molded into comical shapes like those unfortunate children who were said to have been stolen by gypsies and forced to grow up inside of oddly shaped containers so that they could be sold as circus freaks.

On the permanent staff, there were two notable exceptions to this rule. They were J. B. Boothroyd and R. G. G. Price, author of that superb history of *Punch* which is practically the sole source (except for heavily

"I KEEP THINKING IT'S TUESDAY."

Paul Crum, 1937

J. W. Taylor, 1948

"Are you the maître d'hôtel that this is à la?"

biased autobiographies) of inside information about the magazine since Spielmann's book in 1896, excepting, of course, the magazine's own historic pages.

Boothroyd, who is talented enough to have survived the purges and bloodlettings of Muggeridge and William Davis, joined *Punch* in the forties and started out with his successful "Home Guard Goings On" series. His was the humor of outrage. In his essays, a perfectly normal narrator, not the silly-ass chronicler so often depicted in *Punch* articles, but a reasonable man, is done in through no fault of his own by the deplorable ignorance or the lunacy of the world surrounding him. Boothroyd could find funny situations anywhere. His early work reintroduced what had become cliché situations and made them fresh and amusing, as his contemporary Robert Benchley was to do in America. A friend gets wonderful treatment from head waiters and hall porters, taxi drivers and other difficult flunkies while Boothroyd, following his friend's technique, is ignored and insulted by them. How is this possible, the narrator wonders, infuriated but keeping, as always, his gentlemanly temper. Life, in Boothroyd's pieces, was one long frustration. Never mind getting ahead, how does one simply keep one's head above water?

By the fifties Boothroyd had become the most proficient writer of typical *Punch* pieces of all time; except possibly for Wodehouse and R. G. G. Price. He also wrote excellent light verse, topical, up-to-date, and funny. His poem, "And Now . . . ," describes the rumba craze of the thirties, which maddened sensitive radio listeners for years.

"AND NOW . . . "

It's a *rum-*
Ba band another *rum-*
Ba band a never *slum-*
Ba band there's any *num-*
Ba of *rum-*
Ba bands
    Shicker-shicker-shicker.
Turn on the radio,
Mammoth set or midget,
All you'll ever get
Is the everlasting fidget
Of a *rum-*
Ba band another *rum-*
Ba band a pluck and *strum-*
Ba band with a
Shicker-shicker-shicker-shicker

219

Shee shicker-shick and a
Ticker-ticker-ticker-ticker
Tee ticker-tick and a
Boom and a nobble and a clang
And a bang
And a chatter and a natter
Let it clatter
Let it shatter
Let it spatter
Doesn't matter
Getting flatter
It's a *rum*-
Ba band another *rum*-
Ba band another *rum*-
Ba band another *rum*-
Ba band another RUM!
 Shicker-shicker-shicker
Turn on the radio,
Mammoth set or midget,
All you seem to get
Is the orchestrated fidget
Of a *rum*-
Ba band another *rum*-
Ba band another *rum*-
Ba band, there's any *num*-BA . . .
To play the *rum*-BA
Can't someone have the rumba banned?
 (*Shicker-schick*)

When Boothroyd wrote the poem, the rumba was the equivalent of the 1970s rock music. It was impossible to get anything else on the radio. No one who lived then can read the poem without hearing the dreadful rhythm and tapping a reluctant foot.

With Boothroyd writing delightful comedy and Evoe providing counterpoint with verses like

Tom, Tom the piper's son
 Stole a pig and away he run,
The pig was missed, and Tom was hissed
 And sent to a psychiatrist.

Punch could not have been all bad, especially with R. G. G. Price to back them up.

Like Boothroyd, Price is a survivor of many Nights of the Long Knives, and he has lasted on sheer talent. His articles have the ability to adapt to the comic standards of the times. While both Boothroyd and Price still write weekly pieces for *Punch* today, a reader seeing an issue for the first time would never know that they have been with *Punch* for nearly forty years. Anyone trying to place the *Punch* staff in context would probably rate them as contemporaries of Alan Coren's, although both were popular contributors before the present editor was born. Somehow the *Punch* stuffiness passed them by.

Price, like Herbert, Milne, and many other *Punch* writers, recalls wanting to write for *Punch* from his early childhood. Arriving in 1942, after a bad nervous breakdown (he had been an outside contributor since 1935) he got off the ground with the "H. J." series, supposedly written by an eccentric scientist who rambled on about his family in a curious sort of English that the readers loved. After the series ran out Price continued to maintain his high humorous standard, including a touch of the lunatic, and mercifully avoiding the golf course and the other treacherous quicksands of the *Punch* article. His short piece "Quiet Pleasures Are the Best," about an evening at a rectory during which each member of the Baddlebrig family is required to construct and read aloud a piece of poetry, is one of the funniest things I read during my *Punch* researches. Price's schoolmaster reminiscences based on his own experiences as a middle-school teacher are delightful. No one can read his review of *The Blackboard Jungle*, in which he compares the experiences of the harassed ghetto teacher with his supposed own adventures at the hands of horrible English schoolboys, without laughing aloud.

For a long while Price shared the book review page with Anthony Powell as well as contributing weekly articles or poems. His *History of Punch* is beautifully written and invaluable to seekers after *Punch* esoterica. Unfortunately, it suffers from a perfectly natural flaw, the fact that Price himself was and is an active Table member and that many of the people he was writing about in the fifties were still alive when he wrote the book. One remembers Thackeray saying of Jerrold, "How can you carry on a feud with a man if you have to eat with him every Wednesday?"

Except for Knox and Boothroyd and occasional outsiders like Alfred Noyes and Walter de la Mare, the versifiers in the Evoe era can be discounted as interchangeable lightweights. To take a featherweight subject that isn't really very funny and put it into a verse meter doesn't make it any funnier. Patrick Barrington, Justin Richardson, and Richard Usborne could easily have been done away with (and, in fact, in the sixties and seventies a great deal of typical Punch verse *was* done away with). Richardson achieved some popularity with his "Phoney Phleet" series, which dealt with the same joke repeated over and over again in different

"Tell Daddy you're sorry."

Norman Mansbridge, 1950

ways. R. P. Lister depended on tricks. In one poem ("The Human Race") he dug up twenty-four line endings to rhyme with the word *race*. It was clever but it was not poetry. Nor was it humor.

Of the writers, Richard Mallett and H. F. Ellis were better than most. Like Price and Knox, Ellis came from a schoolteaching background, and his series "Assistant Masters, Are They Insane?" was very popular. He was actually, like Eric Keown, a product of the Seaman days, but he did not hit his stride until he was given his head by Knox. He and Mallett shared the assistant editor's duties when the aging and infirm C. L. Graves retired.

Ellis had his special subjects—rugby, which he loved to play, and schoolteaching. He was capable of writing about practically anything, and he was funnier than most of the thirties Punchites, though not as funny as Boothroyd or Price. There was a Wodehousian flavor to his stories that just missed Wodehouse. He wrote a piece in 1948 about washing dishes ("For Men in Aprons") that was made into a highly successful musical revue skit. He had a marvelous knack for opening sentences that seized the reader's interest and put him into a receptive mood, ready to laugh at what was to follow, a technique often used in movie comedies when, for example, the camera shifts rapidly from bulky Oliver Hardy to the banana peel lying ahead of him and back again, telegraphing what is to happen without spoiling it.

Richard Mallett, who did not survive the Davis purges, had been a free-lance journalist since he was sixteen. He was an omnivorous reader, remarkably retentive, and well-versed in art, music, and theater as well as literature and, later on, films. In America as well as in England he was recognized as one of the finest film critics in the world. Price called him the best English parodist since Beerbohm, but I found him no better, if no worse, than many of the *Punch* parodists and certainly not as good as Beerbohm. But he was extraordinarily funny, especially when playing fast and loose with the English language or maintaining a delicate balance between craziness and reality.

Mallett is said to have invented the technique of criticism by parody (although a few attribute this to Evoe). Some of his parodies were magnificent, but he was not able to keep up a constant flow of excellence. He worked hard at it. Some of his pieces are said to have taken as much as a year to write. It was Mallett who wrote most of the superb parody of the *New Yorker* that appeared in *Punch* in 1954.

His poetry was excellent—a cut above Burnand but below Hood—often depending on puns. He had the ability to create a completely lunatic character who was very close to reality and wrap an essay around him that was at once wry and funny. For example, his "Amos Intolerable" about a man who works for weeks polishing epigrams to drop at parties, and who, instead of falling on his face, succeeds in impressing and infuriating everyone at the same time.

Jefferson Farjeon and Geoffrey Williams wrote schoolboy humor around their juvenile characters, Smith Minor and Molesworth respectively, both of whom delighted the older readers. G. H. Vallins, William Kean Seymour, and St. John Hankin were parodists but not first-class ones. In any event they were overshadowed by Knox and Mallett. Their humor doesn't come off in the seventies. H. W. Metcalfe was a one-joke man.

One of the typical *Punch* writers of the period was T. S. Watt, who did occasional verse and short, funny bits about things close enough to home for everyone to understand and enjoy. His "Noël Noël" celebrates the attempt of Big Business to be folksy—a bank manager instructs tellers and cashiers in false heartiness for the Christmas season. Colin Howard, another typical *Punch* writer, specialized in the comic O. Henry type of story—a domestic chronicle with a surprise, funny ending exploding in the last few paragraphs. An elephant follows him home from the circus and he finally gets rid of it when there it is back again. His Saint Bernard pretends to be deaf and has to be tricked into acting in a film. D. H. Barber is the silly man who catches his train at the last minute forgetting that he is carrying an egg in his hand, to the amusement of his fellow passengers and the chagrin of his office boy who inadvertantly mails it to a customer. He and a friend spend a strenuous morning moving all the furniture in order to surprise his wife by turning a worn carpet around, only to find that a local handyman has already done it the day before.

B. A. Young, who still appears frequently in *Punch*'s pages, is a Conservative and former writer of radio scripts. He writes articles of ironical disapproval, less loony than Boothroyd's and also less quivering with outrage. A. A. Milne's niece, Angela, who wrote as "Ande," was *Punch*'s first women's-interest writer. She could be very funny, but would go off on unfunny tangents periodically. She wrote verse and prose and was very popular during World War II. Mary Dunn created an amusing character, Lady Addle, an absurd peeress whose "memoirs" delighted readers in the forties.

Probably the best of the cartoonists during Evoe's reign was Graham Laidler, who used the pseudonym "Pont" and drew the "British Character" series from 1934. He was one of a very few artists to be tied up in an exclusive contract by the proprietors, most others having the freedom to peddle work rejected by *Punch* wherever they liked. Pont, when he signed up with *Punch*, was in precarious health and the proprietors were not really taking much of a risk. In fact, he died at the age of thirty-two. He was already seriously ill when he attended the London School of Architecture, and he had to spend his winters either in the Austrian Alps or in Arizona. He had a tremendous vogue in his years at *Punch*, a tribute, he thought, to the British public's vaunted ability to laugh at its own foibles.

Perhaps even a greater vogue was that enjoyed by Rowland Emmett, who captured the public imagination with his fanciful locomotives, which first appeared in 1939. His wonderful steam engines, "Nellie Neptune" and "Wildgoose," were constructed of curlicues and twine, beer barrels and tea kettles, and decorated with flowers and divers' helmets. They were such a success that Emmett was besieged by advertising agencies to design fantastic machines to promote all sorts of commercial products. Today his drawings are hung in the Smithsonian Institution, the Chicago Museum of Science and Industry, and the Ontario Science Center.

Asked by art critic Bevis Hillier why he chose the locomotive as the vehicle for his fantasies, Emmett replied that it could not be otherwise. "What is more romantic than, say, the late sun burnishing the Afternoon Slow Stopper to St. Torpid's Creek . . . luminous mists up to the axle-boxes, and perhaps first and second seagull obligato?" Apparently Hillier understood and did not press the point any further.

The funniest of the regular social cartoonists were Anton and Paul Crum. "Anton" was the name used by the busy partnership of Mrs. Antonia Yeoman and her brother H. Underwood Thompson. Their jokes are still as fresh and funny as they were in the thirties and forties. They dealt in shady characters: spivs, confidence men, climbers. Crum, whose real name was Roger Pettiward, was killed early in World War II. He began to contribute in 1936 and was responsible for *Punch*'s move into a new kind of low-key fantastic humor that mystified the older readers. His most famous joke showed two hippopotamuses sunk up to the their ears in a jungle stream. One is saying to the other, "I keep thinking it's Tuesday." For some reason, this galvanized the *Punch* readership into violent action. Letters poured in saying it was incomprehensible and asking what the joke was. An equal number of letters arrived from people who said that the cartoon had made them roll about with helpless laughter for hours. It was another of those *Punch* anomalies that characterized the magazine's progress through the years.

Norman Mansbridge and David Langdon are still drawing as much as ever and both are members of the Table. Langdon, who claims to have introduced the open mouth into the funny cartoon to show who was speaking, has contributed to the *New Yorker* as well as other comic papers. Mansbridge is a realistic artist whose jokes speak for themselves.

225

Redigested Digest

ARTICLES OF LASTING COMFORT

THE WORLD'S MOST CROONED-OVER MAGAZINE

Punch *parodies. (Above, 1950; facing page,
1954; following page, 1971)*

PUNCH ★ Apr.7,1954 THE Price 2+ cents

N★W·Y★RK★R

Punch goes PLAYBOY

DO NOT TOUCH

"Ionicus" (J. C. Armitage) and "Acanthus" (F. Hoar) did clear, realistic socials. L. H. Starke specialized in peculiar monks and pompous executives. L. H. Siggs was the suburbia expert, and "Douglas" (Douglas England) illustrated the "Charivaria" page with Fougasse and did full page and color artwork. W. A. Sillince and William Scully were chalk and charcoal artists. Sillince, perhaps the funnier of the two, drew dons and businessmen. Scully's cartoons bore a strong resemblance to Peter Arno's, if Arno had been censored to remove any suggestions of sexuality. Russell Brockbank, who would later become art editor, was probably the most technically proficient of the group. He loved vehicles, as Emmett did, but refused to make them fanciful. He insisted on accuracy and added tiny details to his cars and airplanes as a kind of inside joke for collectors and antiquarians.

J. W. Taylor drew children, harassed little men, and wonderfully funny animals. Best of all, with the possible exception of Brockbank, was Fougasse, who would become Evoe's art editor in 1937 and who was responsible for a great many changes in *Punch*'s format and attitude toward cartoon humor.

In 1939 the Nazis rolled into Poland. Once again *Punch* was faced with a world war.

When Seaman went, *Punch* did not look like having a
future. If Evoe's Editorship had not left behind it something
healthy and capable of growth, no amount of galvanising and
altering would have saved the paper. . . . *Punch* was ready,
perhaps over-ready, for big and apparent changes, but after
Seaman it had probably needed more than anything a period
of convalescence, of almost imperceptible but steady re-
fashioning, and of cultivating the imagination.

—*R. G. G. Price*

n 1941 *Punch* celebrated its
hundredth birthday. It should have been a time for rejoicing: for special
editions and celebrations and acres of space in the press. Unfortunately,
public attention was turned elsewhere. British soldiers were dying on
foreign battlefields. A few months after Mr. Punch's centennial, Britain
would declare war on Japan. Sixty days later Singapore would surrender
to the Japanese. Eight months after that a British army would land in
French North Africa. Winston Churchill, often a favorite target of *Punch*
cartoonists, replaced Chamberlain as prime minister. Evoe's son was
captured by the Japanese and held in a prison camp for four years. How
bitterly Seaman would have envied Knox if he had still been alive. What a
subject for stiff upper lip poems! Knox, who had asked to be excused from
writing funny pieces for a year when his first wife died in 1935, did not
share his personal tragedy with the public.

He wandered aimlessly about in the blackout during air raids, with a
bottle of whisky in his pocket in case someone might need a drink while
the proprietors made ready to evacuate the Bouverie Street building. The
Table was sent to a secret destination in the country, like the treasures of
the British Museum. An emergency office was set up in Manchester, and
another was offered in the United States if it should be necessary to
withdraw before a Nazi invasion. For the first time in a century the
magazine missed an issue, because of the fuel shortage. An old friend
came to the rescue—the *Times* printed the cartoons that would have
appeared in *Punch* that week.

In World War I Seaman's Bouverie Street Roughriders had fancied themselves a kind of guerilla fighting unit. Under Evoe the magazine was more like an elderly ex-officer, knitting mufflers and collecting wastepaper and scrap iron for the war effort. The old hate-the-Germans cartoons gave way to mild jokes about the exigencies of the home front: rationing, air raid wardens, blackouts, and Americans. *Punch* was still a prime morale raiser for British troops abroad, as it had been thirty years earlier. But now thousands of English-speaking, foreign soldiers, to whom the British Isles were very much ''overseas,'' covered the English landscape.

It was during this period that I first saw *Punch*. Like so many other American soldiers, I was barely twenty, three thousand miles from home, surrounded by strangers with strange customs, debarred from steaks and ice cream, bombed, shot at, bewildered, and very, very lonely. Many of us had never lived anywhere except with our parents and had never had an adult experience outside of college, where, we were told, we were expected to behave like grown men, but were not told how. We were turned loose in London with huge wads of money that wouldn't buy anything except whisky and weird strumpets with beehive hairdos and shrill unpleasant voices. We were cut off from news, except for letters that took weeks to arrive. We never saw an American paper or magazine except for *Yank* and the *Stars and Stripes*. But we could get English papers, the *Mirror* and the *Times*, the *Daily Mail*, and, of course, blessed, intelligible *Punch*. The cartoons poked fun at us, but we loved it. They were funny. There was no question but that we were a huge, poorly disciplined gang of ruffians whose appetites rivaled those of Barry MacKenzie, but we needed a laugh almost as much as the poor devils the Japanese had captured in Hong Kong and Singapore, and we got it from *Punch*.

I was not aware, of course, when I sneaked off to the mess early on Wednesdays to be the first to laugh at Pont or Bateman or Fougasse that there was in fact a Table and that I would one day sit down at it between Boothroyd, whose adventures in pursuit of hard-to-get cigarettes and razor blades I so enjoyed, and R. G. G. Price, whose ''H. J.'' had got himself involved with the League of Small Housewives.

Evoe was then in his sixties. He had expressed a desire to retire (flatly refusing to write an autobiography when he was asked by publishers to do so). But once more all the talented young men had gone to war. Dozens of *Punch* artists and writers sent their copy in every week, no matter what remote branches of the service they were working in, but there was no one available to take over the editorship on a permanent basis. Evoe agreed to stay on for the duration.

Evoe and Fougasse had served as officers in the first war, and both had suffered serious wounds. This time there was no reason for *Punch*'s editors to apologize for not being in uniform. The second war was bigger

231

". . . coming over to entertain the American troops, or something . . ."

Punch *and the American GIs in World War II. (Above, Rowland Emmett, 1943; below, Frank Reynolds, 1943)*

"Doc. Wilbur for the Red Sox delivered the pay-off blow—which spelt curtains for the Dodgers——"

than the first one, and there was a bigger *Punch* in which to write about it. Mr. Punch had to reach out to British troops all over the world.

A major source of bewilderment to the aged Sir Bernard Partridge, who was doing the big cut, was the rapidity with which the battle lines changed. In the first war, British and German troops could be counted on to engage in bitter stalemates that lasted for month before an eventual and predictable victory. Now Partridge would prepare a cartoon celebrating the taking of a strategically important beachhead, only to find by press night that it was already old news, that British troops had established six more beachheads and advanced fifty miles. Fleet Street whispered that *Punch* kept in readiness a drawing of the British lion fiercely pouncing on a blank rectangle in which the name of the latest victory could be quickly lettered if necessary. For years critics had been suggesting that there were no military or political matters that *Punch* could not handle adequately with the caption ''For This Relief Much Thanks'' and a drawing of the Walrus and the Carpenter.

Evoe stayed on long enough to point the magazine in the right direction after the war and then became the first *Punch* editor to retire of his own volition. In 1949 he settled happily into his Hampstead cottage for a life of scholarly peace and quiet. He continued to lunch at the Table on Wednesdays, and the Punchites were always glad to see him there. He disapproved mightily when the magazine was acquired by United Newspapers and went home muttering dire predictions about the future of British journalism. He died in 1971.

Faced once again with a brave new world purged by war, the proprietors were given a second chance in 1949 to bring in a vigorous, youthful editor with new ideas. The lesson of the twenties was still fresh in their minds. They remembered what had happened when an Edwardian editor had been unable to cope with the Jazz Age. Evoe's lovable qualities had not improved circulation and *Punch* had been saved from a further decline only by another war.

Once again they let the chance go by. Sticking to tradition, they went to the Table and consulted the seniority charts. The choice fell, for the first time in *Punch* history, on an artist, Cyril Kenneth Bird, whose cartoons, signed with the pseudonym ''Fougasse,'' had been appearing in the magazine for more than thirty years.

Fougasse was another Seaman man. His first cartoon, ''War's Brutalizing Influence,'' appeared in the July 16, 1916, issue. It showed a spit-and-polish young officer metamorphosing into a fierce, unshaven, murderous brute capable of taking on a German division single-handed. Fougasse had drawn it lying flat on his back in bed, where he was recuperating from a spinal fracture suffered when a Turkish shell fragment struck him at Gallipoli.

Because of his pseudonym, many people believed that he was wounded by a mine. A *fougasse* was a treacherously undependable kind of French land mine used in World War I which might or might not go off at any time. But Bird chose the name because the description seemed to fit his cartoons, which also might or might not hit their mark.

Fougasse was the son of a cricket-playing wine merchant who gave his son a good middle-class education at Farnborough Park School and Cheltenham College, and talked him out of art and into engineering because the family could not raise enough money to keep him until he was able to support himself as a painter. He was graduated as a civil engineer in 1908. In the next few years he moved at moderate but acceptable speed up the career ladder, traveling for reputable engineering firms and studying photoengraving and lithography on the side. In 1914 he secured a commission as a second lieutenant in the Royal Engineers and was posted to a naval submarine base in Scotland. There he met and married the daughter of one William Hay Caldwell, a gentleman celebrated for being the first to discover that the duck-billed platypus lays eggs.

Sent to the Dardanelles in 1915, he was severely wounded and sent home to be mustered out. His health prevented his return to the active outdoor life of an engineer, and he had no money to support his young wife. After an abortive attempt at writing, he began to draw, studying techniques from a correspondence course he found in a newspaper advertisement. *Punch*'s art editor, F. H. Townsend, liked his work and got it past Seaman.

Fougasse's style was new to *Punch*, although he admitted being influenced by J. Priestman Atkinson. He drew with odd, jerky lines, "as a canary would draw if it could," first war cartoons and then upper-middle-class jokes about gentlemen's clubs, reunion dinners, golf, cricket, and bridge. He was said to be the inventor (with the help of Atkinson) of the episodic joke, the comic strip series of pictures leading up to a punch line or situation. There is some question as to whether he or Bateman first popularized this style. Bevis Hillier maintains that his draughtsmanship was inferior to Bateman's, and, in fact, it was, though Bateman was no Keene or Phil May. However, Fougasse was funnier than Bateman.

Like May, Fougasse was a devotee of simplicity. He would draw dozens of sketches for a single cartoon, eliminating unnecessary lines until he had reduced a drawing to its absolute minimum, Then he would do the same with the captions. After his work began to appear in *Punch*, his popularity increased at surprising speed. In only four years he was a *Punch* star, and collections of his cartoons in book form were selling very well. E. V. Lucas wrote the preface to his *Gallery of Games* in 1921, and Milne introduced his *Drawn at Venture* in 1922. Offers came in from advertising agencies for posters and magazine and newspaper commercial art.

In 1937 Fougasse succeeded George Morrow as art editor. He modernized the traditional layout, removing the lines between and around the page columns, changing typefaces, increasing white space, and in general making the magazine more attractive and less like a Victorian antique. When World War II came, he was approached by the government to do posters of the ''Loose Lips Sink Ships'' type. His ''Careless Talk'' posters, in which Hitler, Goering, and Goebbels appeared in all sorts of odd places (sitting behind you on a bus, riding near you on an escalator, always listening . . .), were immensely popular. They brought to the attention of the thousands of young men and women in uniform the need for security consciousness. In addition to his other work, he was also an air raid warden, a position fraught with comic possibilities for cartoons.

In 1949 he accepted the proprietors' invitation to become editor, moving to the head of the Table, which had meant little to him since he was a moderate eater, a teetotaler, and a nonsmoker. To celebrate his new appointment he added a red border to the traditional Doyle cover, also touching up Mr. Punch's costume, Toby's collar and hat band, and the jackets of some of the books in the picture. The cover advertisements disappeared and were either placed inside or done away with entirely.

Fougasse was never entirely at home at the head of the Table. He was aware of his limitations as a literary editor, and he was homesick for the art editor's studio with its clutter of sketches and layouts. His editorial policy was simply defined: Keep the magazine as Evoe had left it. He made H. F. Ellis his chief of staff for literary matters and turned over all responsibility for the writing end of *Punch* to him.

The effect that Fougasse's appointment as editor had on Ellis can only be imagined. To be passed over and then immediately given the duties of the senior job without the glory and the perquisites must have been painful to him. He was an established writer and a good one. He could certainly have gone to another magazine or supported himself as a freelancer. Instead, he showed the old *Punch* spirit, the intense loyalty that went back to the days of Lemon and Brooks. Four years later, when Fougasse was succeeded by Malcolm Muggeridge, he would be passed over again, but he does not seem to have harbored any animosity against the proprietors.

Sensing a mystery, perhaps an intramural civil war of the sort that has plagued *Punch* since the Thackeray-Jerrold days, I determined to ferret

THE MONOPOLIST

"How *dare* anybody but me protect anybody?—and what's more, bring them food!"

Bernard Partridge, 1941

Bernard Partridge, 1941

WILL·O'·THE·WISP

out the cause of Ellis's failure to reach the top position, for which he seemed so eminently eligible. I was amazed to find that *Punch* in 1953 had made a complete about-face, reversing the policy of a century. It was not that Ellis had not gone to the right schools, but the opposite. He was passed over because he was too much of a gentleman.

Peter Dickinson, the novelist, who came to the staff and the Table in 1952 and who was himself considered as a possible editor at one time, wrote to me in February 1978, that in selecting Muggeridge to replace Fougasse the proprietors

> were reacting (unconsciously I think) to what was really a class problem, but which they saw as a readership problem. . . . Between the wars our public school (i.e. private school) system had been producing far more people who thought of themselves as gentlemen—honorary leisured class, even though they had to work—than society could support. The second war concealed this for a while, but as peace came society changed, and all these people, who had been our natural readership, tended to put their heads into the sand, and so did we. So we had a paper which was mostly very elegantly done about nothing much. The management, who actually had to sell the thing, were aware of the changes, but when they tried to influence the editorial it only made the editorial retreat yet further. There was a strong undertone that they were gentlemen and somehow the management were not. I now see that even if Muggeridge had not been available it was unlikely that H. F. Ellis (who could have done it very well) would have got the job.

The unfortunate Ellis, who was born half a century and two wars too late, improved the literary standards of the magazine by going back to Seaman's system of finding good young writers in the universities and training them. He also followed Seaman's lead in taking on most of the editing himself, riding herd on lazy writers, rejecting substandard work. Outsiders were invited to come in and discuss their work, to meet the staff, and to participate in parties and outings. Ellis had something of the flair shared by Lemon and Seaman, the ability to spot a winner in the embryonic stage. The credit went to Fougasse.

With Ellis established as his right hand, Fougasse chose Russell Brockbank as his art editor, and began to work on polishing the "elegance" that Peter Dickinson spoke of in his letter. Stories were shortened, and more dialogue was inserted in them along with an almost *Cosmopolitan*-like increase in the use of italics. To the dismay of the staff, who expected an avalanche of complaints from readers, he dropped the Cartoon Junior, the second political cartoon that Raven Hill and Ernest Shepard had drawn for so many decades. To everyone's surprise, there were no complaints. Nobody seemed to notice it was gone.

Fougasse pulled the teeth of the political cartoons. He felt that it was better to mollify subscribers than to be partisan. *Punch* was, after all, a humor magazine and not a political organ as it had been in the nineteenth century. Mr. Punch timidly walked a middle-of-the-road tightrope. In Price's words,

> There was a genuine difficulty here. Roughly half the population supported the Conservatives and half the Socialists. If *Punch* were to be a National Institution, should it take sides? It might have found it easier simply to satirise the weaknesses of both Parties, a plague o' both your houses attitude. Alternatively would it have been necessarily any less of an Institution if it had taken a point of view and stuck to it? After all, this is what it had done at its beginning. The decision was left suspended and *Punch* was, even more than it had been, a Conservative organ without the courage of Conservative convictions.

B. A. Young was appointed assistant editor. Boothroyd was directed to see what he could do about the "Charivaria" page. Kingsmill left the book review page, which was now assigned to Richard Mallett, with Eric Keown and R. G. G. Price to help him. Russell Courtney (Guy Eden) continued the "Essence of Parliament," which he had covered under Knox; but he was not permitted to take sides on controversial issues, so the feature was virtually redundant. Readers could get a better picture of parliamentary doings by reading the *Times*.

Logic and beautiful draughtsmanship vanished from the cartoons. Fougasse demanded that they be funny. Everything else was secondary. "Shorn of glamour" he wrote, "pictorial humor is simply a shorthand by which humorous ideas may be absorbed by the reader with the minimum of effort." He maintained that a man with a good sense of humor and no skill made a better cartoonist than a clever artist with no sense of humor. He insisted on strict propriety, carefully censoring any hint of the risqué, no matter how faint, in prose, poetry, or artwork. B. A. Young remembers him rejecting the title "Country Matters" which seemed to him, for some reason, to be a trifle off-color. He painted out the navels in other people's beach scenes because he found them indecent.

Cartoons about the stupidities of the poor, of miners, of farmers, Irishmen, blacks, and other minorities were done away with. During Fougasse's editorship cartoons dealt with courting couples, unfortunate clubmen, angry golfers breaking or throwing away their clubs, wives infuriated by husbands who read the newspaper at breakfast, and skaters falling through the ice.

To keep *Punch* from becoming nothing but a joke book, Fougasse introduced some serious items. The two center pages were devoted to a serious poem, usually by R. C. Scriven, celebrating the beauties of the Yorkshire countryside or some similar subject, and illustrated by Ernest Shepard, now at loose ends without the second cartoon. Two double pages were devoted to serious articles, dealing with matters of current interest. One of them usually dealt with commerce and industry and was written by Bernard Hollowood. The other, describing newsworthy matters of social significance, was written by Keown. Boothroyd, Young, P. M. Hubbard, and Angela Milne shared a weekly feature describing a visit to some area of current interest. In due course, after much criticism, the serious poem was dropped, to the relief of younger Punchites who found it old-fashioned.

The principal cartoon was done by L. G. Illingworth, a talented artist who had succeeded to the big cut after Partridge's death in 1945. He overcame his aversion to *Punch*'s political blandness by letting off steam with biting cartoons in the *Daily Mail*.

Fougasse grew increasingly bored with the editorship after he had brought *Punch* to what he felt was an acceptable point of excellence. He would doodle dreamily on a pad at editorial lunches (the other Punchites would fight over the discarded sketches after he left). He brought in a number of highly talented young people, among them Peter Dickinson and Ronald Searle.

Fougasse retired in 1953. Not a convivial man, he did not subsequently frequent the Table; but he continued to draw for *Punch* and published a number of anthologies of his cartoons. He died in 1965.

Since Fougasse had inherited most of the luminaries of the Evoe period, he made few major changes in the permanent staff, bringing in new people only when someone left or when they showed unusual talent. A notable acquisition of this period was Alex Atkinson, a former repertory actor, who wrote funny pieces about the theater and then branched out into general-purpose writing about daily life and the traditional *Punch* articles of criticism by parody. Another addition was P. M. Hubbard, a former Indian Civil Servant, who escaped, like Knox, to Fleet Street. An excellent feature writer, he dealt, like Atkinson, with everyday experience. He also did bright, cheery little verses about childhood and summers in the country.

The postwar rise of the female writer was refected in *Punch* by Marjorie Riddell, who did a wonderfully funny series in which she played the role of a single young woman attempting to make her way in London, plagued by the constant unsolicited advice of her overprotective mother. She was sometimes confused with Marjorie Redman, who wrote irritating little pieces for *Punch* about a small child. William Cole, who put together an anthology of *Punch* for Americans in 1953 (and who was himself an

"Well, off-hand I should say we've found one of those deadly German anti-personnel bombs."

W. A. Sillince, 1943

American) dealt with Miss Redman summarily. "I learned early in my *Punch* reading," he wrote, "to pass quickly over pieces that began 'Mummy! Mummy!'—the English are inclined to be treacly about small children, and pieces of this nature make A. A. Milne seem like a four-letter word realist." Another *Punch* lady, Mrs. D. J. Saint, wrote comic monologues about a teacher in a junior school. The only female Punchite who seems to have had anything of importance to write, other than the lightest of light comedy, was Angela Milne.

Unable to escape 'Arry completely, *Punch* had some success with the "Snax at Jax" series which began in 1951. Written by Alan Hackney, it dealt with conversations in a dreadful snack bar.

Of the cartoonists Ronald Searle was the best. He achieved a wide reputation outside *Punch* for illustrations, cartoons, and the famous "girls of St. Trinian's," a pack of little monsters capable of any enormity. The girls were cast in a number of film comedies, and they appeared in a great many anthologies as well. For a while Searle did the caricatures on *Punch*'s theater page. When I asked why he was no longer drawing for the magazine, I was told sourly, "We can't afford his prices now." Searle was made a member of the Table but does not seem to have retained the fierce *Punch* loyalty that transcends money. Or maybe there was something else. . . .

J. H. Dowd did the caricatures for the film critiques. He was eventually replaced by a *Tatler* caricaturist, R. S. Sherriffs. André François brought a new touch of the fantastic with his small French village scenes, his ladies with boa constrictors, and other curious subjects. François could add a touch of madness to any subject, no matter how commonplace.

The Swiss-Italian cartoonist Giovanetti won the hearts of thousands of readers with *Punch*'s first anthropomorphic animal star since Henry Mayhew's *Conversation Between Two Hackney-Coach Horses* in 1841. Giovanetti's Max, a jovial hamster, did not need a joke situation to draw laughs. It was enough to see him joyfully playing with a soap bubble or enjoying a nap in a hammock. Max out-Disneyed Disney in cuteness without the traditional Disney saccharine quality. He went through a number of editions as an anthology and may have been responsible for the hamster craze among children on both sides of the Atlantic. When he disappeared from the pages of *Punch*, Hargreaves attempted to replace him with similar episodic cartoons about little barnyard animals. They were amusing, but there was only one Max.

The Australian George Sprod arrived at about this time, as did William Hewison, who would become art editor in the seventies, and Michael ffolkes with his curlicues and rococo backgrounds. Norman Thelwell brought back the horse and the fanatical rider undeterred by rain, snow, or misadventure. His small girl on a fat pony became a *Punch* tradition. Kenneth Mahood also joined the group, as did Eric Burgin. Since these people are creatures of the present, there is little point in describing their work. They are a part of *Punch*, but not necessarily of *Punch* history, since all a reader has to do is open the magazine any week and see for himself.

Hewison has been a member of the Table for some years. As I write this, Mahood and ffolkes are Table members of only a few weeks duration. Norman Mansbridge, another Table member, Bernard Hollowood, and Roy Davis also contributed a large amount of the artwork. Mansbridge started as an illustrator and graduated into a very funny cartoonist. F. W. Smith ("Smilby") found humor in all sorts of social situations.

In 1953 the proprietors chose Malcolm Muggeridge as *Punch*'s eighth editor. The day of the gentleman-Punchite with the right sort of tie and experience on the *Granta* was over forever. The young men who had tried so hard to write like Wodehouse that they had finally turned into Wodehousian characters became a part of the past.

Punch had declined steadily since Seaman's day. Muggeridge was the supposed transfusion that would bring it back to vigorous health again. It was still a National Institution, there were no worries about that. E. M. Forster, in his *Maurice*, writes of a terrified young man visiting a psychiatrist for the first time to discuss his homosexuality. When he arrives in the waiting room and sees *Punch* on the table, his fears depart and everything is all right. It seems so *normal*. Gordon Lonsdale, the KGB "mole" who stole admiralty secrets in the fifties, would meet his contacts in public places. The recognition signal was a copy of *Punch* in the agent's hand. This was, perhaps, more a sign of decay than of National Institution status. The KGB must have realized that there would not be enough people walking about with copies of *Punch* to confuse the contact.

Muggeridge was an experienced journalist who had spent most of his working life on daily papers. He began as a leader-writer on the *Manchester Guardian* under C. P. Scott, who was already in his eighties. An avowed Communist, he went to Moscow as the *Guardian*'s correspondent. What he saw there soon made him as anti-Communist as he had formerly been a party enthusiast. He followed this experience with a stint on the *Statesman* in Calcutta and then returned to Fleet Street, where Lord Beaverbrook hired him to write the "Londoner's Diary" in the *Evening Standard*. Of this experience he wrote, "No one's education is complete without a spell as a gossip writer. How otherwise is it possible to know the minutiae of human vanity?"

Muggeridge's experience with Beaverbrook was not a happy one. They hated one another. Of Beaverbrook he said, "Those who were privileged to witness it [are not] likely ever to forget the spectacle of otherwise sane and even amiable fellow humans striving to translate into terms of ostensible sense the malignancies, the prejudices, the sheer raving absurdities of their exigent master. I hear it still over the telephone, that raucous Canadian voice—'You've gotta say . . . You've gotta say . . . ' We duly said it."

Muggeridge later wrote a brilliant but biting profile of Beaverbrook in the *New Statesman* which touched a sensitive nerve. Beaverbrook put out the word to his staff: Get Muggeridge. The strategy was not to carp at him in the papers every day until the public had got used to it, but rather to wait for him to do something big and then lower the boom.

The chance came when the *Saturday Evening Post* asked Muggeridge to comment on an article by John Grigg which was uncomplimentary to the Royal Family. Muggeridge accepted and wrote in typical Muggeridge fashion, saying anything he thought would stir up public comment. Reread today, his article is well-balanced and quite harmless. Compared with more recent criticisms of the Royal Family (or with *Punch* on Prince

Albert), it is even tame. The *Post* held it back so that it could be issued during the Queen's forthcoming visit to America, but Beaverbrook's *Daily Express* got a copy. They quoted it selectively, out of context, on the front page, with plenty of editorial comment.

In an article in the *New Republic*, after he had left *Punch*, Muggeridge commented on the great to-do caused by the *Express* feature and by the article itself: "The deadly solemnity with which my article was received, and the furious indignation it generated, made me feel that the Monarchy, at any rate as a social phenomenon, deserved to be taken more seriously than I had previously supposed."

He called in his lawyer to see if the *Express*'s article was actionable, since it was distorted and had been, in his estimation, potentially damaging professionally. He was told that there were sufficient grounds for a libel suit but that in view of the circumstances and the particular matter at issue he could not expect a judge and jury to be unprejudiced. "It was eerie and a little alarming," he wrote, "to have the theory of 'People's justice' as administered in communist countries, thus expounded by this Dickensian figure . . . in the antique quiet and tranquility of one of London's Inns of Court."

The incident was followed by a stream of abusive telephone calls and vicious letters. The disapproval was mostly upper class. One angry royalist wrote Muggeridge's wife to tell her how pleased he was that their youngest child had been killed in a skiing accident.

Muggeridge's background was probably the humblest since Mark Lemon's. He was the grandson of an undertaker in Penge and the son of a clerk in a shirt manufacturing firm who became an alderman and later (1931) a Socialist M.P. Malcolm attended free day schools and Selwyn College, Cambridge. It was a social step upward for the family. In those days, a boy who went to Oxford or Cambridge would always have comfortable work available to him. He could teach or preach or find an administrative berth in the Civil Service. The Muggeridges were relieved that Malcolm was out of the dog-eat-dog search for jobs.

When he left Oxford, he went to India to teach and narrowly missed being recommended as tutor to a young maharajah (the British resident found him "unsuitable"). He then turned to journalism, ending up at "that place of shadows," as he called *Punch*. He was to remain a journalist for the rest of his working life, except for a World War II stint in military intelligence in England and occupied France.

When he arrived in Bouverie Street, he was not favorably impressed with the atmosphere there.

> It was a somber place, haunted by old jokes and lost laughter. Life, as I discovered, holds no more wretched occupation than trying to make the

Eric Burgin, 1954

"Could I have a second opinion?"

A. E. Beard, 1954

English laugh. The portrait of one of my predecessors, Owen Seaman, looked down on me till I had him removed, to be replaced by Leach [sic], a more sympathetic visage. Through the window I looked enviously into *News of the World*. I and my staff, all anguished men, would sit together trying to discover what, if anything, was funny, sadly reaching the conclusion that nothing was.

Muggeridge had little, if any, sense of humor. He liked his jokes earthy and did not understand cartoon subtlety. After a few attempts at trying to determine which of the week's cartoon submissions were funny and which were not (disagreeing with his art editor, Brockbank, on all of them) he gave Brockbank full responsibility for cartoon selection. This was a wise move. As a result of it, Brockbank was able to fill the magazine with a variety of styles, giving the pages a lively appearance, a far cry from the days when every new artist had to draw like Leech or du Maurier.

One effect Muggeridge did have on the cartoons was his insistence on the removal of the ancient taboos. According to him, sex was funny. He drew the line at obscenity, but a gradual modernization of the jokes was begun. In time, sexually oriented jokes became quite common, as did sexually disposed writing. Articles like Alex Atkinson's Jean Anouilh parody, "Pyramus and Thisbe," in which the heroine is told that her breasts are like "tree-ripened peaches against the south wall of a chateau in Provence" (her mother's are described as resembling two socks filled with lard) would never have gotten into *Punch* before 1953.

When he came to *Punch*, Muggeridge was appalled at the staff's inexperience. As a grizzled old reporter of fifty, he had never seen a publication whose writers had been hired while still at college and moved into a one-magazine career. Many of them knew nothing at all about the outside world except what they had heard in the cloistered halls of 10 Bouverie Street. According to him they were not journalists at all. *Punch*'s role, he said in a *New Yorker* interview, was social history—to record the age. Was it possible with such a staff? He seesawed back from incredulity at their naiveté to admiration, claiming that Fougasse had left him with the finest group of writers and artists in the world.

At first there was a period of utter chaos while he felt his way into the scheme of things. He was appalled to hear that A. P. Herbert sent his copy directly to the printer without his seeing it until it was in proof, and he put a stop to it (something even Owen Seaman had not dared to do with the sacred traditions of the Table). He had a strong tendency, not unusual in old newspaper men, to give work to his former cronies, who would submit lengthy bad articles that he would hand over for setting without reading, usually with the comment, "Looks good."

246

In a letter to me, Peter Dickinson, who came to *Punch* in 1952 as assistant art editor, recalls the Muggeridge period with amusement and some nostalgia.

Thurber visiting and sulking because he wasn't allowed to do his usual monologue without interruption. . . . Old ladies who had contributed in Owen Seaman's time turning up with scraps of poems and having to be accompanied up and down in the lift because they were claustrophobic. Distinguished old men coming to hunt up a joke they remembered from their childhood and getting in a huff when they found we couldn't find it from their vague description . . . Muggeridge spending a whole afternoon when we needed decisions, incommunicado with some old crony who thought he could write for us, M. trying to think of something the poor old soak could actually achieve. A young man who sent in a couple of unsolicited articles which were good enough for Ellis to have him in to talk to, only for the young man to tell Ellis that he had better things to do with his talent than writing for *Punch* (I wonder what became of him). Furious ex-army officers ringing up from the suburbs, their moustaches bristling against the telephone, because we'd printed a joke they couldn't understand. (One got in once with the caption ''Not this one, I fear,'' as if spoken by one of the figures in the picture, when it was only Brockbank's note of rejection to the artist.) The mysterious William Whip, whose immensely long and boring article appeared in proof form . . . and no one knew anything about him or it.

After the initial period of confusion, *Punch* turned into a pretty good magazine, lively but messy. As Price pointed out, it was a lot closer to the old *Punch* in Muggeridge's third year than it was in his third month as editor. He knew everybody and he knew what was going on in the world. He was full of ideas, some of them terrible, but enough of them usable once the staff had convinced him to discard the dross. He was willing and able to do things that the staff had wanted to do for years but had been unable to convince the editors of. He was able to bring in outside names, celebrities who formerly would not have been caught dead in *Punch*; and he was forceful enough to break hallowed tradition, such as replacing the old Doyle cover.

Among the people he convinced to write articles for *Punch* were Noel Coward, Angus Wilson, Cecil Beaton, the American writer Willard Espy, and Stephen Potter of *Gamesmanship* fame. He talked Wodehouse into writing for the magazine again after nearly a quarter of a century. He got John Betjeman, a future Poet Laureate, to join the staff and the Table. He added Geoffrey Gorer and Christopher Sykes to the list of contributors.

He made the decision to publish extracts from some recently discovered Boswell papers and some hitherto unpublished limericks by Edward Lear.

The decision that was most popular with the staff was his insistence that articles now be signed with full names. Fougasse had allowed only initials for most, reserving full names for certain writers he thought had earned the privilege by long faithful service. Under Muggeridge, writers received for the first time the same credit that the artists had enjoyed for more than a century.

As editor of *Punch*, Muggeridge found himself a celebrity. He had made a number of radio broadcasts. Now he was discovered by television. He experienced the intoxicating sensation described by Jerome K. Jerome as the joy of "hearing one's name mentioned on an omnibus." With his abrasive manner and his gnomish resemblance to Mr. Punch he was perfect for the home screen. He was offered a job as interviewer on *Panorama*, the first big BBC-TV news-magazine program, where he hobnobbed with film stars and world figures, very like a kind of English Groucho Marx. In no time at all he was a household name. He became the first *Punch* editor to see himself immortalized in wax at Madame Tussaud's.

With two sources in which to invest his creativity, he chose to give his best to TV. Most of his energy and the best of his ideas went into his public appearances. *Punch* got what was left over. At the same time he became more and more autocratic about forcing the staff to use his work. Ellis was heard to remark that arguing with him was like being on a television talk show.

His sneering public style began to get on people's nerves. It was estimated by *Punch* staffers that every time he appeared on television the magazine lost a thousand subscribers. To cap it all, he became religious, sponsoring a series in *Punch* by Dorothy M. Sayers, who was, in addition to being the creator of Lord Peter Wimsey, an ordained minister and brimming with ecclesiastical zeal. A few thousand more readers dropped out. When he was criticized for this, Muggeridge said that they were all over eighty and would have died soon anyway. More readers left because of an Illingworth cartoon urging an ancient, corpselike Winston Churchill to retire.

It became obvious to one and all that Muggeridge's days at *Punch* were numbered. There had been a blowup with one of the proprietors about jokes made about the Prince of Wales being sent to school at Cheam. An Agnew son was at Cheam, and the jokes were resented. When I asked Peter G. Agnew, who is now retired and living in Cornwall, why Muggeridge had not completed the time specified in his contract, I received a brief, cool reply: "Malcolm Muggeridge felt that the proprietors had lost confidence in him and the contents of the issues he was producing. The proprietors felt he had lost the enthusiasm he had initially for *Punch*."

In fact, Muggeridge was engaged in a clever skirmish with the management. It was financially important to him to be sacked, because he would then receive tax-free compensation. If he resigned he would lose this, and his contract was due to run out in a few months. The last straw came with the publication of an article called "A Taste in Wine," by Edward Hyams, which was unnecessarily offensive about the Roman Catholic mass. Muggeridge had probably not read it before it got into the magazine, and no one is sure who did. A new wave of cancellations followed. Probably a great many of them were people who were still getting *Punch* from force of habit and would have cancelled eventually anyway, but it was the end. Muggeridge went.

Commenting on his departure some years after the fact, Muggeridge wrote:

> It was with a sense of infinite relief that I went downstairs, past the figure of Mr. Punch, and out through the door for the last time. A sense of almost mystical exhilaration seized me at the thought that I should never again cross that threshold, never again enter the twilit world within, or find myself under the professional necessity of trying to be funny.

There is no doubt that at *Punch* Muggeridge was a square peg in a round hole. Nevertheless, by sheer brilliance and enthusiasm, he left the magazine better than he found it. He believed that it should be ultratopical rather than humorous, and to that end he dispersed the carefully nurtured stable of outsiders, replacing them with "names." He discontinued the anecdotal sketches entirely, and then relented, allowing some but only if they were in some way connected with current events. He complained that *Punch* was "too well written" and insisted on simplified prose. He reduced the amount of poetry, except for Betjeman's.

He collected all the criticism into a single section, adding a radio and television critique by Hollowood, a stock market article, and art and ballet criticism. G. W. Stonier wrote a series of articles about London, and Patrick Balfour, later Lord Kinross, was assigned to investigative reporting duties.

Unlike his predecessors, he brought in very few new people. Claud Cockburn, an ex-Communist, would-be revolutionary follower of causes, who had been on Senator Joseph McCarthy's list of the 269 most dangerous reds in the world (and had been accused by the Communist government of Czechoslovakia of being a colonel in British Intelligence)

*"**Wow!** One thing that really grabs me today is the way kids can do their own thing."*

"Smilby" (F. W. Smith), 1964

Russell Brockbank, 1950

was described by Muggeridge as "my very present help in time of trouble." Cockburn, who, like Muggeridge, had been a journalist all over the world, turned out to be a humor writer of distinction and a welcome adjunct to *Punch*. Christopher Hollis, who joined the Table in 1955, was Conservative M.P. for Devizes, a Catholic, and an old Etonian. He wrote sharp, incisive satire and took over the "Essence of Parliament" from B. A. Young, who, released from the restrictions of the Fougasse era, had brought it back to the level of Henry Lucy's time.

Muggeridge brought in Leslie Marsh in 1953 to be his deputy editor. Marsh had worked with him on the *Standard*, editing the "Londoner's Diary," and a warm friendship had grown between them. "When I went to *Punch*," Muggeridge wrote in the second volume of his autobiography, "the first thing I did was to ask Leslie to join the staff, which to my great joy he did. When I left he was still there; the only truly useful contribution I made to the magazine's well-being." Other Punchites disagree. One staff member who worked under Muggeridge remembers

a bitter, smiling, destructive, dangerous man. If any man really destroyed the paper, it was [Marsh]. One man without humor can do enormous harm to a humorous paper. As Muggeridge became more and more enamored of

251

TV and got to be recognized in restaurants, Marsh achieved more and more power. He loved to sack people. He wanted desperately to sack Christopher Hollis. Muggeridge said, "He's one of my oldest friends. I'll give Leslie anyone but not Chris." Freddie [B. A.] Young should have been Deputy Editor.

When Bernard Hollowood replaced Muggeridge as editor, he retired Marsh.

Probably Muggeridge's most celebrated acquisition was Anthony Powell, who took over the literary criticism, helped by R. G. G. Price and by J. Maclaren-Ross, an excellent but improvident book reviewer. The proprietors complained to Powell at one time that they could not get in the front door of the Bouverie Street building because of process servers waiting to collect Maclaren-Ross's debts. Powell stood up for him, and Maclaren-Ross stayed on the payroll.

Powell, whose series of novels, *A Dance to the Music of Time*, is a classic of twentieth-century literature, is now writing his autobiography in Somerset. He told me that when Muggeridge suspended the Table privilege of sending copy directly to the printer, he directed that it be sent to Marsh, perhaps a more efficient way of running a magazine, but certainly not conducive to the happiness of the staff. A Punchite who remembered Powell as a book reviewer had said to me, "Every time he kissed a girl in a taxi, if she wrote a book, it was sure to be reviewed in *Punch*, especially if she was the daughter of a peer." I wondered if this was merely spite, triggered by reminiscence of some ancient quarrel (the Punchites are an unforgiving lot), or by envy of his success. I asked Powell.

He replied that in his day the book page, as always, was a poor relation. The books that were reviewed were decided by whoever made up the magazine (probably Marsh), not by Powell.

I am rather mystified by the reference to books of girls I had kissed in taxis being reviewed, peers' daughters or not. This has the air of being a direct reference, but to what, or whom, I cannot fathom. So far from books being chosen on a frivolous or slapdash principle, objection—if at all—was to the 'seriousness' of the books noticed. My own page was in the nature of a feature and would sometimes be a publication not likely to get much attention elsewhere, but the rest were 'what ought to be reviewed,' and it was I myself—so far as it went—who suffered pressure to do books by persons who had written for *Punch*, or possibly been kissed or otherwise manhandled by other members of the staff. I haven't been through my six years of reviews, but I think they will reveal the most routine of publications that seemed 'important.' Nancy Mitford was a peer's daughter, but I never kissed her in a taxi (a syndrome to which she did not at all belong), though, having known each other for years, we used to kiss when we met in later life.

After Muggeridge had departed and Hollowood was in command, Powell left, or, as he put it, ''I stayed on for a year and was then sacked.'' *Punch* could not afford a separate salary for a literary editor who came in two days a week, and there was a strong personality clash between him and Hollowood. Powell was considered to be a Muggeridge man and was too much of an intellectual for the changes that Hollowood had in mind. It is never easy for an editor to cope with a subordinate who has earned international distinction in his own right, and so Powell left.

In 1957 Bernard Hollowood was made editor. The circulation at that time was about one hundred thousand and was decreasing at the rate of two thousand a week. It was generally believed that the job would be offered to Young, who was the obvious choice and who wanted it, but the proprietors thought otherwise.

In appointing Hollowood, the proprietors felt that they were taking no risk. They had had ample time to examine him from all angles. He was a perfectly safe *Punch* man with a sense of humor and the ability to handle a budget. They were combining the old method of selecting a senior Table member with the new procedure of avoiding at any cost the old-style public school and Oxbridge gentleman-editor, unable to communicate with anyone who was not entirely ''our sort.'' When Muggeridge left, Young was made interim acting editor for a short period. Hollowood's appointment was a surprise to most of Fleet Street, including *Smith's Trade News*, the trade paper of the London press. It reported:

> Since Malcolm Muggeridge left the editorial chair at *Punch* I have watched the weekly issues with any amount of care. I thought that the temporary editorial caretaker was doing a fine job. At times it seemed he was providing readers and retailers alike with something as good as—and even better some weeks—the Muggeridge issues. Now comes the news that a new editor has been appointed to start on January 1. He is not B. A. Young (the staffer who has been carrying on so effectively) but Bernard Hollowood.

Young was passed over because he represented the old pre-Muggeridge staff, although he was not in agreement with them in all things and ought not to have been lumped in with them, except chronologically. Nevertheless the taint was there. The proprietors believed that Young would have attempted to make *Punch* more highbrow than it had been under Muggeridge, and that was not what they had in mind.

253

Albert Bernard Hollowood was the son of middle-class working people. He was born in Burslem, Staffordshire, and attended local schools and Cheltenham College, taking a master's degree in economics at London University. He taught school at all levels for twelve years, lecturing on economics at London University and at Stoke and Loughborough College. He was editor of *Pottery and Glass* and, when he moved to *Punch*, was assistant editor of the *Economist*. He is the author of eleven books and the editor of several anthologies. At present he is working on his autobiography, to be titled *Hollowood Be Thy Name*.

During his years at *Punch* he was deputy literary editor and radio and television critic, as well as general-purpose writer on subjects dealing with commerce and industry. He traveled widely as a *Punch* correspondent, reporting on economic affairs in the United States, Canada, Holland, Switzerland, and Brazil. His series, "My Lifetime in Basic Industry," about the mining village of Scowle, was a delightful burlesque of the industrial novel. It was later issued in book form. He was very good at the technique of the workingman self-derision essay, a far cry from the 'Arryism of the past, free of condescension and snobbery, and funny to people of all classes.

"I am no Muggeridge," he said to an interviewer when he moved to the head of the Table. "I doubt whether I shall have time to become a TV personality like him. I think running *Punch* will be a full-time job." Then, realizing that his plain speaking might be considered as harsh or snide criticism (a lesson Muggeridge had learned to his cost), he added, "We all liked Muggeridge. He was a good editor. But I don't think that I shall be getting publicity for *Punch* in the same way that he has. . . . Of course he has been badly misquoted and some newspapers murdered him."

It was wishful thinking on Hollowood's part. TV was unavoidable in the sixties, and he was a celebrity in spite of himself. As soon as his appointment was announced, before he had time to move into the editor's office, the BBC had him up before the cameras.

[DOUGLAS] BROWN: Are you going to be a new broom? Are you going to make any drastic changes in *Punch*?

HOLLOWOOD: That is very difficult—a difficult question. *Punch* is pretty good as it is. I am not sure that it needs a new broom, but of course I've got my own ideas of what I want to do but you will have to wait until January the first for them.

BROWN: Yes.

HOLLOWOOD: I do not take up my duties till then.

BROWN: What is the strength of *Punch*?

"I hope you're not thinking of doing anything silly."

Hector Breeze, 1976

"That's your younger generation today—no sense of social responsibility."

"Smilby" (F. W. Smith), 1974

HOLLOWOOD: Its literary quality—that is the first thing. The fact is that I think it does contain the best literary humour in the world.

BROWN: Does it reflect the age we are living in do you think?

HOLLOWOOD: I should say absolutely certainly.

BROWN: What is its weakness?

HOLLOWOOD: If there is one I think it is the fact that we are sometimes slightly aloof, you know.

BROWN: We go back to the bobby sox, don't we?

HOLLOWOOD: Occasionally I think we are a little incomprehensible to the young, but we can get rid of that.

BROWN: That is one of your ambitions is it?

HOLLOWOOD: That is one of my jobs. That is what I want to do.

BROWN: Getting it towards the teen-agers as well as towards, say, the universities and the professional people?

HOLLOWOOD: Yes. I want to make it absolutely universal.

BROWN: One last question. Why have they made you editor?

HOLLOWOOD: Ah. You have got me. I am completely baffled. I've no idea.

Hollowood made a number of changes, none of them quite as radical as some of Muggeridge's, but changes nonetheless. (He tried to give the magazine a new name, but could not convince the staff or the proprietors to go that far). In a letter to me in January 1978, he explained some of his alterations:

> The changes I made were many. I considered—the first editor to do so—that there is not enough first class literary humour to fill each week's copy of the paper (cf. the *New Yorker*), so I kept the best humour and interlarded it with first class "serious" writing. I launched this policy with a series on the nuclear threat called *East is West*, featuring such writers as Rebecca West, J. B. Priestley, and Professor Blackett. I got pieces from world politicians and editors. I was aware that women had had a poor deal in *Punch*, so I opened a weekly spread called *For Women*.
>
> I deplored the practice of using TV stars as writers and went all out to find new talent. I devised a method whereby all unsolicited manuscripts were circulated separately to assistant editors, and asked each for private comment. I found new ability in such people as Alan Coren (signed on as assistant after seeing two of his articles), Patrick Skene, Alexander Frater, and many many more. I think the quality of the literary humour improved.

Hollowood's new policies were successful. The weekly decline in circulation stopped and sales began a slow but regular climb. Muggeridge

256

had been generous with the proprietors' money, but Hollowood was more circumspect about expenditures. Staff morale improved. Being a cartoonist himself, he expected to have full say over the cartoons chosen for each issue. Brockbank, accustomed to the absolute power delegated to him by Muggeridge, resigned the art editorship and was replaced by William Hewison, who is still art editor today.

During the Hollowood period J. B. Boothroyd, who could now sign his full name to his articles, became Basil Boothroyd permanently. He contributed much to the style of *Punch*, as Ellis had done, writing a great many of the unsigned pieces as well as those for which he was credited. *Punch* had a good deal of unsigned editorial material, and the staff writers competed fiercely for it. Under the Hollowood austerity budget (which the proprietors had forced on him), the *Punch* pay scale was barely adequate, and the writers were paid extra for the extra work.

To Hollowood's way of thinking, it was impossible for *Punch* to succeed as a humor magazine, the character that Fougasse had tried hard to establish for it. He explained his ideas about humor in an article in the *Journal of the Institute of Journalists* in 1962. It is one thing to be funny, he said, and quite another to be funny after *trying* to be funny. It is one thing to be a gifted amateur and another to be a professional craftsman. The criticism is harsher. In Britain humor is an intellectual status symbol. "If we laugh in the wrong place," he wrote, "we betray ourselves utterly, our I.Q., our educational background, our niche in the social system."

Punch was expected to be funny. If it was not funny, it was criticized contemptuously. Nobody, Hollowood said, criticized the *Times* or the *Economist* for not being funny. When the "Parkinson's Law" series appeared in the *Economist*, the readers were delighted. Had it appeared in *Punch*, Hollowood thought, it would not have been greeted with such wide acclaim, because it was the sort of thing that *should* have been in *Punch*. In 1959 Alan Hackney, who had done the "Snax at Jax" pieces in 1951, wrote the wonderful "I'm All Right Jack." It was exactly what Hollowood wanted, brilliant satire—hilariously funny and dealing with a social and industrial problem that was up-to-date. Hollowood was not surprised when no letters came in praising or condemning the series. It was enough to the readers that the series was good enough for *Punch*. Later it was made into a highly successful film starring Ian Carmichael and Peter Sellers. The *Express* had the film version written into a book. Only then did the reading public sit up and take notice.

With respect to cartoons, Hollowood, like Fougasse, felt that the idea was more important than the skill of the artist (he himself was not much of a draughtsman compared to some of the magazine's cartoonists). His own drawings gave the impression, probably deceptive, of having been dashed off at great speed to make a deadline. He encouraged new artists, such as Bill Tidy and "Larry," and he got along well with Hewison, who shared his views.

In his heyday as editor, Hollowood gave complete satisfaction to the proprietors, who asked him to take on the dual responsibilities of editor and managing director. For some years he did both jobs, but found them too demanding and asked to be returned to his former position as editor. Victor Caudery took over as managing director and handled the business end of *Punch*.

In 1968 the proprietors were engaged in negotiating the sale of Punch Publications, Ltd. to United Newspapers. For all of Hollowood's innovations, the magazine was still losing money. Observers who were present at the time feel that he was suffering from the traditional malady of *Punch* editors, loss of enthusiasm. In addition, he was in constant pain from a bad knee. According to Mr. Agnew, "Bernard Hollowood was ill and spending periods away from his office. He tendered his resignation." According to one of his contemporaries, "the management decided to make a change." According to Hollowood, "I retired because (a) I was ill and (b) I wanted to write books." Lord Barnetson, the chairman of United Newspapers, had no comment on Hollowood's departure.

In his letter of resignation to Victor Caudery, Hollowood noted that he was about to go into the hospital for a number of weeks. It seems to me that the suggestion that the management wanted to unload him is a bit harsh on Hollowood. The fact remains that two weeks after he left, the sale to United was consummated and the new management brought in a new editor, quite normal under the circumstances, but there was no animosity on either side. As late as the mid-seventies Hollowood was still writing the television criticism, and he still submits cartoons today. When he left he was made an editorial consultant.

At the end of his letter to Caudery, Hollowood added a postscript, recommending a "short term" appointment as editor for Peter Dickinson, whom he considered to be the "best bet." This time the proprietors were not in agreement with him. As Mr. Agnew carefully phrased it: "Peter Dickinson was not seriously considered at the time Bernard Hollowood was appointed because he was too young and immature. When Davis was appointed, Peter was more mature, but here again he was not considered the best choice."

The Dickinson question was answered with more frankness by Dickinson himself. "Nor was it any surprise when I didn't get the job. I would have been a lousy editor, I now see. Lazy-minded and timid. Lucky for me I had begun writing books which were making enough money for me to give the job up. I'd enjoyed it a lot, but should perhaps have left earlier.''

Dickinson left *Punch* in 1969. The choice between the Davis purges and the attractive life offered him from the sales of his popular and well-written novels was an easy one. He became one of those fortunate ex-Punchites who not only can eat at the Table on Wednesdays, but are also welcome at the Alternate Table. B. A. Young was still around, but the new proprietors do not seem to have considered him this time.

Parts of it are excellent.

—George du Maurier

n 1968 United Newspapers
acquired the firm of Bradbury, Agnew & Company, whose assets included Punch Publications, the *Countryman*, a group of monthly farming
journals, and a number of commercial printing companies. The value of
the purchase consideration was £850,000 (about $1.5 million at the
time) of which £18,800 (about $33,000) was in cash and the rest in
shares. The Bradbury Agnew assets included the building at 10 Bouverie
Street, which was subsequently sold. Obviously, the new owners got a
very good deal on the acquisition.

When United took over, *Punch*'s domestic circulation was 115,758,
about 16 percent higher than it had been when Muggeridge left.
However, the magazine was running at a loss. Within nine months,
according to Lord Barnetson, the chairman of United Newspapers, the
loss had been turned into a profit, and *Punch* has been making money
ever since. Barnetson credits this to management improvement rather
than changes in policy or editorial or artistic quality. He did not fail to
give the new editor, William Davis, his fair share of the glory. "Mr.
Davis played his part in this improved performance," Lord Barnetson
informed me, "and his role in transforming the editorial content of the
magazine was of major significance."

Barnetson is a former leader-writer and editor of the *Edinburgh
Evening News*. His life has been like one of those wonderful old rags-to-
riches movies that aren't made any more. From his desk at the Edinburgh
paper he invested wisely and rose, in spite of the crippling British tax
laws, to become a captain of industry, not an easy thing to do these days.

"What do you mean, no?"

Michael ffolkes, 1977

*"When it come to Love, being a mollusc **and** a teenager is a tragedy."*

Harpur, 1978

He is also chairman of Reuters, of the *Observer*, of Sheffield Newspapers, Ltd., and of Farming Press, Ltd. He is deputy chairman of the British Electric Traction Co., Ltd. His chairmanship of Bradbury, Agnew gives him an automatic seat at the bottom of the *Punch* Table, where he frequently enjoys a Wednesday lunch with the Punchites.

In addition to his chairmanships, Lord Barnetson is a director of a number of other companies, including the prestigious banking house, the Hill Samuel Group. He holds eighteen offices or memberships in professional societies.

Why should such an astute businessman buy an ancient magazine that has been on the decline since 1900 and was still losing money when he bought it? No one seems to know, and Lord Barnetson did not explain, at least not to me. On the financial side, United probably made a profit on the sale of Bradbury Agnew's real estate. But if that were true, why not reinvest in a profitable enterprise and close down the loser, the technique used so successfully by corporate raiders in America? *Punch*'s losses undoubtedly improved United's tax picture, but if that was the reason for the purchase, why make Davis work so hard to make a profit?

It seems to me that United's investment was motivated by an utterly British (even in businessmen) love of institutions. The United Newspapers Magazine Division includes such publications as *Pig Farming*, *Dairy Farming*, and *Arable Farming*. Their newspaper division includes a string of provincial journals. *Punch* is something they can be proud of. It means prestige. Executives of the company can go to their homes or to their clubs without being greeted by a chuckle and a welcoming cry of "Here comes the man from *Pig Farming*." Moreover, if anyone can make *Punch* the success it used to be, Lord Barnetson can.

If the reasons for the purchase of *Punch* are mysterious, what about the reasons for the sale? A family-held company for 120 years, a part of the Bradbury and the Agnew heritages, why did the present members decide to let it go? Peter Agnew answered my question.

In 1966/7 Bradbury Agnew embarked on a fairly large modernisation programme mainly to have the facility to print *Punch* by fast web offset in the country, replacing the slow web letterpress in London.

After deciding this, the National economic climate deteriorated and inflation meant a considerable increase in the investment required. It was discovered that the company was being seriously considered by several publishers with a view to a takeover, and rather than be forced into a situation of not being able to choose, an approach was made to Securities Agency, Ltd, the merchant bankers owned by the Harley Drayton Old Broad Street financial house. They were the financial advisors to United

262

Newspapers, and therefore referred the proposition to William Barnetson, now Lord Barnetson, who negotiated the deal.

The drama that accompanied the sale of a business that went back to the time of Thackeray can only be imagined. Mr. Agnew's calm, unemotional statement reflects, perhaps, an unspoken turbulence between the lines.

The fact remains, *Punch* was sold, and the papers were signed two weeks after Hollowood's retirement. His replacement was a Barnetson man, not an Agnew man.

On November 7, 1973, the word *fuck* appeared in *Punch* for the first time. There was no need for William Makepeace Thackeray to whirl in his grave. The time had long since passed when the dreadful word could bring a blush to a maidenly cheek. William Davis, who had been editor for five years when the breakthrough occurred, told me that there had been a dreadful row with the proprietors, but that he had won in the end. The offending article also included the words *balls* and *arsehole*. It was a review by Clive James of a book by Martin Page entitled *Kiss Me Good-night Sergeant Major*, which dealt with songs sung by soldiers in wartime. Some of the songs dated back to the Afghan campaign and may well have been sung at the *Punch* Table in the old days. But for *Punch* to quote in its austere but somewhat relaxed post-Muggeridge pages:

> Don't want a bullet up me arsehole,
> Don't want me bollocks shot away.
> I'd rather live in England,
> In merry, merry England,
> And fornicate me fucking life away.

was one small step forward for mankind but one giant step forward for *Punch*. From then on, the magazine never looked back. Frontal nudity complete with nipples and penises appeared in the cartoons. There were jokes about gays, sado-masochists, foot fetishists, and anything else that happened to occur to the staff. There was everything except a full-color airbrushed centerfold of a naked lady, but if Davis had thought it would attract new young subscribers, there would have been one.

Davis was thirty-six when he was appointed to the editorship, comparatively young for a twentieth-century *Punch* editor. "I am in journalism to have fun," he said in an interview, "and hopefully to make some money, although I never really thought about that. But I love writing, and I never found it difficult, so I'm doing what I like and getting well paid for it and that's a perfect combination." Those who have read his books and articles may doubt his sincerity, for he never seems to write about anything *but* making money.

Davis got his start in journalism while he was still in his teens by answering a want ad in the *Daily Telegraph*. He was hired by a small weekly, the *Stock Exchange Gazette*, for five pounds a week and luncheon vouchers, to break in and do odd jobs including running out to get the editor's lunch and, after a while, writing. He switched after several years to a new paper, the *Recorder*, where he was given the title (in lieu of a large salary) of deputy city editor. Like many new enterprises of that period, the *Recorder* went bankrupt. Davis, who was twenty-one, moved to the *Financial Times* as night subeditor. Four years later he was financial editor of the *Evening Standard*.

With characteristic efficiency, he took care to move his younger brother into every job he vacated (the brother eventually became business editor of the *Observer*).

Davis is fond of saying that if he had stayed in the city instead of turning to writing he could have made a great deal of money but would not have had as much fun, and "life's too short to pass up all the opportunities to have fun."

In his final article as editor, a piece in the *Punch* Nostalgia Issue of December 21, 1977, called "Good-bye to All This," it is obvious that what he will miss most of all are the traditional *Punch* trips to France or to the various watering places and spas of England.

> As fact-finding missions they were a dead loss. But the purpose was not that serious: I merely wanted to give *Punch* contributors a chance to know each other better and have fun in the process.
>
> You can't produce humour in a solemn atmosphere. Soon after I became editor ... I visited the offices of the *New Yorker*. I found the place depressingly gloomy and resolved not to let it happen to *Punch*. So I didn't protest, in the years that followed, when contributors indulged in all kinds of antics under the editor's nose.

He did not protest, of course, because he was the master indulger in antics, the deviser of practical jokes and pranks of all kinds. It was Davis who thought up the business of A. P. Herbert's check written on the cow. He dressed Alan Coren as a sheik during the oil crisis and sent him out in the Barnetson Rolls Royce with a photographer. The result (duly reported as a comic piece in *Punch*) was noted the following day in the *Times*.

> An Arab Sheikh appeared in the Stock Exchange visitors gallery yesterday morning to see how Western capitalism operates. With his entourage of

chauffeur and personal photographer, and in flowing Arab robes, he was soon recognised, and a chorus of boos arose from the trading floor. He left hurriedly, but according to the Stock Exchange information service, calmly. Another £500 million of foreign investment lost forever?

Coren was also sent to Scotland with William Hewison to see how Scots would react to two Englishmen prospecting for oil on a golf course.

During my first interview with Davis, which I have described in an earlier chapter, he led me down the narrow corridor that bisects the *Punch* area of 23 Tudor Street, flanked on both sides by editors' offices and workrooms. The corridor is on two levels, broken about halfway by a small flight of five steps. Without warning, he broke off our conversation.

"I told our accountants that I wouldn't talk to them unless they could do *this*!" he shouted, and taking a short run, he leaped up all five without touching them, landing on the top step. It was gracefully done for a man of forty-five. I did not care to attempt it myself, especially after lunch. I said I was glad I wasn't an accountant. The lesson was, I assume, that only the young and agile should be allowed to audit *Punch*'s books.

Davis the prankster, who has made *Punch* one big happy, junketing family, was received with a good deal of suspicion when he arrived in Tudor Street. *Private Eye* printed yet another "Dropping the Pilot" cartoon called "Dropping the Jokes" and made a great many humorous references to his German background. Price and Boothroyd, who had seen it all happen before, merely shrugged their shoulders and prepared to accept the inevitable chaos that accompanies a change of administration. Davis called in William Hewison and demanded that no single cartoonist be represented more than once in an issue. Hewison replied that *Punch* printed a minimum of thirty cartoons per issue and there weren't that many first-class cartoonists in London. The subject was dropped.

He refused to read copy, pointing out that his job was ideas, not paperwork. If it wasn't ready for the printer when it arrived, fire the writer. Never use him again. He went back to the Muggeridge system of courting stars and celebrities to write for the magazine. Some of their copy was unpublishable, but he seemed to think it was enough to have a "name." His assistants were appalled. At one point in his first year, the entire staff discussed a mass resignation. On second thought a number of them realized that it wasn't that easy to find other jobs in England. The number of papers and magazines had decreased sharply and working for *Punch* was no longer considered the best possible experience for a British journalist. Nobody left. Alan Coren, who as his assistant worked most closely with Davis, broke out in a nasty skin rash born of pure nerves.

He was hard on the girls. One temporary typist lasted only half a morning and left in tears. Another was fired during one of the office

"Speaking as a professional, I don't think much of your mortice-and-tenon joints."

"Nick," 1977

"Well, let's hope he gets into something soon, because let's face it, Mary, he'll never make a carpenter."

Mike Williams, 1977

outings. I asked Caroline Cook, his secretary, how long she had worked for him. "Six years," she said, "*but it seems much longer.*" The quiet, gentlemanly discussions that had once taken place in the editor's office gave way to screaming rows that moved up and down the corridor. For the first time in a century, voices were raised in anger—and in front of the junior people.

One of the Punchites described Davis to me as a curious combination of absolute brilliance and a four-year-old boy. Another called him a piranha. Yet the prime minister invited him to Chequers to ask his advice on fiscal policy. When the Boothroyds invited him to dinner one evening, he insisted on having the radio on at full volume during the meal to listen to some program that he considered important. At the table he talked loudly over the noise, paying no attention to the program, conversing on matters of everyday interest with his hosts.

After dinner the Boothroyds were amazed when Davis was able to discuss the program in detail, with a great many intelligent comments on its content. He had simply absorbed it and channeled it away for future reference.

Abrasive though he may have been, Davis was also quick to apologize and admit error, something no other *Punch* editor was ever able to do, except possibly Mark Lemon. He was thoughtful and kind when Punchites were in trouble. His manner was undoubtedly part of his big-happy-family fixation. You don't have screaming rows with employees and business acquaintances, but do have them with brothers and sisters. It took a while for the Punchites to realize this.

Fortunately, he got better every year. In time he became quite bearable. The Punchites, realizing that he enjoyed the rows, attacked him fiercely at the Table and on points of editorial content, but defended him fiercely behind his back when he was criticized by outsiders. One tends to wonder what he is like at home (he is married and has three children in their teens and twenties). Does he ever relax? Is the table conversation unfailingly brilliant? Does he talk—or think—of anything but achievement and millions?

While Davis was financial editor of the *Manchester Guardian*, he began to write profiles for *Punch*. He has a brisk, energetic style, light and amusing, but not the warm wonderful humor of Boothroyd, Price, or Coren. He had started a BBC television program, *The Money Programme*, and was already a minor celebrity when he came to Tudor Street.

"What got me interested in humour was that I saw its potential as a weapon," he said in an interview with the trade journal *Newsagent and Bookshop*, the British equivalent of our American *Publisher's Weekly*, "and I've always taken the view that the best sort of humour comes by reporting rather than inventing . . . and I've seen enough absurdity

267

around me in, what, twenty years of daily journalism to be able to be the little boy who says the emperor has no clothes on. . . . When you get the CIA making plots to deprive Castro of his beard—how the hell can you compete?''

Interviewer Steve Harris wanted to know if Davis ever found himself faced with Muggeridge's problem—the painful dreariness of having to be funny every day? He replied:

> You see in Malcolm's day they were rather elderly around here, and Malcolm himself, after all, was no chicken—and they were in a building that I thought was rather gloomy and, as I think Malcolm once put it, full of the ghosts of dead jokes. . . .
> Here there is a different atmosphere. Very young team. Very young crowd, and we have lots of fun—and if you have fun you generate fun.

Davis is right. Under his leadership, the atmosphere of the Tudor Street office was conducive to humor. The people there were relaxed and they did have fun. There was laughter in the offices and in the library. Some of the staff did not understand him, and others disliked what they believed to be his eccentricities, but there was none of the sour, smouldering hatred that exists in an office where the boss is a vicious tyrant. Many of the staff were glad to see him go, but few were sorry to have had the experience of working with him.

When Davis was invited to take on the editorship of *Punch*, the first thing he did was telephone Malcolm Muggeridge to ask his advice. Muggeridge replied that the proprietors were no laughing matter but that journalism, as Davis must know very well, was an adventure. He accepted the job. There is a rumor around *Punch*, undoubtedly apocryphal, that in his last days as editor Hollowood went around inviting young journalists to lunch and absent-mindedly assured each of them that he would be the next editor of *Punch* and that Davis was the only one who believed him. Hence, his appointment. It is a good story, but one learns soon not to believe everything one hears in the corridors of a humor magazine.

In fact, the proprietors, this time United Newspapers, hoped that his financial expertise, more practical than Hollowood's advanced degree in economics, might help the magazine out of the red and attract new advertisers. This was to be done by wooing youthful subscribers who might buy the products in the advertisements. When Davis first arrived in 1968, more than half of the advertising was devoted to liquor and tobacco, an unfailing sign of a middle-aged or elderly readership. ''Advertisers used to say 'All they do is drink and smoke. That's it,' '' Davis wrote. After a decade of his editorship, the advertising is diversified and not dependent on a single or even a few industries.

When Davis left, 15 percent of *Punch*'s readers were over fifty-five. The majority were in the fifteen-to-thirty-four age group. Seventy percent were under forty-four. *Punch* had the highest readership of any weekly magazine in the universities. The dentist's waiting room image was gone forever, and *Punch* was back in the competitive market again.

It is still a National Institution. Major film and television production companies keep a set handy for reference on period films. The costumes for "Upstairs, Downstairs," "The Forsyte Saga," and "The Pallisers" were designed for the most part by Leech, Keene, Tenniel, and du Maurier with minor alterations by present-day designers. Those which were not taken from *Punch* were checked with *Punch* for authenticity, as are vehicles and room furnishings. Many elegant BBC–TV drawing rooms have been based on du Maurier's cartoons of musical evenings, which were modeled on his own Hampstead house. Lamps, shoes, horse trappings, military uniforms, street scenes, all come from *Punch*, because of the insistence of the editors on absolute accuracy. James MacDonald Fraser admitted to an interviewer that a good deal of the excellent background research in his Flashman books is taken from *Punch*, "a very good potted summary of what went on."

Davis's innovations resulted in a number of subscription cancellations, but the defectors, he insists, were older readers the magazine hoped to discourage. "My first avalanche . . . came on the day I devoted an entire issue to a parody of *Playboy*," he said. "There were seventy cancelled subscriptions that morning. The issue was a sellout and our younger readers wrote enthusiastic letters. It was a turning point for *Punch*." Between 1970 and 1972, *Punch* lost three thousand readers, mostly older people. "We lost them because they couldn't keep pace," Davis said in an interview in *Campaign*.

> I think where we've been fortunate is in the way the whole atmosphere in this country has changed—the atmosphere in which a humour magazine operates. These sort of things that Muggeridge tried to do were fairly namby-pamby—they were soft really. But it was a period when people were very easily offended. There was a great deal of hypocrisy about the Empire and all the other things. Then you had the satire period on television, which I think changed the whole atmosphere, certainly as far as the young people were concerned. They are able to take much more and want much more honesty than their parents ever did, and I think that has helped enormously. Without that the gamble might not have come off at all.

Punch's editorial staff is small, and I have described it in my first chapter, so there is no need to repeat. Most of the contributions come from outsiders. Davis even convinced the Prince of Wales to do a book

269

"He's the patron saint of drunks!"

Bernard Cookson, 1977

"Yes, but with the Conservatives one does get a better class of racialist."

McLachlan, 1978

review. Table member E. S. Turner and staff writers David Taylor and Miles Kington are excellent. Turner's parodies are in the best *Punch* style. Taylor, who replaced Alan Coren as assistant editor, does lampoons of phony advertising layouts and occasional interviews among other well-written humorous material. Jonathan Sale covers London as a kind of roving reporter, checking on trends and fashions. Among the cartoonists, in addition to Tidy, Larry, David Langdon, Thelwell, Norman Mansbridge, and an occasional Hollowood or Searle, there are new names: Gerald Scarfe, Michael Heath, Kenneth Mahood, Graham, Honeysett, Mike Williams, Albert, Lowry, and the splendid illustrator Philip Hood.

In short, like Muggeridge and Hollowood, Davis may not have left *Punch* in perfect condition, but he left it a little better than it was when he joined it. In the Nostalgia Issue of January 3, 1978, his first issue as editor, Alan Coren wrote a parody of *Private Lives* which purports to be a dialogue between him and Davis. It ends with a farewell speech, supposedly joking but with a ring of sentimental truth in it.

COREN: I shall miss you at *Punch*, old William. We all shall. I suppose that's all I wanted to say in the article really. All that barmy energy, all that bottomless enthusiasm, all those crackpot jaunts to cockeyed places with the entire staff rolling helpless from booze and hysteria on strange French floors, in Dublin foyers, at truly fearful restaurants with truly appalling people, and all the time we managed to get out close on five hundred issues of the magazine, and most of them were good, and some of them were great, and you whipping us along like a maniac dog-sledder and firing off ideas, great, good, average, bad, and terrible, not so much a sniper as a berserk shotgunner besieged in the Tudor Street office, what on earth will the premises be like without you? It was all so much fun, wasn't it?

DAVIS: Yes, yes, yes, absolutely, yes, yes. What was?

It took ten years, but Coren's rash had cleared up forever.

And what about Alan Coren? In the last days of Davis's editorship, circulation had gone down to an alarming 80,552, but the magazine was making a nice profit from advertising sales. Coren's first two issues were sold out. Lord Barnetson says that when Coren took over, circulation rose four thousand, or 5 percent, in only sixty days.

Coren changed the cover again and inserted *Punch*'s first table of contents. One of his early moves was to bring Sheridan Morley, Kenneth Mahood, and Michael ffolkes to the Table. Alan Brien does a weekly feature on London. Davis still writes articles on money, while running his new publishing firm and editing the United Newspapers magazine *High Life*. Alan Coren has brought *Punch* away from topicality and back toward humor again. He has introduced fiction—each week there is a short story, illustrated by some talented artist.

As an editor Coren was a novelty to the British magazine-reading public, although they knew him well enough as a humorous writer. A lot of new subscribers and readers bought *Punch* out of curiosity and were sufficiently impressed to stay on. By the end of his first year of editorship, circulation had risen to 86,000 and readership had increased from about 900,000 to 1,100,000. Profits for 1978 had risen 100 percent over those of 1977. Although readership breakdown figures were not available when this book went to press, there is every indication that *Punch* has broadened its base in the twenty-to-forty age group. The magazine has proven once again, as it has so many times in the past, that creative people sell more copies than financial experts and economists. It will be interesting to see if the lesson is overlooked by the businessmen again.

A year after Coren's move to the head of the Table, a typical *Punch* issue (October 25, 1978) shows 36½ pages of advertising, and they are no longer devoted to whiskey and cigars for the middle-aged. Twenty-six of the advertisements are full page and full color. There are, of course, advertisements for wine and spirits, but there are an equal number of pages devoted to high fidelity stereo systems. The spectrum of advertisements runs through airlines, watches, clothing, automobiles, perfume, margarine, pocket calculators, television sets and TV game cassettes, building and loan societies, insurance companies, wool, Listerine, and Hush Puppies. The old days of corn plasters, dandruff remedies, and vintage port seem to be over. If, in fact, the quality of a magazine can be judged from its advertisers, *Punch* is aimed at the young again, and the advertisers know it. The reason for the change and for the renewed interest of the British business community, would seem to be Alan Coren.

Coren is thirty-nine, married to a pretty blond anesthetist, and the father of two children. He attended East Barnet Grammar School and won a scholarship to Wadham College, Oxford, where he took a first in English. At Oxford he won scholarships to Yale and Berkeley, becoming a kind of reverse Rhodes scholar.

Coren was quick to see the funny side of American life and offered his views of the United States to *Punch*. Hollowood accepted them and promptly invited him to join the staff. At the age of twenty-four he became *Punch*'s youngest assistant editor. After fifteen years of writing for *Punch*, Alan has kept his sense of humor and his skill. He writes about five thousand words a week, and the quality of his writing remains consistently high. As editor he will continue his large output, but may have to cut down on outside projects such as his delightful children's books. It can only be hoped that he won't have to cut them out entirely. He has told interviewers that he intends to commit himself wholly to the magazine, even at the cost of limiting other activities.

Of course Coren's writing won't disappear entirely. *Punch* has a tradition of participating editors. The editors of American magazines, such as *Esquire*, the *New Yorker*, *Playboy*, *Vogue*, or *Cosmopolitan*, rarely if ever write at all. Coren's contract with *Punch* calls for at least one full-sized article per week, up to the standard of his best work, and good enough for *Punch*.

Some of Coren's extracurricular activities that may now have to be curtailed are television criticisms for the *Times*, his appearances on talk shows (the proprietors are still sensitive about the Muggeridge days), and his pieces in the *Evening Standard* and the *Daily Mail*. On the other hand, as editor his social life will increase. He will probably be expected to appear at as many dinner parties as an ambassador, and he will certainly have to travel a great deal (though probably not as much as Davis). He will keep his job as rector of St. Andrew's University. (The students elected him last year, to succeed John Cleese.)

Many people (I am one of them) think Coren is the funniest writer in England today. His parodies and flights of fancy are the equal of early Benchley and Leacock and in many cases funnier than Perelman. He recently did a short parody of a murder mystery to celebrate the signing of an executive order by New York City's Mayor Edward Koch giving homosexuals equal job rights with other civil servants. The order was widely attacked as the thin end of the wedge for gay infiltration of the schools, the police department, and the fire department. Coren visualized a Kojak sort of scene in Central Park where a recently murdered corpse is discovered by a passerby who reports it and suddenly finds himself surrounded by wonderfully silly gay cops. It sounds like a hackneyed, cliché situation, obvious and overdone, but Coren made it bright, funny, and surprisingly fresh. It was without cruelty and perfectly capable of being laughed at by gays who might read it as well as by *Punch*'s non-gay readership. The old saw about people smiling at *Punch* but not laughing aloud may no longer apply in 1978, thanks to Coren.

His two most famous series were columns supposedly written by the mother of the president of the United States, the celebrated Miz Lillian; and by President Idi Amin of Uganda. The humor depended on contrived funny accents, in Miz Lillian's case a corn pone jargon something like that of Al Capp's Yokum family, and in Amin's, a kind of Stepin Fetchit negro low-comedy dialect.

Each of the series brought him front page publicity for the wrong reasons. In the case of Miz Lillian, Coren offended one of those classic English octogenarians, a certain Miss Alison Oliver, a retired Edinburgh librarian. Miss Oliver took it upon herself to represent the British and American public as arbiter of taste and haled Coren up before the Press Council with a formal complaint, to wit that the series was scurrilous and calculated to antagonize every American who read it. As a librarian, Miss

PUNCH 14—20 OCTOBER 1970
2s 6d (12½ np.) WEEKLY

Punch

MOTOR NUMBER

Inside :
ALAN COREN,
THE SLOWEST MAN
IN THE WORLD

*Alan Coren, Punch's eleventh editor.
(Geoffrey Dickinson, 1970)*

Oliver had only to browse through the stacks and consult old copies of *Punch* to see what earlier editors had said about Queen Victoria, Prince Albert, Abraham Lincoln, Woodrow Wilson, Disraeli, Gladstone, the Duke of Wellington, Winston Churchill, and sundry kings, queens, emperors, maharajahs, viceroys, tsars, and their relations. But it is interesting to note that neither Miz Lillian nor the American ambassador complained. On the other hand, there were a great many letters of praise from admiring American readers.

The Press Council listened politely to Miss Oliver and then found in favor of Coren. In the August 10, 1977, issue of *Punch*, the adjudication of the Press Council was reprinted:

> The readership of *Punch* is by no means limited to those who purchase it in the first instance. It is commonly made available in many places of public resort where it may be read by anyone with time to spare. These will not all be the sophisticated university-educated people to whom its editor assured us the articles complained of were addressed.
>
> These articles may well be regarded by many people as being in very bad taste. They were said by the Deputy Editor, who wrote them, to be a form of satire. If so, the target against which they were directed was not obvious: indeed those who were in fact held up to ridicule and contempt week after week were the mother of the President of the United States and her family. Thus the Press Council did not find very plausible the author's suggestion that allegations of incest against a fictional character called Uncle Fungus Carter (even if recognised by less sophisticated readers as being made merely in jest) were directed against the supposed prevalence of incest in the Southern States.
>
> The Press Council considers that the articles themselves were as pretentious and as unpleasant as the very things the writer claimed to be condemning. The Council also feels that the author's name should have appeared. But, having regard to the general character of *Punch*, the Council, whilst not regarding the articles as useful, cannot see that they fell to a depth below what is admissible in a free society or that any rule of Press ethics has been broken. The complaint against *Punch* is not upheld.

The Amin series (which Miss Oliver apparently did not find in bad taste) is said to have been read with some pleasure by the president of Uganda himself, often aloud to friends. He does not appear to have found it in any way injurious to his dignity. When Coren awarded him the Victoria Cross, Amin had it made up and wears it on his uniform. When Coren suggested he change the name of Lake Victoria to Lake Amin, he did so.

The Amin columns brought on the affair of the mysterious letter, a copy of which is included herein. It seemed that in April 1975, the counselor for education of the Uganda High Commission in London, representing his chief executive, issued a stern reprimand to Coren and *Punch*, but in a spirit of forgiveness, invited him to visit Uganda as a presidential guest:

UGANDA HIGH COMMISSION

Telephone: 01-405 8904 (4 Lines)

Telegrams: STUGANDA LONDON

My ref: M.638/Part II   Your ref:

COLUMBIA HOUSE,

69. ALDWYCH,

LONDON, W.C.2

7th April, 1975.

Dear Mr Coren,

His Excellency President Amin of Uganda has asked me to write to you to express his considerable displeasure at the ill-informed and insulting way in which you have for some time been regularly attacking him and to suggest that you allow him a chance to answer his critics with the truth.

To that end and in a spirit of forgiveness for which the season is appropriate His Excellency would be pleased to accommodate you as his guest in his palace at Kampala so that you may see at first hand the disparity between the propaganda of his enemies and the real benefit which His Excellency brings to our country.

We beg to suggest that you may on arrival so revise your opinions as to wish to settle in Uganda and we assure you that no obstacle would be placed in your path. On the contrary, we should encourage such a decision.

Should you have difficulty in arranging your departure, our Government would be pleased to assist by offering a seat on one of its planes at your earliest convenience.

Yours faithfully,

H.O.DRACHO
For Counsellor (Education)

Alan Coren, Esq.,
"Punch" Publications,
27, Tudor Street,
London, E.C.4.

The letter was a forgery, made up by the girls of the Alternate Table and a friend who owns a small printing press. It fooled everyone, including the arch-practical joker himself, William Davis, who proudly described Amin's invitation in a *Vogue* article about Coren in January 1978. Alan prudently did not accept Amin's supposed offer of hospitality, and the letter became part of *Punch* history.

The Amin and the Miz Lillian columns (published in book form as *The Peanut Papers*) bode well for the future. After generations of see sawing between politics and comedy, Mr. Punch seems to have dusted off his old baton to prepare for some of the old style drubbing. "I have no doubt," Davis wrote in *Vogue*, "that as editor, Alan will continue to offend. It would be sad if he did not. *Punch* cannot—and should not—confine itself to harmless jokes about vicars and landladies, or for that matter set out to pander to the prejudices of a relatively small group of people who like to think of themselves as an elite."

And what of the future? Coren is trying to get serious popular writers—people like John Le Carré or Len Deighton—to contribute, a return to the days when Hollowood preferred Rebecca West to Muggeridge's stars and celebrities. He has Miles Kington and David Taylor to help him on the staff, and Jonathan Sale as well. Robert and Sheridan Morley, Benny Green, and Barry Took are still there, and he has added a London column done by Alan O'Brien. He is trying to get John Cleese.

In January 1978 *Vogue* conducted a survey to see whether people really did read *Punch* in dentists' offices, telephoning ten London dental surgeons. Three had *Punch* in their waiting rooms; seven didn't. As *Punch*'s circulation rises, the readership of its rivals drops. With United Newspapers behind him, Coren is not restricted, as was Hollowood, by an enforced budget crunch. The National Institution has weathered a number of storms in its long life, and fair weather seems to be ahead. The coming year should tell whether a new era is opening for *Punch*, or whether Alan Coren will be the London *Charivari*'s last editor.

Bibliography

The files, letters, records, and unique documents and photographs in the library at the offices of *Punch* at 23 Tudor Street in London.

Standard reference works such as the *Encyclopedia Britannica* (Eleventh Edition), the *Dictionary of National Biography*, the *Oxford Companion to English Literature*, and others.

Adlard, John. *Owen Seaman, His Life and Work*. London: The 1890's Society, 1977.

Adrian, Arthur A. *Mark Lemon, First Editor of Punch*. London: Oxford University Press, 1966.

Anstey, F. (Anstey Guthrie). *A Long Retrospect*. London: 1936.

Bateman, H. M. *A Mixture*. New York: Dial Press, 1924.

Batho, Edith, and Dobree, Bonamy. *The Victorians and After. 1830–1914*. New York: Robert M. McBride & Co., 1938.

à Beckett, Gilbert A. *The Comic History of England*. London: Bradbury, Agnew & Co., n.d.

The Best Cartoons From Punch. New York: Simon & Schuster, 1952.

Blanchard, Sidney. *Mr. Punch; His Origins and Career: With a Facsimile of His Original Prospectus in the Handwriting of Mark Lemon*. London: printed by James Wade, 1871.

Boas, Guy, ed. *A Punch Anthology*. London: Macmillan & Co., 1932.

Buckingham, James Silk. *Slanders of Punch: An Address to the British Public as to the Slanderous Articles of Certain Writers in Punch Against the British and Foreign Institute and its Resident Director*. London: James Ridgway, 1845.

Cole, William, ed. *The Best Humor From Punch*. New York: World, 1953.

Craven, Thomas, ed. *Cartoon Cavalcade*. New York: Simon & Schuster, 1943.

Davis, William. *The Pick of Punch*. London: Hutchinson, 1974, 1975, 1976, 1977.

———. *The Punch Book of Inflation*. London: David & Charles, 1975.

Duff, David. *Punch on Children*. London: Frederick Muller Ltd., 1975.

Du Maurier, George. *Society Pictures From Punch*. London: Bradbury, Agnew & Co., n.d.

The Early Morning Milk Train. London: John Murray, Ltd., 1976.

Ellis, S. M., ed. *The Letters and Memoirs of Sir William Hardman: Second Series 1863-1865.* New York: George H. Doran, 1925.

Fitzgerald, Penelope. *The Knox Brothers.* New York: Coward, McCann & Geoghegan, 1977.

Giepel, John. *The Cartoon.* London: David & Charles, 1972.

Harris, Frank. *My Life and Loves.* Vol. 2. Paris: Obelisk Press, 1945.

Hatton, J. *Journalistic London.* London: Sampson, Low, Marston, Searle & Rivington, 1882.

Hewison, William. *The Cartoon Connection.* London: Elm Tree Books, 1977.

Hibbert, Christopher. *Gilbert & Sullivan.* New York: American Heritage, 1976.

Hillier, Bevis, ed. *Fougasse.* London: Elm Tree Books, 1977.

Holroyd, Michael. *Hugh Kingsmill: A Critical Biography.* London: Unicorn Press, 1964.

Hollowood, Bernard, ed. *The Women of Punch.* London: Arthur Barker Ltd., 1961.

Jerrold, Douglas. *Georgian Adventure.* London: Collins, 1937.

Jones, Michael Wynn. *The Cartoon History of Britain.* New York: Macmillan, 1971.

Kelly, Richard M. *The Best of Mr. Punch.* Knoxville: University of Tennessee Press, 1970.

Layard, George S. *A Great Punch Editor.* London: Sampson Low & Co., 1907.

_____. *The Life and Letters of Charles Keene of Punch.* London: Sampson, Low & Co., 1892.

Lehmann, John. *In My Own Time.* New York: Atlantic Little Brown, 1955.

Lucas, Audrey. *E. V. Lucas: A Portrait.* New York: Kennikat Press, 1939.

Lucas, E. V. *Reading, Writing and Remembering.* London: Methuen, 1932.

Lucy, Sir Henry. *Sixty Years in the Wilderness.* London: 1909.

Mayhew, Athol. *A Jorum of Punch.* London: Downey & Co., 1895.

Mayhew, Henry. *Mayhew's Characters (London Labour and the London Poor).* Edited by Peter Quennell. London: Spring Books, 1975.

Mikes, George. *Eight Humorists.* London: Allan Wingate, 1954.

Milne, A. A. *Autobiography.* New York: E.P. Dutton, 1939.

The Most of Muggeridge. New York: Simon & Schuster, 1966.

Mr. Punch's History of the Great War. London: Cassell, 1920.

Muggeridge, Malcolm. *Chronicles of Wasted Time.* Chronicle 1, *The Green Stick*; Chronicle 2, *The Infernal Grove.* New York: William Morrow, 1973 and 1974.

The New Punch Library Series: *Mr. Punch and the Arts, Mr. Punch's Cavalcade, Mr. Punch in War Time, Mr. Punch's Theatricals.* London: the Educational Book Co., n.d.

Ormond, Leonee. *George du Maurier.* London: Routledge & Kegan Paul, 1969.

Pearsall, Ronald. *Collapse of Stout Party.* London: Weidenfeld & Nicholson, 1975.

Pepys, Derek. ''Bernard Partridge and Punch.'' *Image 8*, Summer 1952.

The Pick of Punch. New York: E. P. Dutton, 1957.

Pound, Reginald. *A. P. Herbert.* London: Michael Joseph, 1976.

Price, R. G. G. *A History of Punch.* London: Collins, 1957.

Priestley, J. B. *The English.* London: Penguin Books, 1975.

_____. *English Humour.* London: Heinemann, 1976.

Punch. 1841 to the present.

The Punch Pocket Book of Fun. London, 1857.

Renton, Richard. *John Forster and His Friendships*. New York: Scribners, 1913.

Repplier, Agnes. *The Pursuit of Laughter*. New York: Houghton Mifflin, 1936.

Ruskin, John. "The Art of England." Slade Lectures. Oxford, 1870.

Silver, Henry. *The Diary of Henry Silver: 1857–1865*.

Spielmann, M. H. *The History of Punch*. New York: Cassell, 1895.

_____. *The Hitherto Unidentified Contributions of William Makepeace Thackeray to Punch*. New York: Harper & Brothers, 1900.

Thackeray, W. M. *The Newcomes*. Cambridge: Heritage, 1940.

_____. *Vanity Fair*. New York: Heritage, 1940.

Viztelly, Henry. *Glances Back Through Seventy Years*. London: 1893.

Ward, Leslie. *Forty Years of "Spy."* London: Chatto & Windus, n.d.

Weintraub, Stanley. *Whistler, a Biography*. New York: Weybright & Talley, 1974.

Welsh, Robert, ed. *Galloping Through Punch*. London: David & Charles, 1976.

Williams, R. E., ed. *A Century of Punch Cartoons*. New York: Simon & Schuster, 1955.

Sources

vii "wear corduroy trousers": P. G. Wodehouse, *The Pick of Punch* (New York: E. P. Dutton, 1957), p. 9.

3 "Why is a chestnut horse": *Punch* (1841): 48.
4 "I was between": Diary of Henry Silver, March 11, 1863.
6 "Once through the door": R. E. Williams in *A Century of Punch Cartoons* (New York: Simon & Schuster, 1955), p. xii.
12 "In 1910 I was allowed downstairs": A. A. Milne, *Autobiography* (New York: E. P. Dutton, 1939), p. 235.
14 "No stranger ever was": G. S. Layard, *The Life and Letters of Charles Keene of Punch* (London: Sampson & Low, 1892), p. 73.
15 "When the slogan": Milne, p. 232.
15 *"Mock turtle, red mullet"*: Silver diary, January 12, 1859.
16 "keep yourself disengaged": Ibid., November 10, 1858.
17 "I recollect": Ibid., August 15, 1857.
17 "Am to dine regularly": Ibid., December 29, 1858.
17 On Post Office prepayment: Entries from p. 17–p. 20 were chosen at random from Silver's diary between 1858 and 1864.

33 *"Punch* keeps up": Silver diary, June 28, 1860.
37 "Well boys, the title": M. H. Spielmann, *The History of Punch* (New York: Cassell, 1895), p. 25.
41 "an extraordinary mop of hair": Athol Mayhew, *A Jorum of Punch* (London: Downy & Co., 1895), p. 94.
41 "If his lines had been cast": Spielmann, p. 269.
42 "Mayhew [made] his personality": Ibid., p. 17.

44 "To me *Punch* was always": Mayhew, p. 121.

44 "M. L. has seen a prospectus": Silver diary, October 12, 1864.

46 "The crowning effort": S. M. Ellis, ed., *A Mid-Victorian Pepys: Letters and Memoirs of Sir William Hardman*. In R. G. G. Price, *A History of Punch* (London: Collins, 1957), p. 27.

46 "I smell lots of tin": Spielmann, p. 269.

46 "His 'air 'ung in corkscrew curls": A. A. Adrian, *Mark Lemon, First Editor of Punch* (London: Oxford University Press, 1966), p. 3.

48 "Come to town": Silver diary, August 4, 1858.

49 "It may not be—at least not yet": *Punch Pocket Book of Fun* (London, 1857), p. 169.

51 "THE MORAL OF PUNCH: Punch 1 (1841): 1.

55 "I was made for *Punch*": J. Hatton, quoted in Price, p. 28.

55 "Glorious imitator": Silver diary, January 5, 1859.

55 "I don't agree": Ibid., February 19, 1862.

55 "His place as editor": Ibid., October 22, 1862.

55 "Show us your cock": Ibid., December 9, 1858.

57 "Wants a piano": Spielmann, p. 311.

57 "We've got the little man": Ibid.

58 "Whilst there's life": *Punch* 1 (1841): 102.

61 "Now, MR. CAUDLE": *Punch* 8 (1845): 135.

63 "Oh Mr. Punch!": *Punch* 1 (1841): 48.

64 "no person connected with": Spielmann, p. 278.

64 "always ready in a": Ibid., p. 273.

64 "so congested with puns": Agnes Repplier, *In Pursuit of Laughter*, (New York: Houghton Mifflin, 1936), p. 166.

65 "talk of G. à B.": Silver diary, April 27, 1863.

66 "Why is a loud laugh": *Punch* 1 (1841): 155.

68 "How many": *Punch* 2 (1842): 20.

68 "Mr. Llewellyn Price": *Punch* 4 (1843): 172.

69 "Ever since the Italian opera": *Punch* 4 (1843): 126.

71 "Considerable sensation": *Punch* 4 (1844): 32.

75 "The Jews govern": Silver diary, February 23, 1859.

80 "No; black are our bosoms": J. Hatton, *Journalistic London* (London: Sampson, Low, Marston, Searle & Rivington, 1882), p. 19.

81 "a very kindly entertainer": E. V. Lucas, *Reading, Writing, and Remembering* (London: Methuen, 1932), p. 322.

85 "the little John Leech": Angela Thirkell, ed. *The Newcomes*, by W. M. Thackeray (Cambridge: Heritage, 1940), p. xiii.

87 "Won't get aristocratic": Silver diary, January 18, 1860.

88 "Of all Leech's work": Spielmann, p. 176.

89 "The poor ask for bread": *Punch* 5 (1843): 22.

90 "Ah! Fanny": *Punch* 33 (1857): 114.

90 "natural simplicity": John Ruskin, quoted in Ronald Pearsall, *Collapse of Stout Party* (London: Weidenfeld & Nicholson, 1975), p. 176.

283

90 "prime exponent": Ibid.
90 "Put him as a line draughtsman": John Sloan, ed. "In Praise of Thackeray's Pictures," in *Vanity Fair* by W. M. Thackeray (New York: Heritage, 1940), p. xiii.
92 "Leech was the very": Richard Renton, *John Foster and His Friendships* (New York: Scribner's, 1913), p. 219.
92 "J. L. still nervous": Silver diary, June 15, 1864.
93 "If ever there was": Leonee Ormand, *George du Maurier*, (London: Routledge & Kegan Paul, 1969), p. 436.
93 "You never saw": Ibid., p. 160.
97 "Meanwhile old Thackeray": E. Fitzgerald to Frederick Tennyson, 1845, in W. M. Thackeray, *Vanity Fair*, J. T. Winterich, ed. (New York: Heritage, 1940), introduction.
97 "talks of using": Silver diary, April 1, 1863.
99 "Upon my word": Spielmann, p. 323.
99 "And now for the gossip": S. M. Ellis, ed. *The Letters and Memoirs of Sir William Hardman: Second Series 1863-1865* (New York: George H. Doran, 1925), p. 120.

101 "He [Mr. Punch] cracks": W. M. Thackeray, "John Leech's Pictures of Life and Character," *Quarterly Review*, December 1854, no. 191.
109 "a most artistic one": Leslie Ward, *Forty Years of "Spy"* (London: Chatto & Windus, n.d.), p. 87.
112 "If only I could": Spielmann, p. 432.
115 "The effect was marvelous": Renton, p. 73.
115 "Somehow, one liked": Ormond, p. 436.
118 "While he could afford": J. B. Priestley, *English Humour* (London: Heineman, 1976), p. 179.
122 "I hate your Blifils": Ormond, p. 165.
122 "Old Mark I like": Ibid., p. 164.
125 "curiously grey in the face": Sir Henry Lucy, *Sixty Years in the Wilderness* (London, 1909).
129 "He is exceedingly amusing": Pearsall, p. 166.
130 "A DOMESTIC DRAMA": *Punch* 43 (1862): 104.
133 "Percival Leigh says": Silver diary, January 25, 1865.
135 "S. B. emits some": Ibid., August 12, 1865.
135 "Discussion on whether": Ibid., March 2, 1859.
135 "Shirley despises all actors": Ibid., February 8, 1865.
136 "Others of us": E. V. Lucas, p. 323.
136 "Oh, by the way": Ibid.
137 "In humour slow": Pearsall, p. 165.
137 "Too scholarly": Spielmann, p. 340.
138 "At dinner his appearance": Ward, p. 57.
139 "T. T. says": Silver diary, January 19, 1859.

140 "You must be clear": John Ruskin, "The Art of England," Slade Lectures, 1870.
141 "The line between": Douglas Jerrold, *Georgian Adventure* (London: Collins, 1937), p. 15.
143 "*Punch* readers are": Milne, p. 236.
143 "Ergo, *Punch* readers": John Adlard, *Owen Seaman, His Life and Work* (London: The 1890's Society, 1977), p. 25.
144 "If 'Happy Thoughts' ": E. V. Lucas, p. 317.
146 "The play was worse": Frank Harris, *My Life and Loves*, vol. 2 (Paris: Obelisk Press, 1945), p. 128.
148 "As a jovial head": Lucas, p. 317.
148 "Not a bad fellow": Silver diary, June 17, 1863.
149 "one of Burnand's happier": Price, p. 135.
149 "no fire and much caution": E. V. Lucas, p. 323.
149 "His political articles": Price, p. 135.
152 "No paper has": Ibid., p. 128.
152 "Brazen, vulgar, unashamed": Spielmann, p. 379.
152 "*the spirit of Caddishness*": Ibid., p. 380.
156 "It was typical": John Lehmann, *In My Own Time* (New York: Little Brown, 1955), p. 23.
162 "Draw firm and be jolly": William Hewison, *The Cartoon Connection* (London: Elm Tree Books, 1977), p. 138.
162 "a veritable coelocanth": John Giepel, *The Cartoon* (London: David & Charles, 1972), p. 86.

164 "*Punch* humor": Jerrold, p. 288.
168 "Verse three": Reginald Pound, *A. P. Herbert* (London: Michael Joseph, 1976), p. 24.
168 "Once he had": *Morning Post* (London), Seaman obituary, February 3, 1936.
169 "All Owen's past life": Milne, p. 227.
169 "Once when George": Price, p. 228.
172 "A kindly old boy": Ibid., p. 227.
174 "He was a strange": Milne, p. 229.
175 "mean, ungenerous": Graves to Milne, 1939.
175 "A nutting went": Adlard, p. 67.
175 "Henry James has": Ibid., p. 86.
176 "Mr. Davidson": Repplier, p. 216.
176 "not since its foundation": E. V. Lucas, p. 319.
177 "of which I": Milne, p. 171.
177 "honor of writing": Ibid., 201.
177 "The new editor": Ibid., 217.
177 "I burst in": Ibid., p. 271.
180 "You know the sequel": Audrey Lucas, *E. V. Lucas, a Portrait* (New York: Kennikat Press, 1939), p. 57.

183 "as many concerns": Milne, p. 239.

183 "on only one day": Audrey Lucas, p. 44.

183 "usually wrong": Price, p. 135.

183 "spared his other": Ibid., p. 242.

184 "More Wise Words on Wedlock": *Mr. Punch's Cavalcade* (London: Educational Book Co., 1935), p. 107.

186 "Dear Bankers": Pound, p. 265.

186 "Dear Sir": Ibid., p. 266.

187 "Your ref.": Ibid.

189 "A valuable youth": Ibid., p. 81.

190 "Let's stop everybody": *Punch* 175 (1928): 48.

190 "The portions of a woman": Pound, p. 95.

191 "Oh seagull": Ibid., p. 96.

191 "I went to the palatial": *Punch* 175 (1928): 163.

193 "In the shock of discovery": *Mr. Punch's History of the Great War* (London: Cassell, 1920), p. xv.

193 "Honorary Cornet-Major": *Punch* 147 (1914): 545.

195 "I tell you": Ibid.

195 "shirkers, slackers": *Mr. Punch's History*, p. xv.

196 "not only a privilege": Ibid., p. 24.

196 "a handful of": Ibid.

196 *"C'est magnifique"*: Ibid., p. 156.

197 "cartoons are lacking": Ibid., p. 30.

197 "A new and dangerous ally": Ibid., p. 32.

198 "The cheerfulness of": Ibid., p. 54.

199 "As to Punch": Rudyard Kipling, to E. V. Knox, quoted in Penelope Fitzgerald, *The Knox Brothers* (New York: Coward, McCann, 1977), p. 209.

203 "A dog": *Punch*, January 16, 1924, p. 49.

203 "Much sympathy": Ibid.

203 "say what you think": Price, p. 231.

205 "What is the matter": Pound, p. 203.

213 "I am very glad": Penelope Fitzgerald, p. 126.

213 "Two of the brightest": E. V. Lucas, p. 320.

213 "At times": Price, p. 196.

215 "man of rueful": Pound, p. 112.

215 "You have saved me": Penelope Fitzgerald, p. 168.

219 "And now": William Cole, *The Best Humor From Punch* (New York: World, 1953), p. 101.

220 "Tom, Tom": Ibid., p. 100.

225 "What is more romantic": *The Early Morning Milk Train* (London: John Murray Ltd., 1976), p. 83.

230 "When Seaman went": Price, p. 259.
235 "as a canary": Bevis Hillier, *Fougasse* (London: Elm Tree, 1977), p. 5.
238 "were reacting": Peter Dickinson to Arthur Prager, February 4, 1978.
239 "There was a": Price, p. 301.
239 "Shorn of glamour": Hewison, p. 138.
241 "I learned early": Cole, p. 38.
243 "No one's education": *The Most of Muggeridge* (New York: Simon & Schuster, 1966), introduction.
243 "Those who were": Ibid.
244 "The deadly solemnity": Malcolm Muggeridge, "The Queen and I," *The New Republic*, 1961.
244 "It was eerie": *The Most of Muggeridge*, introduction.
244 "it was a somber place": Ibid.
247 "Thurber visiting": Dickinson to Prager.
248 "Malcolm Muggeridge": Peter G. Agnew to Arthur Prager, February 1978.
249 "It was with a sense": *The Most of Muggeridge*, Introduction.
251 "When I went to *Punch*": Malcolm Muggeridge, *The Infernal Grove* (New York: William Morrow, 1974), p. 157.
251 "a bitter, smiling, destructive": Conversation between a Punchite and Arthur Prager, September 1977.
252 "Every time he kissed a girl": Ibid.
252 "I am rather mystified": Anthony Powell to Arthur Prager, January 17, 1978.
253 "Since Malcolm Muggeridge": *Smith's Trade News*, December 21, 1957.
254 "I am no Muggeridge": *Daily Record & Mail* (Glasgow), December 12, 1957.
254 "Are you going to be": BBC Television News broadcast, December 13, 1957.
256 "The changes I made": Bernard Hollowood to Arthur Prager, January 25, 1978.
257 "If we laugh": Bernard Hollowood, "Humour in Journalism," *Journal of the Institute of Journalists*, April 1962, p. 48.
258 "Bernard Hollowood was ill": P. G. Agnew to Arthur Prager.
258 "Peter Dickinson": Ibid.
258 "Nor was it": Letter: Peter Dickinson to Arthur Prager.

260 "Parts of it": *Punch*, Caption of a cartoon familiarly called "The Curate's Egg," November 9, 1895.
260 "Mr. Davis played his part": Lord Barnetson to Arthur Prager, March 23, 1978.
262 "In 1966/7 Bradbury Agnew": P. G. Agnew to Arthur Prager.
263 "Don't want a bullet": *Punch*, November 7, 1973, p. 707.
263 "I am in journalism": Interview with William Davis, September 1977.
264 "As fact-finding missions": William Davis, *Punch Nostalgia Number*, December 21, 1977–January 3, 1978, p. 1204.
264 "An Arab Sheikh": *Times* (London) in "Spotlight," *Vogue* (London), January 1978, p. 94.

267 "What got me interested": Steve Harris, "Punch: Into the World, Out of the Waiting Room," *Newsagent and Bookshop* (London), December 19, 1975, p. 24.

268 "You see in Malcolm's day": Ibid.

268 "Advertisers used to say": Interview with William Davis, "The Life of Mr. Punch," *Campaign* (London), November 30, 1973.

269 "My first avalanche": William Davis, *Punch Nostalgia Number*, p. 1205.

269 "I think where": William Davis, *Campaign*, Ibid.

272 "I shall miss you": Alan Coren, "Private Lives, Partly," *Punch Nostalgia Number*, p. 1206.

276 "The readership of *Punch*": Adjudication of the Press Council, reprinted in *Punch*, August 10, 1977, p. 223.

278 "I have no doubt": *Vogue* (London), January 1978, p. 94.

Index

Edinburgh Castle (tavern), 37, 45
Edinburgh Evening News, 260
Edison, Thomas, 157
"Editha's Burglar" (Benchley), 153
Edward VII, King, 4, 109
"Effect of the Antigarotte Collar On a Garrotteer" (Keene), 106
Ego 3 (Agate), 181
Egyptian Hall, 84–85
Ellis, H. F., 13, 216, 223, 236–238, 247, 248, 257
Elliston, R. W., 57
Eltze, Fritz, 171
Emmett, Rowland, vi, 225, 229, 232
Enchanted Doll, The (Lemon), 49
England, Douglas, 229
English Encyclopedia, 81
"Entertainments at Which We Have Not Assisted" (Morrow), 210
Espy, Willard, 247
Esquire, 216, 274
"Essence of Parliament," 129, 135, 137, 143, 150, 151, 203, 216, 239, 251
Etchings and Drawings by A. Pen, Esq. (Leech), 87
Eton (school), 145
Evangelical Penny Magazine, 64
Evans, F. M. "Pater," 12, 13, 15, 17, 18, 19, 21, 30, 33, 40, 44, 47, 48, 65, 79, 81, 84, 93, 99, 122, 139
Evans, William F. M., 81
Evans family, 81
Evening Standard, 103, 243, 264, 274
Evoe, *See* Knox, Edmund George Valpy
Examiner, 79
"Experientia Docet" (du Maurier), 121
"Extra Pages" (feature), 156

Fadebray Ltd., 6
"Fair Offer, A" (Thackeray), 96
Fallen Idol, A (Guthrie), 153
Family Failing, A (Oxenford), 108
Family Herald, 81

"Fancy Portrait of My Laundress" (Reed), 159
Fantoni, Barry, 27
Farjeon, Eleanor, 204
Farjeon, Jefferson, 224
Farming Press, Ltd., 262
Farnborough Park School, 235
Farren, Nelly, 146
"Faux et Preterea Nihil" (Guthrie), 153
"Federal Phoenix, The" (Tenniel), 110
Fetchit, Stepin, 274
Ffolkes, Michael, 24, 242, 272
Field, 81
Figaro in London, 41, 64
Financial Times, 264
Fitz-Boodle, George Savage. *See* Thackeray, William Makepeace
Fitzgerald, Edward, 85, 97
"Flattering!" (Keene), 116
Fleet Prison, 42
Fleet Street Bistingo (restaurant), 7
Fleischmann, G. A., 5
"Flippancy" (du Maurier), 167
"Foreign Affairs" (Leigh and Leech), 87
"For Men in Aprons" (Ellis), 223
Forster, E. M., 243
Forster, John, 46, 79
"Forsythe Saga, The" (television series), 269
For Women (*Punch* column), 256
Foster, Birket, 37, 126
Fougasse. *See* Bird, Cyril Kenneth
François, André, 242
Franco-Prussian War, 193
Fraser, James MacDonald, 269
Fraser's Magazine, 42, 95, 96
Frater, Alexander, 256
Freaky Friday (motion picture), 153
Freischütz, Der (Weber), 57
Friendly Town, The (Lucas), 183
Frith, "Sissie," 129
Frith, William Powell, 88, 90
"From the Cross Benches" (Lucy), 149
Fun, 103–104, 125, 126, 143, 145
Furniss, Harry, 10–11, 13, 150, 151, 155, 156–157, 159, 180, 196, 202

303

304